Gwen Harwood was bor
in music, she was to teac
at All Saints' Church, Brisbane. Married with four children, she
is now a grandmother and pursues many interests including the
study of modern philosophy and working with composers.

Poetry awards received by Gwen Harwood include the Grace
Leven Prize 1975, the Robert Frost Award 1977, the Patrick White
Award 1978, the Victorian Premier's Award 1989 and the South
Australian Festival Award 1990. In 1988 she received an Honorary
Doctorate of Letters from the University of Tasmania.

Alison Hoddinott, the editor of *Blessed City,* is a senior lecturer
in English at the University of New England. She was born and
raised in Tasmania, winning a scholarship to Oxford in the
mid-1950s. Her friendship with Gwen Harwood has spanned
almost forty years.

IMPRINT

BLESSED CITY

The Letters of Gwen Harwood
to Thomas Riddell
January to September 1943

GWEN HARWOOD
Edited by Alison Hoddinott

ANGUS
& ROBERTSON

A division of Harper Collins *Publishers*

Collins/Angus & Robertson Publishers'
creative writing programme is
assisted by the Australia Council,
the Australian government's arts advisory
and support organisation.

AN ANGUS & ROBERTSON BOOK

First published in Australia in 1990 by
Collins/Angus & Robertson Publishers Australia

Collins/Angus & Robertson Publishers Australia
A division of HarperCollins *Publishers (Australia) Pty Limited*
Unit 4, Eden Park, 31 Waterloo Road, North Ryde,
NSW 2113, Australia

Collins/Angus & Robertson Publishers New Zealand
31 View Road, Glenfield, Auckland 10, New Zealand

Angus & Robertson (UK)
16 Golden Square, London W1R 4BN, United Kingdom

National Library of Australia
Cataloguing-in-Publication data

Harwood, Gwen, 1920-
  Blessed city.

  ISBN 0 207 16587 4.

  1. Harwood, Gwen, 1920- — Correspondence. 2. Riddell,
  Thomas — Correspondence. 3. Poets, Australian — 20th
  century — Correspondence. I. Hoddinott, Alison,
  1931- .II. Title.
A821.2

Typeset in 11/12 pt Times Roman by Midland Typesetters
Printed in Australia by Globe Press
Cover painting: Vida Lahey — Springtime in Brisbane (1932),
Queensland Art Gallery

5 4 3 2 1
95 94 93 92 91 90

To Thomas Riddell
and Alison Hoddinott

INTRODUCTION

All Gwen Harwood's volumes of poetry are dedicated to Thomas Riddell. The letters in this volume provide a large part of the explanation.

Brisbane during the war years was full of Australian servicemen. In his recollection of his childhood at 12 Edmondstone Street in South Brisbane, David Malouf remembers seeing transports "ferrying troops across the city from one station to another on their way to Townsville and the far north". At the beginning of 1943, the year in which these letters were written, Gwen Foster was twenty-two and living with her family at 14 Grimes Street in Auchenflower on the northern side of the Brisbane River. During the week she worked as a clerk in the Public Service, at the War Damage Commission (WDC). On Sundays, she was the organist at All Saints' Church, where her friend Peter Bennie was the curate. He had come to Brisbane from Melbourne, where he had been at school and university with Thomas (or Tony) Riddell.

In late 1942, Tony Riddell, then a lieutenant in the RANVR, was stationed in Brisbane for several months before being sent on to Darwin. Peter Bennie introduced him to Gwen Foster, and when Tony left Brisbane early in 1943 he and Gwen began to write letters to one another. The friendship and the correspondence have lasted, with some interruptions, for over forty-five years.

The value Tony placed on Gwen's letters from the beginning is evident in the care with which he preserved them. He received them when he was on active service and he kept them safe despite the conditions of war and the moves from one battle area to another. After the war he kept them for thirty years until, in the early seventies, he decided to move, more or less permanently, to England. This meant selling his house and disposing of many

1

of his personal and family possessions. By this time, Gwen Harwood had achieved the literary success he predicted for her in 1943 and was one of Australia's best-known and most highly regarded poets. He therefore decided, with Gwen's permission, to give his collection of letters to the Fryer Library in the University of Queensland.

Very few of the letters are dated. Most begin "Monday, 1943", "Thursday, 1943" or, sometimes more precisely, "St Valentine's Day, 1943". The order in which they are catalogued in the Fryer Library bears little relationship to the order in which they were written. They have been ordered chronologically and dated by the editor of this volume on internal evidence – reference to birthdays, Easter, the weather, happenings in the family or at the War Damage Commission. Dates that have been supplied on this conjectural basis are given in brackets. From March to September there are entries for almost every day, so the letters, read sequentially, have the interest of a diary. The total length of the correspondence between January and September has been reduced by approximately one third. Omissions are indicated by dots.

Most of the letters are typed, often on WDC typewriters in office hours. A few are handwritten – sometimes because the subject matter is particularly personal, but usually because there was some difficulty in finding a typewriter that was not being used. The typewriters themselves sometimes assume personalities ("DOG of a machine – there we go again" (58)) as they produce Joycean variants of the words she intends. "I wonder if James Joyce invented his new language by typing in bed," she wonders (62), intrigued by the typographical extravagances she is producing while confined to bed with a sore throat.

There are two main settings for the happenings and human relationships described in the letters. The family house at 14 Grimes Street is ruled by Mrs Foster, who organises committees, welcomes servicemen, friends and relatives into the hospitality of her home and cuts down trees when they threaten to interfere with the drains. Father Foster, huge and cheerful, improvises on the piano, indulges his little dog, Gretchen, and tells tales of his youth

2

in Nottingham. Brother Joe (Hippo) does body-building exercises and is an expert on aircraft of the First World War. Young naval officers, some of them later to become distinguished in Australian academic and political life, appear briefly as guests of the Fosters and disappear again. (There is an intriguing glimpse of Zelman Cowen striding through the rain with his eyes fixed on some goal that blinds him to his surroundings (21).) The other setting is the office of the War Damage Commission in Creek Street, a kind of wartime Circumlocution Office weighed down by its own files and tied up in its own red tape. The contrast between the two settings is indicated by the variations in the letter headings. The house at Auchenflower is sometimes "Crimes Street", "Grimy Street", or "Chez Agens" but, more usually, it is enveloped in a celestial aura as "The Holy City", "Urbs Beata", "Visio Pacis", or "Mansions of the Blest". The War Damage Commission, on the other hand, is the "Kriegschaden-Kommission", "Cretins' Rest Home", or "Sunshine Home for Cretins".

The last letter in this volume was written on 3 September. In it, Gwen looks forward "with great joy" to Tony's return on leave on the 9th. The last few letters before Tony's September leave mark the end of the first year of the friendship and the end of the first phase of the correspondence. At Grimes Street the family is broken up by the successful outcome of Joe's physical training programme when, shortly after his eighteenth birthday on 23 August, he is accepted into the Air Force. At the War Damage Commission, Gwen achieves a minor triumph over the forces of bureaucracy as she reports that the examining department has "lost its fighting spirit", and one of the bureaucrats is overheard to remark wearily to his secretary that: "*That girl* has the audacity of ten men . . . She would talk her way out of gaol."

The most far-reaching change that came about as a result of Tony's leave in September was one that could not have been foreseen. On his return to Brisbane he brought with him a friend, who was also a lieutenant in the RANVR and a graduate of Melbourne University. Bill Harwood, briefly mentioned in letter 72, was introduced to the family at Grimes Street. He and Gwen were married at the end of the war, on 4 September 1945. In October of that year they moved to Hobart, where he took up an appointment as a lecturer in the Department of English at the University of Tasmania. They have lived in Tasmania ever since. In the late seventies Tony Riddell, having abandoned his plan to settle permanently in England, moved to Tasmania, where he now lives.

The letters Gwen Harwood wrote to Thomas Riddell in 1943 can stand on their own as a contemporary account of a particular place and time, captured by a perceptive observer with a satirical eye for the ridiculous and an enormous enthusiasm for life. The lyrical glimpse of "a little seaside place called Yeppoon" in the opening letter, as well as the descriptions of a wartime Brisbane of rationing and peanut shortages, record a world that has vanished forever. The letters are additionally important in that, although the writer was unaware of it at the time, they are the first significant literary production of someone who was to become a major Australian poet. As Thomas Riddell says, "My early collection of letters has a special interest in that they show a facet of Gwen's life when she was young, many years before her name became known as a poet." In fact, they record a crucial year in the development of a writer. They illustrate her growing pleasure in giving her daily experiences a written form and, in response to Tony's encouragement, her dawning awareness that she might write well enough to consider submitting her stories and poems for publication.

A number of the letters can be related, directly or indirectly, to poems written many years later. In an early letter (7), she recalls her childhood at Mitchelton in a passage that evokes "the heavy perfume of the orange and lemon trees in bloom" and "little gullies running down to a lovely creek bordered with yellow and blue flowering trees". This Garden-of-Eden-like world of childhood forms the central subject matter of several poems of memory written from the seventies onward: "The Violets", "The Blue Pagoda" and "The Wasps" for example. Sometimes, an unusual

4

phrase or a vivid image from a poem can be found in the letters. (The adjective, "bird-befouled", used to describe statues in a public park in "Guardian", was originally Peter Bennie's (41).) The description of the photograph of "Joe at an early age, standing on a rock by the seashore and apparently defying the laws of nature by leaning at a perilous angle towards the sea" (27) suggests the attempts of the child in "At Mornington" to deny the laws of nature and thus to conquer time and mortality. The dream of effortless artistic creation attributed to A. D. Hope in the poem addressed to him is strikingly similar to the description of the film, in which "a composer composed a waltz at the piano and walked back to his stand, waved his baton and led his orchestra magnificently through the unwritten and unorchestrated music" (56). In the poem "Barn Owl", a child creeps out at dawn to kill an owl out of an impulse of wilful destructiveness and comes as a result to an awareness of the pervasive cruelty of the world of nature. In letter 16, Gwen tells of the horrified pity that caused her to chop the head off a dove that had been mutilated by the family cat, and the protective gentleness of her attitude to doves contrasts strikingly with the thoughtless cruelty of the child in "Barn Owl".

The wartime letters foreshadow many of the characteristics of her later poetry. The music, folklore, philosophy and literature of Germany are pervasive influences in all her writing. Many of the songs for which Gwen Foster played Thomas Riddell's accompaniment were German lieder. In the letters, she repeatedly records a romantic longing for the snow and fir trees of Germany. In the second letter, she speaks of her intention to escape from the boredom of the WDC by teaching herself German. She is drawn to the romantic, idealistic, philosophical side of the German character at a time when her country is at war with Germany. At the same time she is aware of a darker side, and it is this other side, the authoritarian and militaristic one, that she makes fun of in some of her satirical descriptions of Joe's body-building activities and of the regulation-dominated bureaucracy at the WDC. In letter 47 she remarks:

The Germans seem to mix up the most amazing inconsistencies in their nature. I suppose the mixture of opposing characteristics accounts for their fanaticism when they are caught up by an idea.

These two opposing sides to the German nature underlie the characterisation of the two professors with German names she later created as poetic representatives of some of her beliefs about science and art. Professor Eisenbart, the apparently rational scientist intent on dominating the world of nature through the power of his intellect, represents one side. Professor Kröte, the drunken, failed musician who despite his failures keeps alive his love of art and music, represents the other.

Throughout the letters of 1943, we are made aware of Gwen's rebellion against the boredom of convention and respectability. Her fondness for alter egos, for masks and disguises, is an aspect of this revolt. In the 1943 letters there are many examples of the use of masks. Theophilus Panbury, Fred Hackleskinner and Tiny Tim (who becomes Tinny Tim through a typographical error), all foreshadow the pseudonyms under which she hoaxed a generation of editors in the sixties and seventies. She frequently rebels against boredom by assuming a role and acting a part. Weddings, musical afternoons and other occasions on which music is betrayed by affectation particularly evoke this impulse to rebellion. The role of the "Disillusioned Musician" (one of the "three characters – which I play at weddings" (40)) is one that Kröte often plays at meetings of the Arts Club and musical afternoons. In letter 34 she wishes she were "a young man, because then I could get gloriously drunk before playing at musical afternoons; it must be wonderful to be drunk in the society of a Christian body devoted to eliminating drunkenness from the community". In letter 60 she records with incredulous delight the incident in which the soloist engaged to sing "Because" at a wedding *was* in fact, drunk. ("Oh Tony, I wish you'd been there.") The comic sources of Kröte's character and the closeness of his rebelliousness to Gwen Harwood's own are strongly evident in the letters of 1943.

So, too, are the sources of the images of light and darkness that recur throughout the poetry. The titles of many of her poems reflect her preoccupation with the transition of light between day and night. Her poetry records shafts of light in darkened rooms, the dazzling play of light on water, light refracted through glass, treetops flaring briefly as the sun sets behind them and the flash of a dragonfly's wings as it hovers over a blazing stream. The positive assertions of her poetry are most characteristically expressed in images of light. In the letters of 1943, a particular awareness of the changing sky at night and at dawn is related to the fact that she always slept on the veranda of the house in Auchenflower. Throughout the letters there are many beautiful, lyrical passages of description of the night sky and the changing patterns of light and darkness, and these passages are frequently associated with mood and feeling; particularly with the release from loneliness, with spiritual aspirations and with romantic longings for wider horizons.

Throughout the letters, the reader is aware of the writer's need to share her thoughts and feelings with a friend who will understand. Tony's friendship allows her to describe the daily incidents of her life and her reactions to them. Her vitality and enthusiasm for life are evident in the delight with which she ridicules the absurdities around her, describes lyrically the delicious meals provided at 14 Grimes Street ("I cannot see how anyone can fail to be interested in food" (23)), observes the beauty of the night sky or a rainy day, or speculates about metaphysical and theological questions. The prolonged argument with Tony about the difference between and relative importance of individuality and personality (in which it is clear that their disagreement results from the definition of the terms rather than any real differences) reveals a concern to affirm life and the joy of being oneself. "Still, being young, I prefer being Gwen to watching the grass grow", she concludes a solemn discussion of this question (61). To be fully oneself involves the giving and receiving of friendship and love. Her objection to the philosophies of the east, which she discusses frequently, is that they are "devoid of love", by which she means love for a person. "St Simeon on his pillar may have been a bit queer, but he was doing it for a person, not for the sake of re-absorption into universal nothingness", she observes (39).

The affirmation of the value of friendship is one of the most striking characteristics of Gwen Harwood's poetry. Poems dedicated or addressed to particular friends pay tribute to the qualities of the person and the unique nature of each human relationship. In 1980, Gwen Harwood wrote:

> My life is linked together by very long friendships. It is good in your sixtieth year to have friends who love you still in spite of your faults and shortcomings . . . I would discard last those poems dedicated to friends. (*Southerly,* No. 3, 1980)

Supreme in this chain of friendship is that with Thomas Riddell. In one sense, all her poems are dedicated to him through the dedications of her volumes of poetry. In addition, some poems are particularly addressed to him. The fine poems "Winter Quarters" and "At Mornington", written in the early seventies, pay tribute to his lifelong affection and his power to liberate in her "the pulse of song". They are "friends long enough to show/the heart's true gentleness". The letters in this volume trace the first year of this friendship.

Alison Hoddinott

BLESSED CITY

(1)   Crimes Street,
                                                Wednesday.
                                                [January]

My dear Tony,

It is nearly five years since I visited Vaucluse House,[1] which I did
in the company of Mamma Agnes whose voice drowned that of
the guide during the whole pilgrimage. Your letter brought it all
back to me, and I think it may be xaid that my notice-collecting
days began then in earnest. (You will notice that my typing is far
from perfect; I can7t be bothered breaking down my speed for
a few paltry spaces and gadgets.) I remember being dragged back
from a spinet which I wanted to play—in fact my general
impression is of ropes twisting and running round everything like
the wool of Priscilla's sampler. There was a marvellous bath in
the Roman style which was (at that time, perhaps they have
cleaned it) coated in about three layers of cementy-looking dirt,
and was full of rubbish. There was also an old man in the party
who leant on his stick and regarded various objects with tears in
his eyes, and said from time to time "Oh God. Ooooooh
Gooooood."

   Let me say, if I have not said so before, that you are a Great
and Good Man. In fact, you eclipse all history-book greatness.
I don't know what they would have done to you if they had caught
you stealing the notice.[2] As it is, I'm afraid some horrible doom
may follow you, and all those who have the notice in their
possession. Or perhaps it will have its effect on me, and you will
find me in the evenings embroidering "God is Love" on Agnes's
bright red shawl.

[1]Vaucluse House, in Sydney.
[2]The notice: "Please keep moving, others wish to see"—a handpainted notice Tony
stole for me from Vaucluse House. (GH)

Poor Peter[3] has had dengue, and is going down to the clergy Summer School at Southport covered in a puce rash which he will give to all the clergy of the diocese. The last time he was sick he imagined that he was Pope Alexander VI, and had to cover up his traces before he died. If he had any delirious ravings this time he doesn't mention them. When I had dengue I imagined that the Pope (someone should go into the question of why the C. of E. becomes delirious about Popes) wanted me to distribute pamphlets about Anti-Christ, who was a Chinaman. But I told you about that.

A number of unexpected hook-ups have taken place over Brisbane telephones during the days since you left.

A University Professor and a Beauty Shop.
The A.B.C. and Jenyn's Corsets.

(This marvellous dialogue had to be intercepted at an early stage.)

The town's leading undertakers, by a stroke of luck, in person.
A prominent society matron and the "Telegraph".

This was really funny, because the matron thought the Telegraph had rung up for news of her social activities during the past week, and the Telegraph thought she had rung up to give them the details, and tried to explain tactfully that they really hadn't room, whereupon she became most annoyed and wanted to know what they'd rung up for if they weren't going to print it.

Two branches of "Fresh Food and Ice".

(This was in Italian, or Greek, and I couldn't follow it, but it ended up with receiver slamming.)

Two Methodist clergymen, who became most unchristian.

The undertakers were too good to be true, and began, when they

---

[3] Peter Bennie came to All Saints from Melbourne, where he was a friend of Tony Riddell at school and at university. He introduced Tony and Gwen when Tony came to Brisbane at the end of 1942.

10

discovered who they were talking to, "and what can I do for you, Mr Cannon?" and because neither would come to the point they talked for nearly ten minutes about how good business was, and how they were kept "busy". And then when one of them ventured to say "Well, Mr Hislop?" or "Well, Mr Cannon?", the other would say "Well, ah, yes, well, er, . . ." until finally Cannon had the courage to say "And by the way, what can I do for you, seeing that you rang me up . . .". I really think that by this time they had forgotten who rang up, and Hislop said vaguely "but, er, I thought that you rang me". And then they both denied each other with gentle negatives, and tittered about there being "something wrong with the line" and "how funny".

As I always add a few hundred on to any orders that come through my hands, enormous piles of stationery and Forms A, B, C and D are arriving day by day. They come in huge packages from the stores, labelled "NOT FRAGILE". Of course nobody can remember anything about them, so they all pass the baby and the last man out calls the Office Boy and says "Norman, take those things to the store-room". Also a number of letters were sent in complaining that completely unintelligible correspondence had been received . . .

I really do envy you your visit to the breeding-ground of notices. Five years ago I was too immature to appreciate them fully, and somehow I've never gone back there when I've been in Sydney. Sydney Museum, by the way, contains the loveliest notice in the world, framed.

LADIES' AND GENTLEMEN'S LAVATORIES ARE ON GROUND FLOOR, NEAR SKELETON GALLERY.

. . . Agens and Joe are going to Noosa for a short holiday at the end of the month. When Dad and I are alone, we usually dine on porterhouse steaks and beer, and pray hard for bottle-men to come round in the morning before Agnes gets back, because she is sure to ask in her well-known style: "And where did all these bottles come from?"

I rather like looking after the house, as long as nobody lets father into the kitchen. He uses six plates where a normal person uses one, and always sweeps the pea-pods behind the kitchen door. His behaviour in a kitchen is erratic to the point of madness. Our washerwoman told us that when he was left alone he used up the whole dinner service until no plates were left, and then washed up everything in the bath. I can remember how annoyed she used to be on Saturday afternoons to find his horrible little Flossie, a pom, sitting in the wash-basin in the bathroom. Papa would often start to wash her and then forget, and the poor woman (who came on Saturdays to clean up) would find a dog sitting in the basin smothered in soap. I get on extremely well with my father when the others are away. It is then that his greatness becomes apparent.

The nights are very lovely here now. I went down to the river after tea last night just before sunset, and found the water with its coat on. One night I must bring you home by the river — it's rather beautiful, and the darkness hides the ugliness of the banks which the City Council uses as rubbish dumps. One council fills the bank in, and the next one cuts it away again. We don't deserve a river.

Up in north Queensland there's a little seaside place called Yeppoon, with a small steep hill just beside the town. If you climb the hill you can lie in the long grass on the top and look down on the flat beach. At sunset, if the sand is wet, every cloud and colour of the sky is reflected there and the colour stretches right over the sea to the islands, which seem to stand quite out of the water and float in air. And on the other side of the hill the beach stretches back for miles, curving round until it is lost in the sea.

Gwen

(2)

Crimes Street
Thursday.
[7 January]

Dear Tony,

The bright young fellow who fixed the ice-water machine was none other than Norman, the office-boy, a perfect specimen of Public Servant embryo, or rather, miniature, since all the features are perfectly developed. He always wears braces, and puts on his hat and coat when he goes out to post a letter or buy a meat pie for Crowle's lunch. In order to keep himself occupied he goes out and posts one letter at a time, and sits in the lunch-room in between times eating hunks of dreadful cake, while the office girls titter around him experimenting hideously with sixpenny lipsticks.

As for myself, who knows? I think that my decline has set in, and my fall (which took place in the metaphysical order long ago) is dreadfully near. While I carved away the box the great men would come and stand near me, and look on. Nobody said anything. When half the side of the box was gone, I was sent for, I mean Sent For. Battersby said, "Well, er, Miss Foster, perhaps we could find another job for you. You see, we're rather short-staffed at present, and naturally we haven't as many people to do the work. So we thought . . . " The result was that I was put down at the end of the office outside Battersby's quarters with a desk in front of me, a counter by the side of me, and the telephone at the back of me. All these change their positions relatively because I have a swivel-chair, quite professionally publicservantish. I have enormous resources under my control, and sway the lives of a great many people. Those who are lucky enough to get past the army swarming round the entrance counter are sent to me. It takes them a long time to reach me, because they have to travel by a side corridor, and wander into the Electoral Office. When they get in there nobody takes the slightest notice of them for about ½ an hour. When I get familiar with the telephone I am going to hook up sets of people and listen in—

13

say, Archbishop Wand and the Proprietress of Mullhollands.[1] Perhaps you have some suggestions. In my present position I have to interview about 3 persons per week and the phone hardly ever rings, except when the P.S.'s make calls. I always check up on the numbers, and today's list is

3 calls to wives
2 calls to women unknown
Wintergarden Theatre
Sam Butler's Hotel
Truth Newspaper

. . . I have bought a lovely German reader (quite easy) with pictures, and when I am tired of German I look out of the lavatory window and watch the traffic in Adelaide Street—the foreshortened view is most entertaining.

Your letter was really delightful. I haven't read *Maurice Guest,* but at present I am reading a book of stories by H.H.R. I tried to get *The Fortunes of Richard Mahony,* but could only find the sequel *The End of a Childhood,* and some stories. They are most interesting; some of them have an air of savagery that women don't often express in writing. There are some sketches of young girls amazingly well done, though perhaps they mightn't mean as much to a man reading them.

I also picked up a copy (printed in Holland) of Joyce's *The Mime of Mick, Nick and the Maggies.* (Part of *Finnegan's Wake.*) The cover says ". . . the poet presents in nuce his vision of the childhood of mankind." That may be so. Parts of it are most amusing, but the general theme is not apparent.

He would fire off his farced epistol to the hibruws.
No more turdenskaulds! Free leaves for ebribadies!

[1]Mulhollands: Drinking place of intellectuals, students, musos—a seedy pub in Queen Street at the Victoria Bridge end. A piano-accordionist played there; he'd play requests for a silver coin. (GH)

All tinsammon in the yord! With harm and aches till
Farther alters . . .

I gave it to Agnes, who read it right through, and elucidated
it for me. She read "Monsaigneur Rabbinsohn Crucis", and yelled
out in true uncontrollable Agnesian manner "Gwen! Gwen! Gwen!
Here's Robinson Crusoe." She was stumped by "Lukkedoeren-
dunandurraskewdylooshoofermoyportertooryzooysphalnabortan-
sakroidverjkapakkapak", but promises a reading "as soon as I
can find where the accents fall". I don't know whether you are
one of the people who can read *Finnegan's Wake*. I met a madman
in Kings Cross who claimed to have read it constantly for a year.
For mayself (Good God, I'm becoming mahd 2) I can only say
with Joyce

if Lubbernabohore laid his harker to the ribber he would not hear
a flip flap in all Finnyland. Witchman, watch of your night?

It is unkind of you to refer to those occasions when my
performance in the Wolf[2] lapsed a little . . . Somehow I just

---

[2]"The Wolf": this song is mentioned frequently in the letters. The words are by John
O'Keefe and the music is by Shield. It is included in Boosey and Hawkes: *Baritone
Songs*, Vol. 1.

At the peaceful midnight hour
Ev'ry sense and ev'ry pow'r
Fettered lies in downy sleep
Then our careful watch we keep
While the wolf in nightly prowl
Bays the moon with hideous howl.

Gates are barred a vain resistance
Females shriek but no assistance
Silence, silence or you meet your fate
Your keys, your jewels, cash and plate
Locks, bolts and bars soon fly asunder
Then to rifle, rob and plunder.

haven't the heart to practise the Shell[3] without you though I realise its worth is independent of either of us. The Honourable Mrs Norton appears in the Nuttall Enclycopaedia between Northwich (town in Cheshire, Salt Springs) and Norway (kingdom of north Europe).

> NORTON Mrs., English novelist and poet, nee Sheridan, grand-daughter of Sheridan, authoress of *Lost and Saved*, etc., described by Lockhart as "the Byron of poetesses". 1808–1877.

I then looked up Lockhart:

> LOCKHART, John Gibson, man of letters, born in Cambusnethan; bred for the Scottish bar and practised at it.

After that I began looking at Logarithm, Lockout, Loki, Long Tom Coffin etc. Once I start looking up something in an encyclopaedia I finish up with Zwingli and Zymotic diseases.

---

[3]"The Murmur of the Shell", a Victorian song; words and music by Mrs Caroline Norton.

A sailor left his native land,
  A simple gift he gave,
A sea-shell gathered by his hand
  From out the rippling wave.
"Oh, love by this remember me,
  "Far inland must thou dwell,
"But thou shalt hear the sounding sea
  "In the murmur of the shell."

Ah! woe is me, with tattered sail
  The ship is wildly tossed,
A drowning cry is on the gale,
  They sink and all are lost!
While happy yet, untouched by fear,
  Repeating his farewell,
Poor Mary smiles, and loves to hear,
  The murmur of the shell.

The tidings wrecked her simple brain,
  And smiling still she goes,
A mad girl, reckless of her pain,
  Unconscious of her woes;
But when they ring the village chimes,
  That tolled her lover's knell,
She sighs, and says she hears at times
  The murmur of the shell.

Thanks for interring me decently (and cheaply). Your epitaph was wonderful, especially the masterly rhyme of breath/G.N.F. The In Memoriam column people have had a fit of Angels recently:

Just one year, little darling,
Since God called you away.
But we know you are happy Jimmy
With the Angels in the sky.

Released from sorrow sin and pain
And freed from every care;
By Angels' hands to heaven conveyed
To rest forever there.

The remembrances of sorrowing relatives run in cycles. Last week it was "Sad and sudden was the call". Already it is changing to "Safe in the arms of Jesus". Here's one for you.

God has took our dearest Tony
  Though his real name was Tom.[4]
And the face that once we used to see
  The Angels look upon.
A better ~~mother~~ person never lived
  To hear him sing was bliss,
But now he sings The Wolf on high
  In a better world than this.

Inserted by his loving mother, father, brother, sister, uncles, aunts, Flossie, Gretchen, Hippo[5] and Gwen.

  or Passers-by from near and far
      Say a prayer for T.F.R.
      God heard The Wolf and thought it best
      To grant dear Tony eternal rest.

[4]Thomas Riddell, known to his friends as Tony.

[5]Flossie was the Fosters' recently deceased dog. Gretchen was a dachshund and the family dog in 1943. Hippo was the nickname given to Gwen's brother Joe by his scouting friends.

17

. . . It is raining again. I went to Mass early yesterday morning because it was the feast of the Epiphany; it was raining so hard that the rain rose in a mist from the roofs and leaves floated in the pools on the roadway. The trees and the sky and even the air seemed grey, and then I went into the church, and found it in darkness except for the crib, which was lit up and shining away there with the three kings kneeling down and little robins in the straw. How lovely it was! It made me very happy.

I can't tell you how much I love things that shine like that. When I am in Sydney I go to the aquarium at Taronga Park, and spend hours looking at the coloured fishes. You'd think that they had lamps inside them, they are so bright.

Two years ago at this time I was in Melbourne.[6] I remember walking over to St Peter's through the Fitzroy gardens. There are some splendid gargoyles at the east end of St Patrick's. I used to walk by very often just to look at them.

With my love,
Gwen.

(3)

Sunday Evening,
Crimes Street.
[10 January]

My dear Tony,

The most excellent sun is shining again in Brisbane and all the trees and plants are standing quietly, as if they were glad to feel sunshine again.

The rain has beautified the air-raid shelter (or rather the raised mound above it) with thistles, cobblers' pegs, chickweed, and many other weeds unknown by name to me.

Today has been hot with a kind of still, soaking heat, so that the perfume of flowers seems to stand still in the air around them. I feel very lazy — it's too hot to sleep, so I've been walking round the garden with bare feet, feeling the grass. During a long and commonplace sermon this morning I read *Maurice Guest,* which I got last week. Perhaps it was reading about Germany, anyway,

[6] In January 1941, GF was staying in a guesthouse in Melbourne near Fitzroy Gardens.

all day long I've had a longing for fir trees. All I've got is a picture of one, which I've propped up in front of me. As a rule I hate sermons, though I know some people who go to church simply for the sake of the sermon. There is an old lady at All Saints who always walks out straight after the sermon. Sometimes when I really can't be bothered I go out and stroll round under the trees on the terrace, but usually I read a book. You see, if I go for a walk, there is always the danger of the preacher stopping suddenly, and then someone has to run out and bring me back for the hymn which the C. of E. thinks must follow the sermon; if I've been reading, sometimes it takes me several minutes to get back to the situation, and I start off the hymn in a dazed way with strange harmonies.

I don't know why it is, but a place like All Saints seems to gather around it an appalling number of madwomen, or fanatically one-sided women. I had a dust-up with one some time ago because she had the fiendish idea that I ought to help her clean the church brass on Saturday afternoons (this was a couple of years ago) as (in her opinion) I "did nothing" all the week. I explained reasonably that on Saturday afternoons I gave myself up to heathen practices entirely, generally to beer-drinking with a bunch of Germans chez Mullhollands. This lopsided creature has regarded me as one of the handmaidens of Satan ever since, and accuses me of ill-treating animals (because I turned out a dreadful cat which was going to have kittens, or looked as if it were, on somebody's cassock in the vestry) . . . These women can always quote large chunks of scripture at you. They have me there, because I can't, except for the Psalms out of the Breviary offices we had at the Convent. (I once knew a violent communist woman, the sort that wear clog-like boots and shaggy jerseys and short-cut hair and goggles, who read a chapter from one of the Gospels every night before retiring, and yet professed Atheism. When I asked her about it, she said "Well, it does no harm!".) Peter was much more effective in dealing with these people than I was, and am . . . A lot of people blame All Saints for the collection of madwomen, but I don't think that's right, I think they go there, because I've seen numbers of them arrive, and stay put. They're all right until they get on the subject of religion and then they gibber. I prefer the "Flip-flaps of Finnyland". By the way, the Public Servants call me "Bishop Foster", I can't imagine why. I discovered this by listening to a phone conversation. There is nothing episcopal about my air or speech.

This is a quiet house, by itself. Sometimes I am surprised at its quietness. It may be the trees around, perhaps. It's a very old house (for this part of the world) and last year it began to sag on one side, so that balls on the billiard table would run to one side. They had to move out some of the posts and jack it up and put new ones in. I was sick at the time, and every now and then the place would heave slightly. Peter came out to see me, and we tried to play records, but when the house moved the pick-up arm would be thrown to the side.

It's exactly a year today since I left the Convent[1] (or rather, walked out of the convent). Agnes, who brought a taxi for me, came dressed like an arch-duchess, bosom and all, and sailed up the steps of the convent to show her triumph. (She took all the credit for my departure.) Agnes had never been in a convent before, so it was perhaps not surprising that she mistook the lowest novice for the Mother Superior, and began making a speech to her. Of course, nobody could get a word in, so Agnes departed without the mistake being put right.

Did Peter tell you about my "Reminiscences"? Whenever I walk out of anything, they ask me what I'm going to do next, and I say, "I'm going to write my Reminiscences." But they never get written, and so of any unwritten but notorious scandal they say "It's in Gwen's Reminiscences" . . .

. . . Well, Tony, it's time for me to depart in my capacity as a member of the organ-playing public. I love *Maurice Guest*, and shall take it with me.

Love from
Gwen.

[1]From August 1941 to January 1942, GF was a novice in a Franciscan convent in Toowong.

(4)   Monday morning,
                                        As from Crimes St.,
                                                    [January]
(Typed on official War Damage Commission notepaper.)
Dear Tony,

I hope this paper doesn't fall into the wrong hands before you get it, but if it does you can always come to see your little musical companion in gaol, or wherever they put public servants who abuse the King's notepaper – perhaps there is a Commonwealth reformatory somewhere.

My friend the most excellent sun is obscured by a dirty clogging mist that is all over and through the city, even inside rooms. It makes even the young girls, who are in freshly ironed dresses for Monday, look soiled and limp. It shows up the filthy and greasy stains on the pavements, and seems to hang dust in the air. I've never seen Brisbane look so drab and dirty. At night, if you know where to walk, Brisbane can be lovely, but this morning it's repulsive. Two years ago I was in Melbourne, and I can remember the freshness of the parks in the early morning, and the bells ringing for Mass, and the frogs croaking away in the little ponds. I wish I were there again. When I was in Melbourne I used to write a great deal. My room looked out on to a little inner courtyard, and over this to a big hospital, where I could see the nuns walking to and fro on the veranda. I was writing a play called *The Sparks Fly Upwards*, full of men with beards and suicidal photographers, and very Dostoievskian. In the evenings I used to sit in the Fitzroy gardens until it was quite late, and I could see the spire of S. Patrick's shining over the trees. How lovely it was!

Old Mr Coar (who swallowed the kookaburra),[1] brings us copies of the Rockhampton Bulletin. I was disappointed to find that it contains no In Memoriam notices, though the death-rate

[1]My mother put silver tokens in the Christmas pudding so that everyone got a piece of silver. She put them in the portions in the kitchen. Mr Coar bolted his down and said, "I didn't get one." My mother said afterwards, "He did. I gave him the kookaburra." (GH)

21

in Rockhampton is enormous. I think somebody suggested that a great many people are dead in Rockhampton but still walking around. When I was there the highlight of the city's entertainments was a troupe of Performing Goats, which my great-aunt prophesied would be a failure. They were . . .

I love *Maurice Guest*, and stayed up reading it till quite late last night. I have had always a longing for Germany that amounts sometimes almost to homesickness. When I was a little child I had an old book of *Grimm's Fairy Tales*, and I used to sit under the orange trees in our orchard and read about the Black Forest and the fir trees and snow (which I have never seen). All these things are bound up with the moving basses of Bach and Lubeck and Pachelbel. Perhaps some day I shall see the Black Forest, and Strasburg:

O Strasburg, O Strasburg
    Du wunderschone Stadt
Darinnen liegt begraben
    So mannicher Soldat.

The Grimm used to have all the verses printed in Gothic letters which I found strange and difficult to read, so I learnt them by heart from my grandmother's reading, and used to sit, fascinated, for hours. That, and a translation of the *Iliad,* were the only books I had for a long time, and I used to like visiting old Mr Coar, who had some beautifully illustrated copies of Goethe's *Faust* and Shakespeare.

Somehow it has managed to be lunch-time, so I'll go out and post this.

With love from
Gwen.

(5)

14 Crimes Street,
AUCHENFLOWER.
St Valentine's Day.
[14 February]

My dear Tony,

. . . Agens[1] arrived yesterday morning and immediately began talking. She had plenty of material and continued for several hours. Both she and Joe are dark brown and full of energy.

Eliza[2] was most depressing when I consulted her about your journey.

(1) Ye braid the dank weed in his hair,
   And deck him with jewels pure and rare;
   Ye keep the record of where and when
   The brave ship sunk with her braver men.

(2) She dances out to the ding-dong tune,
   She laughs with raving glee;
   And Death endeth the dream in her requiem scream,
   'Tis a wild night at sea.

(3) opened at "Song of the Dying old Man to his Young Wife."
   But that generally happens, as the pages are loose there.

I attach no importance whatever (as Eliza herself would say) to the "Song of the D.O.M. to his Y.W." because the book falls

---

[1]Agens: GF's mother Agnes Foster, née Jaggard. The spelling Agens was originally a typographical error, which Tony suggested was appropriate because of the Latin meaning "busy", "active". The spelling stuck. See (1).

[2]Eliza: Eliza Cook (1818–89), Victorian poet. In her youth her writings were published in periodicals and attracted a great deal of notice. She conducted *Eliza Cook's Journal*, a weekly periodical, 1849–54. Her complete collected poems were published in 1870. The most popular of these was "The Old Arm-chair" which begins:

I love it, I love, and who shall dare
To chide me for loving that old Arm-chair?
I've treasured it long as a sainted prize;
I've bedewed it with tears and embalmed it with sighs.

GF and TR were in the habit of consulting this oracle for advice on important occasions by opening the pages of the collected works at random. Extract (1) is from "The Waters". Extract (2) is the final stanza of " 'Tis a wild night at sea".

23

open there naturally. I shall be relieved to hear from you and learn that I don't have to dance to a ding-dong tune (the Boogie-Woogie Organist?) and I swear that if Eliza proves false this time I shall abandon her as a Sybil.

Last Monday when I arrived at the W.D.C. I found people rushing around with sheaves of papers, dropping cards on the floor and picking them up, unloading boxes of final notices and Form As and generally going on quite madly at a speed not seen before (by me). I watched this for some time from my little corner and presently all was made clear. The Secretary of the W.D.C. was flying up from Sydney to visit us, and was expected "any day". The staff received orders (verbal) that they were to look "intelligent and industrious" and that everyone had to have a job and be found doing it. Well, when jobs were being handed out it was soon found that there weren't enough to go round.

Word "came through" that the great man was to be expected on Wednesday morning, and on that morning the girl was sent out to buy six penneth of scones . . . When the poor little thing came back with six pikelets (she couldn't buy scones) it was found that we had no suitable plate to put them on for the celebrity's morning tea, so she had to go out again and buy a cheap but good plate at Penney's. After all this, he didn't arrive. As soon as I learnt that he wasn't going to arrive until the afternoon I went into the kitchen to look for the pikelets, but they had been locked up in a cupboard of which I have not the key. Very sad . . .

. . . You may have noticed that I often address inanimate objects aloud. The other day one of the plugs on the phone was out of order, and I spoke to it frequently. Then I put a call through to a certain Robert Mafeking Reed (don't say "Liar", it's true) and forgot to push back the switch which enables the telephonist's voice to be heard by the people talking to each other. I said "What's bitten you!" (to the plug) "Why can't you behave like a normal plug?" This went right into the ear of Robert Mafeking, and proved so successful an accident that I have repeated it (varied, of course) many times — for example, I say something outrageous in a strident voice and then ask softly, "Are you getting through?"

It was interesting to note the bearing of everyone towards the "Secretary", though of course none of this is new to you. The accountant, for instance, used to wait for a nod of recognition from the great man when he saw him coming up the office, but generally he got a properly admiring smile ready about 20 seconds too soon, so that it had a cracked appearance by the time the S. was in range! Or else he would try to time it so that his smile coincided with the S.'s approach, and look up from his papers a moment too late, smiling at the place where the S. had been just before.

I read another book by H. H. Richardson called *The Getting of Wisdom*. It is a study of a young girl's life at school and certainly captures all the appalling atmosphere of a girls' school. I thought it was written before *Maurice Guest*, but it was written later. Richardson is extremely good in her studies of girls and women and once I start reading one of her books I find it very hard to put it down.

Last Friday after sunset there was a most unearthly light — the kind of light that comes only after there has been a storm leaving clouds in the sky. The clouds were of quite unimaginable colours and the light seemed to fill the air with almost tangible colour; it turned the grass and trees a strange green and took away the sense of distance, so that all the houses around us looked like the flat painted backcloth of a stage; the people in the street looked like actors walking to and fro and everything was quite unreal. It made me terribly unhappy because I was alone, and I wanted most of all to have someone there who would say, "Look at the strange light." It was like a dream.

When Joe and I were very young we were fascinated by the light on Sundays, which we both agreed was quite different from the light on other days. It seemed to us to be whiter. I know that Joe has not forgotten this even now, because not long ago he said, "You know, when I was little I thought the light on Sundays was funny."

I hope you are well and happy.

With my love,
Gwen.

(6)

My dear Tony,

<u>HISTORIC MANGO TREE DESTROYED.</u>

Last Saturday in a, for this time of the year, cold drizzling rain,
an historic tree crashed to the ground.

DRAMATIS PERSONAE: Joe (Hippo) Foster, chief axeman.

Agens (Air-raid) Foster.

Bishop Foster, representing the War Damage
Commission.

Beneath the stately tree, in the shade of which generations of
Fosters have lived and died, there gathered a small, sad group,
and from the mouth of Agens there fell the fatal words: "The
damn tree's full of borers. It'll have to come out."

BISHOP FOSTER: What do borers look like?

AGENS: Get out of the way. All you do is talk.

BISHOP FOSTER: What do borers look like?

AGENS: Of course you know what borers look like.
You've seen them.

BISHOP FOSTER: I have not.

Some hours later, standing amongst the fallen branches, Hippo
Foster spoke a few words in his native tongue. He said: "Er(;;
jsbr jp foh yjr dyi,7/8 pih ypp/.2"

BISHOP FOSTER: I haven't seen any borers yet.

AGENS: Look, the tree's alive with them.

BISHOP FOSTER: I can't see any.

AGENS: You don't want to, that's what it is.

Eliza (Arm-chair) Cook, who was present, waved her bonnet
and began to recite:

ODE WRITTEN UPON HEARING THAT A MANGO TREE
HAD BEEN CUT DOWN.

I love it! I love it! It was to me
A home, as well as a mango tree.
My mother beneath its roots is laid,
I nursed my boy in its welcome shade.

Lo! under its boughs in the heat of day
The Poet-one sits and sings his lay,
And there on the grass, to a gipsy's tune
He dances at night by the light of the moon.[1]

They returned home tired but happy, and a good time was had by all.

The absence of the mango tree means that the neighbours have a much better chance of looking into our back windows, but the sun comes in while we are having tea in the evening, and that is delightful. Agens is already making plans for a lawn tennis court after the war, but Joe and I would sooner have a swimming pool for we both love swimming. We worked out the cost by arithmetic (at which neither of us is very good) and it seemed tremendous. And when we thought of the people who would want to come and swim in it we decided to abandon the scheme.

I have got a record of Kipnis singing "Der Wanderer", and "Qui Sdegno" from *The Magic Flute* on the other side (I can't remember the German), which is my favourite song.

Will you tell me which of these songs you sing or would like to sing. I think I could manage the accompaniments.

[1]Eliza Cook was accustomed to refer to herself as "the Poet-one". Her poem "The Dreamer" contains the stanza:

And thus, where the mallow
Was fringing the shallow;
The Poet-one sung (*sic*) to the summer-lit stream,
And then he grew dizzy
With watching how busy
The swallows were, chasing the gnats in the beam.

The poem "Type of the Poet-one", addressed to the "River, Sweet River!", contains variants of the refrain:

Type of the Poet-one! So let him be
Pure, simple, and strong, gentle River like thee.

27

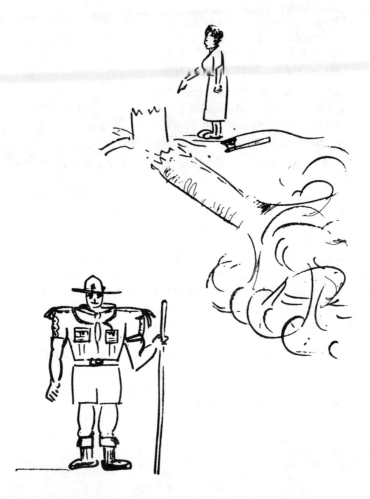

[Illustrations accompanying letter (6)]
Top: *Agens' declining years*
Agens is looking at the stump of the last tree left in Auchenflower

Bottom: *Hippo's declining years*
There is little to say: he has attained great muscular development at the expense of his brain and remains a simple Scoutmaster

Top: *Tony's declining years—blowing up schools*
Bottom: *Miss Gwen Foster's declining years*

"Why do the nations", "Che faro senza Eurydice", "Honour & Arms", "Arm, Arm, ye brave", or any out of the Handel (Randegger) book you have. If I don't do some work of some kind soon I shall become unhinged. I have lost all desire for learning. I recite what I can remember of "The Twelve Red-Bearded Dwarfs"[2] to people who pester me, and think how much better it is to be acquainted with them than with the works of M. Jacques Maritain. Probably I am suffering from several years' overdose of Maritain, and Nature is taking her course of reaction. Lately I have taken to drawing[3], but I am so unskilled (in spite of having been taught to draw plaster casts for many years) that the result is rarely what I hope for.

Tell me about any songs you have in mind and I will learn them. I do miss you in the evenings and repeated performances of "Rule Britannia" and "The Wolf" as solos don't entirely comfort me. Even Joe, who as a rule goes around singing "Daddy" or "In the Mood", sat on the back steps and practised the shriek in "Females shriek . . .". He said that he regarded you as a master of shrieks and envied your blood-curdling effect . . .

With my love,
Gwen.

(7)   As from 14 Crimes Street,
AUCHENFLOWER.
1st March. (Beware the Ides)

My dear Tony,

I haven't heard yet whether you are getting Arm-chair's friends to braid the sea-weed in your hair. I hope not. This is Monday. I have nothing at all to do, and before I go into the contemplative

[2]TR introduced GF to the comic writings of J. B. Morton who, under the pen-name of "Beachcomber", wrote the "By the Way" column in the *Daily Express* for forty years. Selections from his sketches were published in book form and thus reached a wider public. Some of the funniest of these concern the courtroom dramas of Mr Justice Cocklecarrot and the twelve red-bearded dwarfs who plague him. These dwarfs and the anarchy they create recur throughout the correspondence of GF and TR. Occasionally they invade the War Damage Commission with chaotic results. Their adventures have been editorially curtailed in this volume, but cannot be entirely omitted.

[3]See illustrations pp. 28-29.

trance peculiar to red-headed public servants on Mondays I shall write to you . . .

. . . The tree-cutting mania has bitten Agens, and the loquot (is that how you spell them?) tree outside the window of the dining-room has gone. When I got home from Mass yesterday there was only a stump. The back of the house looks horribly bare, and Agens will start taking out the camphorlaurels if nobody stops her. She gets terrible fits of cutting-down and tearing-out and nothing is safe. If I had a house I should surround it with trees and make a small forest in the grounds. When I was a child we had a small citrus orchard out at Mitchelton on the other side of the range. Now it is a fairly big suburb, but twenty years ago when we first went there we lived in the middle of flat fields with little gullies running down to a lovely creek bordered with yellow and blue flowering trees.

I shall never forget the heavy perfume of the orange and lemon trees in bloom, and the rows of mandarins and oranges laid out under the house. We used to pack some of the oranges in barrels of sand to keep them. But the place is quite changed now. The wonderful Brisbane City Council cut down all the trees from the bank of the creek and took the gravel from its banks. They put tons of gravel in the fields nearby and left it there for years. We left Mitchelton about sixteen years ago, and I haven't been there since then. There used to be Chinamen's gardens not far from us, and the Chinamen gave me wonderful ginger out of big jars and pretty little fans from China painted on silk. I remember that all our cats used to run away in the end and live with the Chinamen.

It was an unhappy day for me when I had to go to school. I would much rather have stayed under the orange trees and I'm sure it would have been much better for me in the long run. I'm sure you can't realise the dreariness of a Queensland State school. But enough of these reminuisances, as Peter used to call them.

Joe is going to build boat models now. He also has a scheme for making a huge scale model of the trench system on the Western front 1918, with British and German trenches, soldiers of all nations (I think you saw his model soldiers), sentry-boxes, crashed aeroplanes and "border incidents". (You will notice how fond I am of that phrase, but it seems to express certain situations better than any other.)

I was surprised to find out the other evening that neither Joe nor Agens has forgiven me for entering a convent two years ago. I really thought they had forgotten all about it, but during one of those family rows when everyone gets terribly personal and under no circumstances resorts to reason it all cropped up again. They can't see that it was a necessary thing for me to do. I knew I had to test my vocation and so there was only one thing to do. I didn't really want to leave my contemporaries (though I had a merry enough time at the convent, and some day I will tell you about it) and the pleasant house in Crimes St., but I had no intention of abandoning an essential experience for the sake of family peace. I learned a great deal more in the convent than most people imagine, including

How to make a cupboard from boxes.
How to eat porridge.
How to sweep fast and thoroughly.
How to darn black stockings over a milkbottle (quite useless to me now).
How to stop a wasp from starting a nest in the keyhole.
How to be silent for twenty hours a day.
How to saw wood.

Old Fr Eldershaw[1] (William Harry Frederick Newton) about whom I told you, and whose copy of *An American Tragedy* you borrowed from Peter, is dead. He died in Bundaberg last week . . . I'm terribly sorry about Fr E. He used to take me to the Royal National Show and we'd see Fire-eating Pygmies, Pin-headed Chinamen, Spider-women, Giant Drummers, Biggest Negroes in the World, Hypnotists, Dare-devil Riders of the Globe of Death, Largest Dogs in the World and Ladies Sawn in Half. Once Fr E. poked at the Lady in the Sword Cabinet with his walking-stick,

---

[1]Old Fr Eldershaw: see memoir, *Southerly*, No. 4, 1986.

and the showman got very angry and shouted at him. (Quite useless, because he was stone deaf.) One night we were having dinner in town, and carrying on a long conversation on bits of paper. When the town hall struck eight I remarked aloud to myself "Eight o'clock", and a woman sitting at the next table said "Excuse me, I'm so glad, I thought you were a poor dumb girl!" Another time we were sitting in the grandstand waiting for the results of a trotting race. In the silence that preceded the judge's announcement Fr E. remarked in a most loud and penetrating voice "I say, why don't you wait till the motor trade revives and marry Mr Evers?" (Harold's father owns a motor business.) This amused everyone within earshot immensely.

Well, Thomas Frederick, I'll be glad to hear from you.

With my love,
Gwen.

(8)   14 Crimes Street,
Auchenflower.
1st March.

My dear Tony,
Only this morning I sent off a reminiscent sort of letter to you, and was delighted to find your letter in the box this evening. I'm glad to know that you are safe and have lived through a journey with a juke-box without being mentally unhinged. Probably this note will arrive before my other letter which went by ordinary post anyway. I'll answer your most welcome letter tomorrow in the W.D.C.'s time. When I learnt that you were safe I ran and jumped on "Arm-chair" Cook (in her office of Seer) and have had her formally excommunicated. I'm glad to know that the authorities recognise "Crimes Street".

With my love,
Gwen.

(9)   As from Crimes Street,
                                                           2nd March.
Thomas F. Riddell, Doctor Signorum,
Canonised 1943.
<u>The Heavenly Jerusalem.</u>
Dear Sir, St.,
<u>RE YOURS REF. NO. Z2p/1/4/(b)</u> as far as we can decipher it.
We beg to advise you of another St. in the Kalendar who may
possibly have escaped your celestial notice.

GWENDOLINE, Bd. Patron of telephonists. Mart. 1943. While
she was connecting an Archbishop to his dustman her enemies
electrocuted her and stowed her body in a filing cabinet, where
it was miraculously preserved. Gwendolina.

I do envy you your journey up the coast. I know how lovely
it must be, though I haven't seen it from a ship. I have been to
Sydney by ship and was enchanted with the strange diaphanous
green of the water breaking away, veined with white like marble,
when it became calm again. The evening star is very bright at sea.

I knew that you wanted to be an actor, but I don't know very
much about you at all, really, in some ways. You are a most
mysterious person. Your saying that I will probably find you
changed makes me think of Kirillov in *The Possessed,* who said
that "there are some things a man can't live through and not be
changed. Even if it were only a moment of time . . ." My memory
fails here, but Kirillov saw Shatov experience this when Shatov's
wife returned to him and their child was born. *The Possessed* is
the most powerful of all Dostoievsky's books, I think, and
certainly the most "Diabolical". Shatov and Kirillov are most
lovely characters, in their way, and though Kirillov's lonely
suffering and his suicide were necessary it seems to me that
Shatov's death was not. Kirillov said that there were moments
quite above ordinary joy or happiness which outweighed all the
rest of man's life, and gave it significance, and man had either
to refuse them or suffer them and be changed. The most
wonderful scene in the whole book is the reunion of Shatov and
his wife, and his joy when he sees the little baby.

I found that when I was in the convent and the outside world dropped away, so to speak, a lot of things that seemed to be important dissolved and vanished and didn't matter at all. Six months of silence and having literally nothing, not even a piece of soap, of one's own, showed me that the whole meaning of life is lost to most people who go rushing about madly trying all the time to do something or other instead of to be something. In a convent or a monastery, as you said yourself once, time has a different meaning. I think John Donne said something like this: "days, weeks, hours, these are the rags of time."

I was delighted with your description of the shooting episode—it sounds rather like one of those serials they show on Thursdays or Saturday afternoons at suburban theatres. As for the "juke-box", you were fortunate to escape with something less than boogie-woogie. I have heard "Blow, blow", and "It was a lover and his lass". I was listening idly to the radio with half an ear one Saturday afternoon, and heard some dreadful female . . . pouring forth words that sounded familiar. I remarked to Joe "I say, I thought she was singing 'Blow, blow thou winter wind!' " "She was," replied Joe. Wait till they get on to "Come unto these yellow sands", and "Fear no more". When Shakespeare is exhausted they will probably attack Nashe and Beaumont & Fletcher. Anything may happen. But I should be really interested to hear what the authors of "Scrub me Mamma with a boogie beat" and "Potato Pete" could do with Alfred, Lord Tennyson . . .

. . . "Literary Lapses"[1] is delightful. I discovered a copy in the school Library when I was in Sixth form, and promptly removed it to my own desk . . . I'll send you *I, Claudius* when I remember to tie it up for posting—probably tomorrow. Is there anything you would like me to send you? I'll be glad to do so.

Joe has decided to become (at some future date) a swing pianist, and last night he began learning his major scales again in readiness. "Working up his technique", I believe it's called. Joe in his childhood was a sort of infant prodigy, and played a prelude

[1] *Literary Lapses* by Stephen Leacock.

35

and fugue by Bach at the age of nine, dressed up in a horrid little "ranger suit" (do you know what I mean? They have buttonholes under the belt, and the shirt has buttons that go into them) and a bow tie. This odious boy appeared at students' recitals and bowed in a superior manner to the audience. He abandoned the piano entirely for the sake of drumming, and later appeared marching through the streets with a drum half his own size in the rear of the Brisbane Citizens' Band on public holidays. Did you see Stanley Laurel's masterly style of marching in "Bonnie Scotland"? The shortness and fatness of Joe in his childhood forced him to march in a similar manner. His technique appears to have disappeared, so his appearance as a swing pianist will be at least a few years from now, thank goodness. Joe was so fat at the age of 12 or 13 that people used to laugh at him, except my father, who takes a secret joy in being fat, I think. I do love my father, and it is one of the sad things in my life that for certain inexplicable reasons we have been rather remote from each other. I don't know why it has been so. Perhaps it was my fault as a child. I feel very sorry for him sometimes when Agens tries "to make him see sense", but I can't help him much when he falls into her clutches, because we can never quite reach one another. He has the most amazing generosity, and is always happy when he is giving things away as fast as he can, or buying things for us. Unfortunately he is always being taken in by people, and this makes Agens furious, but I love him all the more for it because it never makes him bitter or savage. I think the fact that he is an Englishman makes it harder for me to get close to him, but we are always happy when we are "keeping the house going" together by ourselves. I admire the English a great deal, but they have some funny ways . . .

Well, St Thomasius, I'll write again soon. I'm going out to post this now.

With my love,
Gwen.

(10)

The Heavenly Mansions,
Crimes Street,
AUCHENFLOWER.
[5 March]

My dear Tony,

Agens' fit of tree-cutting has spent itself, thank God, and she is devoting herself to the Propagation of the Manufacture of String Shopping Bags, Opportunity Stall, to be sold on. This morning (Friday) I left her explaining to the washerwoman that there were subtle differences between a brown string bag (5/6) and a white string bag (6/-) . . .

Peter wrote to me this week, and has returned to the rural simplicity of Imbil[1] with great joy. I suspect, however, that he is going to break out in Thomism shortly as he has commissioned me to rescue Maritain's *Degrees of Knowledge* from the scholastic Harold. He remarked that as he couldn't be definite in his political views he always votes U.A.P. so that things will remain static until he makes up his mind. I have never had occasion to vote although I was twenty-one in 1941. In my childhood I remember my grandmother warning me against the Labour Party, who were dirty, ill-clothed, ill-fed, uneducated and treacherous (according to granny) . . . [2]

With my love,
Gwen.

[1] Peter Bennie, at this time, had moved from All Saints' in Brisbane to a ministry at Imbil in rural Queensland.

[2] The rest of this letter is a parody in dramatic form of one of the cases of Mr Justice Cocklecarrot in which a "mad poet-one", Eliza Cook, is charged with having tried to smother one of the red-bearded dwarfs in an arm-chair. At the end, the prisoner is acquitted and discharged and exults in verse:

What a glorious thing, What a glorious thing!
At last I'm free, I can dance and sing,
The poet-one laughs, to be set free.
Was ever a poet as happy as me?

37

(11)

As From Mansions of the Blest.
Crimes Street.
Monday, March 8th.

Dear Tony,

It will be Ash Wednesday on Wednesday, the beginning of Lent. On Wednesdays in Lent I play for the Stations of the Cross in the evening, so I escape Old Coar, the Demon 500 Player. He trades on his deafness, and pretends he doesn't know what's trumps, and starts gathering up tricks in a heap so that it's quite impossible to sort them all out again — or else he saves up all his trumps till the end and this sort of conversation goes on:

FATHER FOSTER:	Mr Coar, you played a trump.
OLD COAR:	Yes, plenty of trumps, had a hand full of 'em.
FATHER FOSTER:	But you didn't play trumps at the beginning!
OLD COAR:	Oh yes, dreadful hand, God alone knows how I did it.
AGENS (Bellowing):	SPADES ARE TRUMPS, Mr Coar.
OLD COAR:	Oh yes, plenty of spades.
AGENS (Frantically):	NO, SPADES ARE TRUMPS.
OLD COAR:	Clubs?
AGENS & FR FOSTER:	S P A D E S.
OLD COAR:	Oh, hearts?

At this stage everybody sinks back and gives up.

Joe and I both love Old Coar, for when he lived out near us at Mitchelton he used to take us for long walks, carrying Joe, and when he moved to Auchenflower we used to spend some of our holidays with him. He would take us up the Taylor range and boil the billy, which we thought was wonderful. Once when he was cutting a stick for himself he bent down a young sapling, and Joe and I held the end with him. Mr Coar and I let go together and Joe sailed up into the air on the end of the tree, and Joe began to howl with that particular fierceness peculiar to small children. Joe had a frightening way of crying that he knew how to turn on and off at will. I was once locked in a small room with him for several hours and had the full benefit of it. We were playing

38

in the room near our dining room where Joe's drums and the typewriter stay, and quite accidentally locked ourselves in. It was the sort of lock that locks itself from the inside if you turn the key a bit too far, and can then only be opened from the other side. After about half an hour of imprisonment Joe began to get alarmed, because Agens was out and nobody was likely to come home for some time. I wasn't strong enough to push up the window, and anyway there was a huge rosebush outside that would have made exit painful. Joe turned on his frightening wail and kept it up, saying between wails "We're locked in. We're locked in. We're locked in" or "Let's break the window, let's break the window." Fortunately a chance visitor arrived halfway through the afternoon and was amazed to hear horrible screams coming from the back of the house. When she came within conversational range I explained what had happened and threw the key through the fanlight to her.

The Stations of the Cross is a most moving devotion, and the part I like best is the singing of the Stabat Mater as the procession moves from one Station to another. Of course it has to be conducted properly, without the senseless gabbling that seems to be dear to our Roman friends. The Stations in All Saints were done by Daphne Mayo, a Brisbane sculptress, and they are very well done, very simply modelled in blue white and gold for the haloes. (Some of the Stations in Roman churches are too hideous to mention.) . . .

Have you seen the Good Friday liturgy? It is the most moving thing, but we can't do it properly at All Saints because we have no singers. The Reproaches are sung by Harold (solo) and they recite Crux Fidelis instead of singing it, but even the absence of a proper choir can't destroy the beauty of the liturgy. I think I should like best of all, if I had a vocation to the religious life, to belong to an order that devoted itself entirely to the singing of the Liturgy, like the Benedictines of St Pierre de Solesmes. I feel more and more sorry as time goes on to see and hear the rubbish that people are content with. The monks of Solesmes sing beautifully because the interior spirit of the music is not lost to them: they are not a picked choir, everyone has to sing. There are no Benedictines (nuns, I mean) that I know of in Queensland. At our Franciscan convent in Toowong we did not sing the office as a whole, but only the office hymns, and because our numbers were so few we had to omit the night office and also Lauds. Perhaps one of these days the people here will wake up and stir themselves into life. Most people have the idea that music of the liturgy is like "In a Monastery Garden", by Ketelby, and probably their ideas of monasteries are not much different. It is very sad.

Last Saturday my prize soprano, the famous Ethel, sang at a wedding for which I played. She missed a top G, so calmly took a deep breath and had another crack at it! The congregation were slightly concerned, and did not seem happy during the rest of the song. Ethel's voice is not a restful one! My most delightful recollection of her is on a night when a "sacred concert" was given in All Saints church, and Ethel appeared dressed in a peach-coloured evening dress and *a green hat* and sang "With verdure clad", standing on a footstool in the back of the centre aisle.

Tell me when you are coming back to Brisbane; I'll be delighted to have the company once more of

THOMASIUS BD.   Little is known of this Saint, except that he is reported to have been accompanied everywhere by a savage wolf. The story that he came to the assistance of shrieking females is quite apocryphal.

With my love,
Gwen.

(12)   14 Grimy Street.
                                                    [15 March]
My dear Tony,
The fact that the authorities recognise Grimy Street shows that they have some knowledge of its nature. Joe and I were examining the children of Grimy Street yesterday afternoon (I forgot to put on the top this is MONDAY) and we were distressed at their appearance, although we were probably just as bad, or possibly

worse, many years ago. The nicest child in the street is a small wench who does the most marvellous acrobatics on a strip of grass across the street when she thinks she has an audience. She also has a fancy for dressing up and often appears in a bright yellow evening dress, trailing fantastically behind in a sweeping train that mops up the grime of Grimes Street. This dress is the envy of her companions, and on one occasion a small half-demented boy tried to take it from her by force. Her spirited defence of the imperial robe was a joy to watch, and she "packed a sock" with a style that even Joe might envy. Joe and I were extrememly (good God, what a funny word) fortunate in our childhood because when we came here the street was just bare earth, without bitumen. After heavy storms the street became "dangerous" because deep ruts appeared down the middle and a bed of sand formed outside our gate. Joe and I used to collect this, not for any particular reason, and we piled it under the house with repeated journeys of the late Flossie's personal vehicle, a small wooden cart. When the City Council finally decided to bitumen the street a steam-roller was necessary, and I think you must have some idea of what a steam-roller means to children. Even now I cannot pass a steam-roller without wanting to talk to the "man". The steam-roller continued to come to Grimy Street for many years, on and off, because of the Council's well-known habit of leaving a job partly done. At night the gods saw fit to let it be parked outside Fosters', and Joe and I used to explore it secretly. If only we could have started it going!

Joe has a very strange "destructive" streak that gets hold of him at times. Last Saturday he found an old telephone dial and destroyed it systematically. The durability of the wheels and gadgets of the telephone company is incredible. I saw Joe hammer a round plate affair for minutes on end with a hammer and make hardly any impression on it. When the wheels and plates had been battered out of shape Joe turned his attention to a metal-encased battery. I think his physical perfection is being attainted (good God, a "t" crept in to attained) at the expense of his reason. Of course, I can understand the lust to batter useless things out of

41

shape. I should love to batter Mafeking's filing cabinet . . . while Mafeking stood by, helpless . . .

I have bought a Mozart quartet for piano & strings played by Schnabel, Mass and Prevost (can't remember the fourth) in G minor. It is a most beautiful recording, and I listen to it in the evenings, sitting on the back steps watching the darkness come into the garden. I'm sure you will love it . . .

I'm sending you *I. Claudius,* and another book which I hope you like.

With my love,
Gwen.

P.S. . . . What does "dinaric" mean?

(13)
As from Agens' House of Rest,
Crimes Street.
[16 March]

Oh Tony!

A BEARD! The first words I saw in your letter were "I am growing a beard . . ." I was filled with joy, the most complete and intense joy. You can have only the faintest idea of what a beard means to me—I have never in my life had a bearded companion. I shall sit opposite you in trams, and look at your beard.

A sort of heavenly justice has descended upon Agens for her wicked fit of tree-cutting. All the gas escaped from the cylinder in our refrigerator yesterday, and we have to wait until forms are filled in and petitions lodged before it can be mended. Of course the innocent have to suffer with the guilty, but that is not the point. Agens must remain without a refrigerator. (Of course, being Agens, she has already made steps towards the purchase of an ice-chest.) I am convinced that until she propitiates the gods with trees, planted and watered, the refrigerator will not be mended.

It is getting cooler in Brisbane now, and I sought for some slippers last night. It appears that I have three slippers all for the right foot, so I shall probably have to shuffle round in an old pair of father's—I have his dressing-gown and his chinese pyjamas as it is.

42

I know exactly how you feel when your "hands are tied". At the convent I suffered from that feeling most of the time. The Mother Superior allowed me to bring my pictures with me, but when I got there she announced that I could "Tie them up in newspaper and put them somewhere out of the way". And then, oh Horror!, she produced from some unknown recess two appalling pictures of angels both "Done by hand" by some minor artist of last century, and said "I'm going to hang these in St Clare's Chapel, one on each side". Fortunately God stopped her by sending a lot of rain, so much that the chapel walls got damp and we had to take all the pictures down.

The stump of the mango tree has been taken out and nothing is left but a large crater, about seven feet in diameter. It looks as if a small land mine exploded there. It breaks my heart to see a tree cut down, and if I made laws I should make one that nobody could cut down a tree unless they planted three others first; as you may have learnt, Brisbane is the worst city in Australia for tree cutting. As a child I used to dream of a dark forest, and I have always lived with trees. At night now, before I sleep, I lie in bed on the veranda and watch our trees through the opened blinds. I can see the stars too from where I lie. I find it hard to sleep inside a room. Over at the convent my cell doors opened out so that I could see the trees outside, and in S. Clare's chapel a young silvery gum tree grew next to the window nearest to me.

I don't think I have ever forgotten a tree that I really knew. I can remember the shapes of the orange and lemon trees in our little orchard, and all the trees Agens has had cut down. We used to have a tiny orange tree in the garden that had the sweetest oranges I have ever tasted — only three or four a year grew on it, but they were delicious. Agens rooted that out, too. She cuts down the yellow climbing rose that grows in front, quite mercilessly. There are some lovely trees round All Saints. Trees bring a wonderful air of quietness around them, even in the city. Wickham Terrace is quite the loveliest street in Brisbane because of the trees there. In the early morning or in the evening when the sun is slanting down the trees seem to have light around them, and in their leaves. In Melbourne I spent hours in the gardens and parks, just sitting there. I'm always happy with trees, and in peacetime Gretchen and I used to go away in the morning (Gretchen isn't much of a companion, but she likes the walk) up into the slopes of Mt Cootha, and eat our lunch there. I could write a lot then, but now I seem to be "dried up", as if I had no blood left in me, as far as writing goes. I think perhaps it is a good thing because now is a rich time of experiences and I can store them up. There is plenty of time, it seems, and nothing is really ever wasted unless you choose to waste it. I was most interested in your remarks about "saving up" one's feelings and experiences. I think that they become part of you, and change you—or rather, enrich you—and so you don't lose them or their value.

(This reminds me of a rather amusing incident. Bill and Manfred, both Germans, were discussing the poem "Excelsior", in Mullhollands, where a picture on the wall of snow and ice reminded them of the closing scenes. Bill, who was rather violent at times, said that the poem was rotten, and on that account he was going to smash the picture, but Manfred said "Don't, Bill, that young man stands for the higher values".)

I'm going out to post this now, I'll finish answering your letter tomorrow . . .

With my love,
Gwen

(14)   Urbs beata Hierusalem.[1]
                                            Crimes Street,
                                            AUCKINGFLOUR.
                                            [17 March]

My dear Tony,

. . . Joe and I are "going through" his twenty volumes of war books, and they afford endless amusement. We have found some marvellous Russian Generals and some "border incidents" (the real thing). Also we have acquired another book in the series so

---

[1]Urbs beata Hierusalem: the blessed city of Jerusalem.

well known to all lovers of Palmistry and Fortune Telling—it's called *How To Tell Character,* and is fearfully and wonderfully illustrated. Is there time for me to send it up to you? Joe found that his head contours revealed him to be intellectual and romantic, inclined to dream, poetical rather than practical, fond of the beautiful, and a lover of nature; but alas! his ears showed him to be coarse and brutal. I have some bumps which indicate that I am *not to be trusted*; I am also frivolous, thoughtful, unstable and constant. Red hair is not a bad sign, apparently, unless you have some suspicious bumps. I have. And where the "line of reflection" should have been I could find nothing. However your own very weak head line (revealed by the Palmistry book) does not entitle you to say "I thought so". *How To Read Character* will give you (if you are a business employer) power to select the right applicants, and will enable you to add several pounds to your income. It says so in the front . . .

I'm glad that you like *The Snow Goose*[2]; I think it is most beautiful. As you say, it reminds one of Mozart.

It seems to be impossible to get a good edition of Schubert songs. Arthur,[3] who has been in Sydney for a couple of weeks, looked round there for me but returned empty-handed. For himself, however, he bought an immense leather bag with inner compartments and a magnificent lock. He carries it under his arm and looks rather like a minor but most efficient inquisitor on his way to a secret meeting. He also got a harpsichord record of Bach's "Chromatic Fantasia & Fugue" which I shall borrow from him. Arthur's behaviour when he is with his friends having supper in town is a source of amusement to all. When he is seated he handles his pipe lovingly, leans across the table and says, in a solemn whisper, "When you are able, observe the man in the corner wearing a green tie." When everyone has observed the man in question, Arthur says in a most confidential manner: "I think he's a secret service agent. Be careful what you say." And then he leads

[2]*The Snow Goose* by Paul Gallico.
[3]Arthur Cran, who worked in the Public Service.

the conversation through "guarded channels", and carefully avoids politics or international disputes. Arthur shines his brightest away from home, because his mother and father quickly dispel any illusion of deadly efficiency, and have a picture of him as a child pushing a small wheelbarrow. Anyone who wants to build up a reputation for himself as a spy, secret service agent or inquisitor should first obtain and destroy all photos of himself as a child and, if possible, live alone . . .

I was most interested in the Cigar That Breathes. Does it? The Americans are an extraordinary race, and their advertisements are marvellous. Have you ever seen the little pictures of the Clark Grave Vault Co.? They show a cross-section of ground in wet weather, with water soaking all round a six-feet hole containing a Clark Metal Grave Vault ("bone dry"), and underneath, in Gothic lettering, it says:

ARE YOUR LOVED ONES SAFE FROM THE RAVAGES OF
BAD WEATHER?

Has it ever seemed to you that some scenes have an air of utter unreality? There are some things which make me feel that I am only looking at them in a dream, or on a stage set before me. One of the scenes that seem unreal to me is a fire in the evening after sunset. Agens and Joe were burning off the leaves of the doomed mango tree just before nightfall, and as they walked round in the half shadows and passed across the flames I found it impossible to believe that the scene was real. I felt almost as if I were apart from my body, looking at another world in which all these things were, and had a curious sense of time being suspended or not existing. I remembered the strange light one Friday evening and many other times when I had been standing round a fire with Joe when he was quite small. Sometimes a city looks quite unreal, and seems to be only part of a dream . . .

I told you that I had been filing by a "fool-proof" system, and remarked on the simplicity and trustfulness of the W.D.C. in allowing me to juggle with piles of cards. An interesting conversation revealed that my efforts are appreciated.

X: This is most extraordinary, Mr Y, I understood that all the B's had been filed alphabetically.

Y: So they have, Mr X.

X: Who did them?

Y: Well, really I have no idea.

X: Dreadful, dreadful, it's quite impossible to look up a card in this file, here's a number of Barnes in among the Browns.

Y: Probably a mistake made in gathering them up, Mr X.

X: No, that's quite impossible, they are sprinkled all through the file.

Y: I really can't understand how that could happen!

X: Dreadful, dreadful.

Today is St Patrick's day, so a number of green ornaments and ribbons are to be seen in the streets. I am reminded of the story of the Scotch taxi-driver who was taking his English fare past Knox's house. "Look, mon," he said, "John Knox's auld hoos." "Who's John Knox," enquired the Englishman. "Hoots, mon," replied the Scot, "Dinna ye ken the Bible?"

I am nearly asleep, and too tired to be anything but dull, so I'll write you some more when I've had some sleep.

With my love,
Gwen.

(15)
Urbs Coelestis,[1]
Crimes Street,
Saturday 20th March.

My dear Tony,
This morning it promised to be the loveliest day one could hope for. When I woke up the trees were standing in sunlight so golden that it seemed to be lighting up each leaf. I had spent an unhappy and restless night, but all my sadness just melted away in the thin cold air. Everything looked clean and fresh and sparkling.

At midday the organist of Holy Trinity church drove me down to see the organ, and let me play on it and monkey with the stops.

[1]Urbs Coelestis: the heavenly city.

I love playing on a pipe organ, and I don't often get the chance, so I was delighted.

The air grew warmer and the sunshine more intensely bright, and as I went home for lunch I said, "This is a most beautiful day, I shall spend the afternoon in the sunshine."

And when I got home I found that Agens had cut down the little grapefruit tree. She didn't cut it right down, she sliced it in half, leaving a stump and a little branch sticking out helplessly. The tree was only small, not more than three or four feet high, but it was lovely. It was so laden with fruit that its branches bent right down to the grass. I saw the cut branches lying on the lawn with their heavy green fruit, and the leaves drooping already in the hot sun and turned on Joe with fury. "Don't blame me," said Joe, "I didn't plan this. I'm only a poor workman. Agnes told me to do it. She's going to put up some wire-netting here and the tree was in the way." I fled inside to find Agens, as angry as it is possible for me to be, and when I found her I began to say "How can you cut down trees like this. Aren't you going to leave anything alone?" and suddenly I burst into tears because the thought of the little tree lying there, and the mutilated branch left was more than I could bear. So I just sat down and cried for a time, thinking how pretty the tree used to be when the fruit was ripe. It was such a small tree that Agens could surely have left it alone—the trunk was no thicker than my arm. I knew its shape by heart. Now it is night-time, and everyone but me is out; I went downstairs to look at the tree and saw the branches still lying there, but I am not angry only sad. I cannot be angry long, anger leaves me.

A sense of insecurity has invaded our home. The recent felling of trees that have been a part of my life for nearly fifteen years makes me feel this, but there are other things. Because there must be peace within a family everyone must make tremendous allowances in one way or another. Agens' fear that "Gwen will write it down", is as real to her as my fear that she will cut down the trees I love is real to me. Agens has never been able to help me in the ways that I most need help. In material things her generosity exceeds anything one could imagine or deserve. Outwardly I have all I could wish for, and it means almost nothing to me. In many ways it's a lovely sort of house and people more or less attach themselves to us—sometimes Joe's friends, sometimes mine. Last year, as you know, I brought Robin home because he was such a miserable sort of boy out at the rotten school.[2] . . . Although Robin started off by being a jolly schoolboy who was rather fun, he and Agens together make a combination that I cannot bear because I feel it disturbing the family, and Agens has tried to make him a sort of extra brother without realising that the entire spirit of our family as such is foreign to him. Of course he is only eighteen, and most boys of that age ought to be put in a sort of sound-proof, heavily barred enclosure. (Forgive me for being so long-winded and probably boring, Tony, probably you are saying to yourself "all young women of twenty-two should be put in a sort of sound-proof etc".) He and Agens have a great deal in common in that they hate poetry, talk loudly through string music and are tree-cutters, three things which receive my utter condemnation. And though I can stand Joe's brand of fooling because I love him exceedingly (Joe and I are experts in some forms of nonsense which appear to be funny only to the two of us), Robin annoys me most of the time. Still, he's too young to expect much else from, I'm sure I was appalling when I was eighteen. If I remember rightly, I used to go round like a scarecrow reading *The Education of Cyrus* (in English, I know no Greek) and trying to make people listen when I proved the existence of God to them by St Thomas Aquinas's approved methods. I also used to engage people in French conversation of the school-book type and work out innumerable schemes for living on 10/- a week which never worked out in practice although in theory they were infallible. I had in addition that common failing of young people—omniscience; it's a wonder my family didn't go crazy. My father patiently rescued me from

---

[2]The school: in 1942, GF was teaching music at St Christopher's boarding school, Brookfield.

insolvency and Agens quietly took away the worst of my clothes and burnt them (I can't help loving her when I think of what she has had to suffer from me at times) and Peter let me have his books. The family are coming home from the pictures now, so I'll continue this tomorrow afternoon.

Sunday afternoon
... Yesterday afternoon I walked round the Auchenflower Croquet Club and watched the fat ladies playing croquet. Croquet is a game which intrigues me because, though the weapons are so deadly in themselves, nobody ever gets hurt, whereas though a football is harmless almost everybody gets hurt. Just imagine what would happen if someone pulled a hoop out of the ground, spiked her opponent and cracked her brain with a mallet. The mallets, when not in use, are encased in little covers made to fit the hitting end. What purpose does this serve? Do they have to be oiled, like bats? I studied the players carefully and saw that they were *all* fat, with no exceptions. Perhaps the dazzling whiteness of their frocks against the flat green gives one that impression ... After some metaphysical speculations on the Nature and Purpose of Croquet-playing, and The Significance and Future of Croquet in Modern Life I moved towards the park, where I saw a most inviting seat under some trees.

As I approached the seat, however, I almost stumbled on a sleeping soldier who did not appear to be an ideal companion for such an afternoon, so I walked to the top of the little hill in the park where there is a small monument; there I sat on the stone warmed by the sun and looked down on to the Toowong football field and the bowling club. There was no football match but a few players were practising at the goal, and some small boys ran round under the willow trees that grow in the damp ground near the field. The bowling green was dotted with balls (is that what you call them, or are they bowls?) and men in white with coloured blazers clapped occasionally as one of them achieved success. How excellent it would be to substitute the balls of the croquet ladies for those of the bowling club! By looking round I could see a glimpse of the croquet lawn between the trees of the park. The flat green of the fields and the slender willow trees, the hills in the distance and the neat whiteness of the players, all lying in the bright sunshine made a lovely picture that fitted in with the day itself. How nice it would be to be God, and grow forests and willow trees. How angry I should be if anyone cut down my trees needlessly. Can you remember a story in which the stumps of a woodcutter's home began to grow and blossom? How enchanting to have a green branch shooting out from your wall.

I'm tired, so I shall sleep for a while. Take care of your wonderful beard.

THOMASIUS, the Ven.
The beard of this Saint was said to have healing properties, and is preserved in three portions: one in Spain (light gold); one in France (dark brown and silver) and one in his shrine at Melbourne (Aust.) (nut-brown and golden), the last portion being carried in procession through the streets on his feast-day with the singing of his office-hymn "Barba magnifica".

With my love,
Gwen.

(16)

As From Light's abode, celestial Salem,
Crimes Street.
[23 March]

My dear Tony,
Yesterday I had to kill a dove, and that is a most ill-favoured thing for me. When I was a child doves used to build their nests in a little barn where we kept the food for our horse and cow. I used to sit among the straw and chaff and hold the birds in my lap; they were so tame that I could stroke their feathers. Doves have always been under my protection. Yesterday morning as I was getting dressed I heard Agens' screaming voice "Stop Spondulix from getting into the house, stop Spondulix" etc. As I had only a singlet on all I could do was to stand in the hall and make a lot of noise. Sponny (he is the black cat) ran out and down the front steps. He had a dove in his mouth, alive. Agens pursued

him, but she is not built for chasing cats. I put on father's dressing gown and fled downstairs, but by the time I caught Sponny he had torn the bird's side open horribly and bitten its neck. It was still alive, but couldn't have lived so I begged its pardon and cut its head off with the axe. This made me feel rather wobbly and I have been uneasy ever since, though it wasn't my fault I had to kill it.

We had a magnificent thunderstorm last night with cracks of thunder like pistol-shots. When there is a storm I like to be out in it, to feel the water running over my face and feet. I should like to go barefooted all the time, if I could. Don't you like walking on sand with bare feet?

Robin took me to the Cremorne on Thursday, where we saw sights both strange and wonderful. There was a trapeze team called "The Darwinians". The lady was dressed as usual in pink spangled tights, but the man was dressed as an ape, only instead of eyes in his mask he had two little electric light bulbs, which he lit up by a concealed switch somewhere on his person. This appealed to me tremendously and I became wild with joy every time he switched his eyes on. As he turned somersaults on the trapeze he gibbered magnificently. His tail came off, and he took another out of his pocket and pinned it on. There was a "Strong Man" act, with another of the pink spangled tribe and a wonderfully muscular man who stood on one hand, and did a pull-up with one hand, then raised himself until he was upside down again. In normal circumstances I regard all strong-man displays without much interest, but on the stage I am invariably thrilled with them. The comedian did a dance on a large xylophone with the hammers fixed to his shoes. I could have watched the electric-eyed ape all night.

Agens lied to me about the wire-netting. They are putting it up because Robin is going to get an alsatian dog, and it will have to be kept in the back yard. I extracted this news from Robin, who says Agens told him not to tell me, though why I can't imagine. I am not likely to start a row over an extra dog.

Agens likes to build up a reputation for herself as one who

knows all and sees all. She keeps a close watch on everybody and finds out their movements by sinister questioning. When she has any information she hoards it jealously until she can use it with someone in her power, like the villain in the melodrama. She has a list of Black Deeds in her mind (everybody's) and keeps the list in wonderful order. Her favourite statement is "I can read character at a glance." I questioned her about the wire-netting again this morning, but she still lied to me, so I can only imagine that mischief is afoot. Either she is going to take out another tree, or she is going to pull out what remains of the poor grapefruit. God bless us all, cried Tiny Tim.

I don't know how Gretchen will respond to the presence of an Alsatian — some terrible situations may arise. Perhaps it will make a sensible dog of her. What will probably happen is that they won't be able to buy one, and the wire will just stay there anyhow serving no purpose. Agens is going to grow chokos on it for a start.

A gradual decrease in intelligence (due no doubt to my presence day by day in the W.D.C. here) is making itself manifest in me. Is there no cure for this? What are my surroundings, after all, but scenes calculated to deaden everything original, spare, strange, peculiar and curious. People actually walk around with pens held sideways in their mouths, and when you speak to them they nod, or wag their heads from side to side without removing the pen.

TYPICAL CONVERSATIONS

A: Mr B., have you done anything about those files?
B: Yes, I have.
A: What?
B: Nothing . . .

X: What happened to that letter from Charleville?
Y: Oh, somebody wrapped a pie in it, they thought it was an old circular.
X: Did you get it back?
Y: Oh yes, here it is. It's a bit greasy. (It certainly was.)

I also heard the accountant ordering his lunch from the office boy. "Bring me back a jam tart, Norman, and two dirty big pies." The same person, fed on jam tarts and "dirty big" pies, heard me talking about Ben Jonson, and said "Oh yes, he wrote the Pickwick Papers, didn't he!"

This is a poor effort, but it's 12 o'clock now and I'll post this on my way home.

I'll write soon.

With my love,
Gwen.

(17)   As from HIERUSALEM LUMINOSA.[1]
                                             Crimes Street.
                                     Wednesday 24th March.

My poor Tony,

Of all illnesses I think dengue is the most distressing—it resembles a great many things, all very unpleasant, and has a character quite its own. I thought the red cross on your envelope was ill-omened. Please take care of yourself and don8t get up too soon because you are quite likely to think you8re better when you8re not (something has gone wrong with the device that should print an apostrophe and it prints 8 which is it8s lower half) and a relapse is much worse than the original disease. DO NOT LET ANYTHING HAPPEN TO YOUR BEARD. While you are in a weak state any number of secretly jealous and envious people may destroy the beard, or dye it black, or cut it into peculiar shapes.

For your profit and instruction during your period of recovery (please recover, do not join the ranks of the blessed sts and marts too early) I am sending you a little book in the well-known yellow covered series called "Etiquette in Everyday Life". I'm sorry I haven't had time to read it properly myself, but I have glanced through it as you will see by my delighted pencil-markings. The book deals with all departments of life, and ends up rather

[1]Shining Jerusalem, Jerusalem the Golden.

54

suddenly with two chapters on Courtship and Marriage and Training the Children, and has a marvellous index containing such things as Boredom, 27 Bread, 15 Fidgeting, 20 Fork, 16 and so on. I really did try to get you "Amusement for Invalids", but couldn't (the apostrophe gadget has stopped superimposing 8s) find one in town. Your letter arrived yesterday evening and I said to Agens, Tony has dengue. She is very sorry, and hopes it's not malaria! She will probably cut down a memorial tree in your memory.

On Sunday after Evensong I came home in a tram which contained three mothers with young babies. One mother had a little boy; he was sleeping soundly wrapped up in an old woollen jacket. Another had a little girl, screaming like fury. A third mother got in with a baby most beautifully dressed; the mother herself was young and most fashionably dressed, and her own mother was with her. They seated themselves. The third mother pulled out a "dummy" (you know, those rubber things with flat pieces at the end to stop the baby from swallowing them). The second mother (with the screaming baby) remarked in a loud voice to her friend, "I wouldn't give a baby one of them. It spoils the shape of her mouth, the doctor says." The third mother looked angry, but said nothing, and stuck the dummy more firmly into the child's mouth. The poor mother with the little boy just grinned. The mother of the screaming child remarked in a louder voice (because of her infant's screams, I suppose) "Most unhealthy, too. They pick up germs." The beautiful young mother looked angrier, and more aloof. The child of the other stopped crying, and a few minutes later its mother remarked in an ordinary voice to her friend, "You should see how our dog tries to play with baby. He loves her!" Then the beautiful young mother broke silence:

"By Jesus," she said, "I'd be damned if I'd 'ave a
dorg in the 'ouse with a kid."

. . . Joe has a swing record featuring the unusual combination of harpsicord + swing orchestra. The effect is amazing — and seems to be a continuation of the idea of "Blow blow thou winter wind" and "It was a lover and his lass". Truly one feels sorry for the harpsichord; it "takes punishment".

I went to see "Mrs Miniver" at the Elite on Monday night. It was very well done except for the ending. The singing of "Onward Xtian Soldiers" while bombers pass over a hole in a ruined church does not seem to me to be an ideal ending. The Dunkirk episode was most moving.

There were some amusing short features in the first part of the programme. For instance, there was one about Abraham Lincoln's dream of death, and at the end a nasal drawling voice announced: "Perhaps the interpretation of dreams lies hid with that mysterious powerrr which is recognised even by moderrrn science, and which Abraham Lincoln simply called 'Gard'." And in a travel talk showing Monte Carlo: "Here we see the Cathedral, built last century." One saw the Cathedral facade outlined from an angle common to travel talks against the blue sky, and suddenly a choir of unseen voices burst out in the Hallelujah chorus, fortissimo. The effect was ludicrous and all the Fosters burst out laughing. Nobody else seemed to think it was funny, and several people turned angrily upon us. Miss Cottew was with us, and her mother, who is a most delightful person, said in a loud voice that she wasn't going to stand for The King because it was long past her bedtime. Vera said "Mother, you'll have to, I'm afraid," and Mrs Cottew was dragged, resisting, to her feet. As the last chord sounded she dropped back into her seat and announced "Good night, everybody, I'm going to sleep now." She did nothing of the kind of course and remained awake, giving most wonderful comments on the pictures, typically Victorian, and occasionally addressing one of the characters on the screen. A visit to the pictures with one's whole family and some friends means that you must surrender yourself to the atmosphere of the group or become annoyed, I think. Agens was constantly trying to feed the people across me with a huge slab of chocolate, or relay bits of information about those present, or find out the recipe for a new biscuit. When Dad goes to the pictures and sits in the canvas chairs nobody wants to sit with him, because he takes up nearly all of it and one is likely to get pushed on to the wooden supports or out into the aisle.

Brisbane staged a "Chinese pageant" on Monday, but I didn't go to see it, knowing full well that it would be in the style of the "Cup-Day Carnival", if a little more oriental. It featured "Miss Pat Mead's Chinese Ballet", all dressed up in coolie pyjamas, I suppose, and unnamed Russian and Chinese artists. You can stand such things with the right companion, but it's not much fun by yourself. Brisbane's worst is very bad indeed, almost unparalleled, I should think. I can remember when an adagio dancer at a charity concert in the city hall lost his red silk pants and crashed his partner into an ornamental palm tree growing in a pot. I can remember when I was playing at a municipal concert a number of pigeons flew out of the dome and circled round the hall to the obvious apprehension of the audience. On another occasion (many years ago) the whole audience clapped loudly when a man came out to open the piano, mistaking him for Leff Pouishnoff. They tell me also that in a religious or "Sacred" play, the part of Christ was taken by a Scot with a distressingly thick accent, who had to be prompted all the way through, and remarked in a loud whisper to the prompter, "Speak up, mon, I canna hearrr ye."

Do not try to get up too soon, and rest as much as you can. I hope that by now the worst is over, and that your beard is as beautiful as ever. You have an excellent chance to brush and comb it for hours!

With my love,
Gwen.

(18)   The Holy City,
Crimes Street,
Sat. [27 March]

Thomas Riddell,
Sir,
I see that you administer rebukes to me. Now, while I am quite content to be rebuked about my infantile attempt at spelling "locquat" I AM NOT PREPARED TO ACCEPT any rebukes on the

57

matter of "denaril" because I did not ask you about them. The word I wanted to know the meaning of was D I N A R I C. My handwriting is perfectly legible, and I see no reason for your misreading DINARIC as DENARII, except that you don't know the meaning of DINARIC any more than I do, and purposely mis-read it. I looked up DINARIC in all our dictionaries at home, and of course it wasn't there. Our dictionaries all belonged to grandfather and are used to sit on by people typing letters because the chair is too low (I am sitting on Webster at this moment). I think you had better look up DINARIC in Pears.

Pears is wonderful! I was once staying with an appalling woman who used to push back the chairs against the wall after you had sat on them and who owned a hideous red carpet that gave me a headache every time I walked through the house. She knitted incessantly and made horrible biscuits out of wheatmeal flour that tasted like sawdust. I should have gone mad had it not been for Pears, which became my companion day and night . . .

The woman . . . also used to tell character from handwriting (with the aid of a large book wonderfully illustrated). It was a strange thing that her and her best friends' writing revealed them to be generous, loving, trustworthy, clean-living, kind to animals, and possessed of amazing brain, while her enemies revealed themselves to be mean, low, base, ignoble, dissolute, cruel and full of unsuspected vices. I pointed out to her that you could change your handwriting, but not your character, at will, whereupon she examined mine more closely and found that I was unbalanced. Since then I have maintained correspondence on a typewriter.

. . . Your revelation that your own father is a treecutter shows that the disease is not transmitted from father to son, or from mother to daughter, and leads one to interesting speculation on whether it is hereditary or acquired. You will find no bushes at all in our garden, because Agens regards bushes as mere nothings, and deals with them in the same spirit as an elephant eating buns. Bushes merely whet her appetite for the real thing. I'm very gald (glad) that our trees are camphorlaurels, because of all threes (trees) they are the hardest to get rid of. Agens has cut them all ruthlessly from time to time but they grow again. I can remember watching the stumps anxiously for the first green leaves to reappear, and my joy when I saw the little shoots creeping out of the chopped limbs. We used to have a peach-tree with marvellous blossom. Agens excuse for that was that the peaches (which nobody wanted anyway) had grubs in. We had a yellow flowering tree. Agens said it was "diseased". A big locquat (earlier than the recent one I couldn't spell) was "in the way". Another doomed tree "brought caterpillars", and the camphorlaurels that she plucked out root and branch either "brought mosquitoes" or "might have set fire to the house". The hard part about my protests is that they only react on myself. When I rebuke her, Agens says "You wouldn't care if the house got borers in," or "It wouldn't matter to you if the house got burnt down," or "You don't care if the tree brings caterpillars." She takes the attitude of an entirely righteous person who has saved the house from destruction, improved the landscape and secured great benefits for the family.

Agens isn't allowing the loss of the refrigerator to punish her. She is "borrowing" the refrigerator of the little shop across the road. Only this afternoon I walked over with a great leg of mutton on a plate inadequately covered with waxed paper. My shoe lace came undone, and a horrid little dog called "Victory" smelt the leg of mutton and came snapping about my heels. I shall be glad when our own refrigerator is mended and I don't have to walk about with practically naked legs of mutton, while the neighbours peer out of front windows and scratch their heads.

This interesting correspondence will shed further light upon the activities of the W.D.C.:

The W.D.C. receives an official envelope from the Mulgrave Shire Council, unstamped. Tax (5d.) being paid, the chief clerk opens the envelope and finds it empty.

We send the Shire Council a letter: "Contained herein please find one envelope on which we paid tax, and which we found to be empty."

Shire Council then answers our letter: "Received yours of 6th ult.

and contents noted. Error regretted."

W.D.C. writes again: "Please forward original contents of envelope mentioned in our letter of 6th ult."

Shire Council replies that envelope had no original contents, but was forwarded by mistake.

We thank them for their letter and acknowledge contents.

Of course, all these replies took nearly half a page of the terms considered to be "business English", and were full of mutual expressions of satisfaction at the good work being done by all.

A more horrible development of my career is the experience of "working back". It is a complete loss of time for me, for even if I don't work I can't spend a very pleasant evening with a number of people who regard "working back" as a serious affair. The whole staff was involved, and (I suppose none of this is new to you, but it is new to me) a number of them "stayed in" for tea and ate pies of a disgusting nature and various iced cakes which seem to appeal to public servants. "The men" gathered round a small table and became jocularly familiar with those of the opposite sex who came within their range, and "the girls" discussed working back as if it were a legitimate part of human life and something on a level with birth, death and such great mysteries. I was given a bundle of cards to sort alphabetically (see what confidence they repose in me!) and someone painstakingly explained to me an elaborate and "fool-proof" system of sorting. It may have been fool-proof, but it wasn't Gwen-proof and I found some lovely names on the cards, such as Mrs Herodias Smith, Mr Archelangelo Piccolo and William Ewart Gladstone somebody. And then the sight of twenty people all sorting cards frantically and seriously under electric light at long tables, and wearing those funny eye-shades, struck me as being so ludicrous that I started to laugh and they looked at me suspiciously and resentfully. I was sitting at a separate table with a girl of my own age I rather like—Diana[1] is her name. She shares my attitude

[1]Diana: Diana Gill—we met one another at adult education classes and remain friends, writing now and again, though we haven't seen one another since 1945. She was one of the witnesses at our wedding. She married Manfred Ritter c. 1946. (GH)

somewhat and is interesting because she is a lapsed Roman who has taken to Yoga. Her mother is an Italian, and she's given to reading Thomas Aquinas of all people. She's a pupil of Ernest Watson's (I think you met him) and spends most of the day writing harmony exercises behind the cover of an enormous number of big files. She reads a good bit, and so I lent her *Maurice Guest* which she loved . . .

I read a book by P. C. Wren last night – it was in Agens' library books, which I always examine for unexpected treasures. I was just reading it idly and I got interested. It was about a boy who suffered from "mother complex" – his mother had stifled his will and brain from birth. She removed him from the contaminating influence of prep. and public school (because she found the boys reciting "rude" limericks) and from his college at the University because the young men talked about "sex". He fell in love with the violent daughter of a dissolute artist, and his mother intervened and married him to a bloodless fish called Agatha. Giovanna, his former sweetheart, took cyanide, after having written a letter to him, and locked herself in a self-locking box of huge dimensions. The letter told him to remove the box to his house, which he did, not knowing Giovanna was dead inside it. His wife discovered Giovanna's body and became hysterical, calling the police at once. He was convicted of the murder of Giovanna and was hanged. The whole book was overdone, and the characters were exaggerated, but it "had zomezing".

Sometimes in the evenings I walk down to the river before sunset. I love the time just before sunset best of all, I think, because of the yellow light slanting down through the trees and lighting up stones and houses and windows, almost soaking everything with glowing colour. Down by the river I can see the city in the distance looking almost like an enchanted city, and the trees by the water's edge full of light, and all the shining water, and it moves me almost to tears, though I am full of joy at the sunshine and the gentle quietness.

It is a great comfort to be able to write to you, Tony.

With my love.
Gwen.

(19)

My dear Tony,

   . . . Now Tony, you have misjudged me in the matter of my joy over your beard. I would no more engage in "tomfoolery" with a bearded friend than I would . . . (I am trying to think of something to say here, but find it difficult, so I'll merely state: I wouldn't dream of any tomfoolery in the matter of beards.). You don't seem to realise that I have never had a bearded friend, and therefore I shall regard you with awe, admiration, reverence, love, bliss, pride and wonder. The people you will really have to watch out for are Agens and Joe, though Joe is a good man at heart and will probably envy you. Last night I told them "Tony's growing a beard." Agens immediately launched into a sea of abuse concerning beards large, small, plain or coloured, and a ridiculous scene took place to which I cannot do justice. However, here is the substance of it.

SCENE:	Fosters' Heavenly Mansion. The tea-table. Hippo is reading a book on the back steps, Bishop, Father and Agens are eating fruit.
AGENS:	Dirty filthy things, when you have them you can't wash your face.
FATHER FOSTER:	(Grinning at me) I think I shall have to grow one.
AGENS:	You couldn't grow one if you tried. You couldn't even grow a moustache.
BISHOP FOSTER:	Why?
AGENS:	Oh, he just can't.
FATHER FOSTER:	Gwennie, did you ever see that picture of my grandfather's beard? It was magnificent.
AGENS:	It wasn't anything like Grandpa Jaggard's beard, his came right down to his waist. It was snow white and spotlessly clean. He used to brush it and comb it.

[1]Visio Pacis: vision of peace.

62

FATHER FOSTER: Grandpa Jaggard was so mean that he used to go round Rockhampton picking what he could out of the wire baskets on the corner of the streets.

AGENS: (Mad with fury) He never did. You leave my family alone. At least they were famous.

BISHOP FOSTER: Dishonest booksellers.[2]

AGENS: You shut up. That's only one man's word. Masefield might have been wrong.

FATHER FOSTER: Yes, Grandpa Jaggard used to go around picking things up out of litter. He was so shameless he didn't even bother to look round and see if anyone was coming.

AGENS: (Incredibly angry) You stop saying things like that. It's not true.

HIPPO: (Rather suddenly, from the back steps) Of course it's not true: they didn't even have wire baskets to collect rubbish in Grandpa Jaggard's time.

FATHER FOSTER: (Not at all put out) That's right. I remember now. He used to pick them straight out of the gutter.

HIPPO: They didn't even have gutters then.

FATHER FOSTER: That's right. They didn't even have gutters in Rockhampton.

AGENS: They did so.

FATHER FOSTER: Yes, they did, and Grandpa Jaggard used to go round picking things up out of them, he was so mean. What did he do with all his money?

AGENS: I don't know. And stop saying things like that in front of people. You know what Gwen is. She'll write it down and tell all her friends.

BISHOP FOSTER: Any incident at all is legitimate food for a writer.

FATHER FOSTER: By the way, where is that picture of my grandfather?

[2]Dishonest booksellers: in one of Masefield's works there is a reference to Isaac and William Jaggard of London in the time of Shakespeare as "dishonest book sellers". Jaggard was the family name of GF's mother.

63

	(Reminiscently) By Jove, Gwen, you should have seen his beard!
AGENS:	It wasn't <u>nearly</u> as long as Grandpa Jaggard's.
FATHER FOSTER:	Go on with you! It was far longer. Where's that picture, and we'll have a look.
AGENS:	I don't know where the picture is. I suppose it's with all the others.
FATHER FOSTER:	The only pictures you keep are those of <u>your</u> family. You throw all mine out.
AGENS:	Oh shut up.
BISHOP FOSTER:	What sort of things did Grandpa pick out of the gutters, dad? Food or threepences.
AGENS:	You shut up too. All you think about is making fun of my family.
FATHER FOSTER:	(Roaring with laughter) I don't blame her. By Jove, Gwennie, you should have seen old Grandpa Jaggard . . .
AGENS:	(Raging mad) Shut up.
FATHER FOSTER:	And even if he didn't pick things up out of the gutter he was mean enough to do it. You told me yourself how he used to take your Sunday School pennies out of the plate and give them back to you to put in the next week.
BISHOP FOSTER:	That's right, you did, too.
AGENS:	Well, at least he put something in the plate. Some people don't put anything in.
FATHER FOSTER:	(Piously) Stealing from the Lord, that's what it was.
AGENS:	Well, at least he put them back again. That's not stealing.
FATHER FOSTER:	What would you call them, Gwennie, perpetual pence or perennial pence?
BISHOP FOSTER:	Peter's pence, perhaps.
FATHER FOSTER:	Hardly, they always came back to the original owner.
AGENS:	(Seething with rage) You leave Grandpa Jaggard alone.

64

FATHER FOSTER:	By jove, Gwennie, you should have seen my grandfather's beard.
AGENS:	Grandpa Jaggard's beard was snow-white.
BISHOP FOSTER:	I thought you didn't like beards.
AGENS:	Ugh! I hate them. (Savagely) Now, I wonder who Tony will look like? Did Charles Darwin have a beard?
BISHOP FOSTER:	Definitely.
AGENS:	Then Tony will look like Charles Darwin.

There you are! Probably Agens' brain has simplified her notions of bearded men to a great extent, and probably she dimly remembers Charles Darwin from one of her school-books. I did not think it was the time to mention that your beard has rainbow hues of a beauty unknown to Darwin. (By the way, a beard will get you into the highest and most princely offices of the Greek Orthodox Church, and its variegated colouring will ensure your reputation as a saint.) When I'm in Sydney I go to the Greek Orthodox Church in Darlinghurst and listen to the endless Kyries; they used to have two splendid cantors a couple of years ago. In the Greek church the priest is veiled from the congregation during the consecration. I was there on the feast of the Purification once; the church was full of people and there were dozens of little dark-eyed children. They have pictures of God the Father on the walls, and he has a magnificent beard. When the children and their mothers came in the mothers lifted the smallest ones up so that they could kiss the ikons. They had a beautiful picture of Our Lady of Perpetual Succour, covered with fine silver lattice work.

Your limerick about Energetic Ag. is the first successful one I have seen on the "Foster" rhyme. Your eccentric editorial notes on the sad little poem about Bishop F. touched me deeply, at least the poem touched me deeply. Your mother's remark, "At least you'll always look clean," is wonderful. You don't know how much I would love a "motherly" mother. Agens is very fine and energetic and dashing but she is not motherly . . . It would have been good if my father had been my mother, if you can see what I mean.

You say "it is a wretched thing to idealise one's powers and set a goal to life". But it seems to me that it is the only way to live if one is to achieve integration of personality, and by that I don't mean individuality, I am using personality in its full sense. Do you know the lovely hymn "Urbs Beata"?[3] — one of the verses says:

Tunsionibus, pressuris
    Expoliti lapides
Suis locis coaptantur
    Per manus Artificis
Disponuntur permansuri
    Sacris aedificiis

[3]Urbs beata: blessed city. The English words of this hymn (No. 396 in *Hymns Ancient and Modern*):

Blessed city, heavenly Salem,
Vision dear of peace and love,
Who of living stones art builded
In the height of heav'n above,
And with Angel host encircled
As a bride dost earthward move;

From celestial realms descending
Bridal glory round thee shed,
Meet for him whose love espoused thee,
To thy Lord shalt thou be led;
All thy streets, and all thy bulwarks
Of pure gold are fashioned.

Bright thy gates of pearl are shining.
They are open evermore;
And by virtue of His merits
Thither faithful souls do soar,
Who for Christ's dear name in this world
Pain and tribulation bore.

Many a blow and biting sculpture
Polish'd well those stones elect,
In their places now compacted
By the heavenly Architect,
Who therewith hath will'd for ever
That his Palace should be deck'd.

The Latin quoted is from the final stanza.

That, in a way, expresses what I was trying to say to you before about being changed by experiences and so not losing them because they become part of you. It is different, naturally, for a woman. But in any case, if one's life is to be made to fit into its own pattern, and if one's personality is to achieve wholeness and not be torn apart there must be a great many "blows and biting sculptures" before the stone is polished. Since everything in itself is good and can only become evil by being wrongly used it seems to me that one must learn first to use things and not be bound by them. Also it seems to me that all hurry is useless and harmful, because personality cannot be ripened in a hothouse like bananas. But that view may be a result of my own extreme laziness. At present I am unsettled and do not know which way my life will turn. As you know, I thought for a while that I was destined for a convent. Anyhow the experience in itself was most excellent. Do you know the person I admire most (among women, I mean)? That lovely saint, Teresa of Avila. I remember how she used to tell her novices when they were troubled and unhappy to give up trying to pray and go for a walk in the fields instead. She was a wonderful combination of true mysticism and good sense. Another person who achieved this was Walter Hilton, an English Carthusian monk who wrote the Scale of Perfection. His teaching is much the same as that of S. Teresa, and his book is beautiful in every way. At present I must wait in patience to see what I shall do. And after all, wonderful things do open out suddenly when you least expect them. I hope I don't bore you. Anyway, it is 5.15, that mysterious hour when the War Damage awakes from sleep and goes homeward. An irate person is waiting to take away my typewriter from me and lock it up for the night.

Goodbye for the present, Tony, I'll write again soon.

Gwen.

(20)
As From Urbs Hierusalem Beata,
Crimes Street.
Monday, 29th March.

My dear Tony,

Daylight saving has ended, thank God. Joe and I had an extra hour to monkey with this morning, and spent it in the garden watching our black cat, Spondulix, who is the most theatrical animal I know. He did amazing tricks in one of the trees, balancing himself on incredibly thin boughs, climbing vertically, descending with a rush and stopping suddenly and washing his face with one paw while he sat on a narrow branch. He always welcomes applause, and looks round at his audience as if to say, "Am I not wonderful?"

It is pleasant to lie in bed in the early morning and watch the trees with the sun shining through. I hate to get up early and crawl round half-asleep. It's unnatural. Man was not made to get up until after the sun has warmed everything. That is what the sun is for. As for the extra hour of light in the evening, who wants it? Evenings and nights were made to be dark. When I think of the happy days I used to spend up in the hills or out by the Kenmore creek I could almost weep. Still, there are other days . . .

We have got a new maid called Daphne — it remains to be seen whether she'll stay, or whether manpower will take her away from Fosters' bosom. We really need one, because Agens is out managing Brisbane all day, and everyone else is out "working", especially the Bishop, who, after a hard day at the W.D.C., hates to go home and dash round looking for the things Agens has lost or forgotten. Daphne is rather pretty, with long brown hair and an oval face. Gretchen loves her, and walks round under her feet all day. As a rule we have bad luck with "Mamma's helps". The great Booth was six feet high and dominated the household. She terrorised the shop-keepers of Auchenflower by appearing in a housegown as big as a tent and criticising their goods in a merciless voice. Her cooking was excellent, but as she always did her own ironing before ours we were always short of clothes. She used to go out as soon as Agens went out, and come home when she pleased. She was fond of the late abominable dog Flossie, and took pleasure in pointing out the obvious defects in Agens' bringing-up of her children. The only person who wasn't under her thumb was Manfred, who used to adopt tactics of an intimidatory nature. One of his most annoying habits (for Stella – incidentally he was the only one who dared to address her as Stella) was to lean over the ironing board while she ironed and say in a voice of super-enthusiasm, "I say, Stella, aren't those pretty? Did you make them? What nice lace, Stella!" and so on, with infinite variations. When I left for the convent Agens pushed Stella off as a relief to her outraged motherly feelings.

Mavis, our next "help", didn't help at all. She used to sit in the pantry reading *Peg's Paper*, or *The Millionaire Sweetheart*, and leave strings in the beans. Fed on the futile imaginings of *Susan and the Earl* and such 2d. novels, her ambition was to make a wealthy marriage.

The next one, Gloria, was immense. She modelled herself on screen stars and her efforts were rewarded. She left us to marry a wealthy American soldier (they all seem to have enormous incomes) and occasionally comes out to spend the afternoon with Agens. She had a drastic method of "tidying". For instance, she put a silver chain which I left in the dining-room into a disused tea-strainer when she "tidied up" for Agens last week. Joe and I got Daphne on Saturday and warned her of the punishments falling on those who "tidied up" our things.

Agens heard Daphne say she was fond of reading, so provided her with *Murderers' Crescent*, or some such book.

TUESDAY

We are going to keep Daphne; that is a blessing. There seems to be just as much work to do as ever at home, but the optical illusion of having an extra person in the kitchen has some effect on one, I suppose.

I do hope your dengue is getting better and that it hasn't left you too wobbly. You will probably feel dreadful for several weeks yet. How I dread to think of that "cheek so cruelly fair", and your

69

splendid beard possibly turned white. Do take care of yourself, Tony.

I've missed your company in the evenings. Fortunately I've had plenty of work to keep me occupied, as I've had to write out copies of most of the music for Lent and Holy Week. The departing organist took most of the mss. with him, and they have to be done again, and as nobody can buy books of plainsong in this barbaric town I have to write that by hand too, though I don't really mind doing it. I should like to have been the illuminating Abbess of a mediaeval order. I should have spent my time including the faces of my ecclesiastical enemies among the devils in my mss. The nuns in those times seem to have enjoyed themselves thoroughly (in some convents). They even used to go out hunting, and a law had to be drawn up to stop them from wearing too much jewellery . . .

It's getting cooler here now; by the time you are back winter will be nearly here. When Joe and I were children we used to have a fire in the fireplace on wintery evenings. Now that the wretched billiard table is there we can't have fires. How lovely it was! Joe and I used to sit with father in the light of the fire and listen to the blood chilling tales of Maria Marten & the Red Barn, Sweeny Todd the Barber, Dr Crippen, Brides-in-the-Bath Smith and Mrs Lovatt's pies. Dad had a realistic touch in story-telling that made our blood run cold. Old Coar used to tell us stories, too, full of Coarish horrors such as gigantic spiders and mad gorillas from which two childen (much like ourselves) escaped always in the nick of time.

When it was bed-time we used to make toast on the coals which seemed to us to taste more delicious than any ordinary food. Agens was never much good at story-telling and used to chide father for filling our minds with horrible murders. I know that daddy remembers those times too, for last year he brought home a terrible yellow 3d. thriller about the ill-fated Maria Marten and gave it to me with a smile. I never liked dolls, but Joe had a terrible collection of ugly creatures made out of black stockings (by me). He used to bring me dad's old cast-off socks and say "We'll call this one Stanley Wiggimartini." I wasn't too good at sewing in those days, and the unfortunate dolls usually looked like hunchbacks or cripples. They had amusing names, and very definite characters assigned to them by Joe. The late Flossie hated them, and would occasionally dismember and de-stuff one. Joe once cut all the hair off her tail as a punishment, and she went around for several months looking frightful.

Well, Tony, it's time to arise from my hard morning's toil and have lunch.

With my love,
Gwen.

(21)   As From Jerusalem the Golden,
                                                        Crimes Street.
                                             Wednesday 31st March.

My dear Tony,
I have just spent some time putting a new ribbon on this infernal machine, and the lovely black type inspired me to write to you.

Thanks so much for sending me the Schubert. It was very good of you to send it.

So far so good, but inspiration has fled.
Let us examine the weather.
It is raining.

ELIZA COOK: The poet-one laughs to see the rain,
               She)
               he) dances along the street.
               He)   her)   )
               she) blesses the drops that drench his) hair
               And the puddles that soak his)
                                          her) feet.

BARON VON SCHLUTENHEIMER: Ach! Hoch! Gott strafe England! Ja,
                            liebe mutter, wo ist meiner
                            Regenschirm? Gott mitt uns.

(The Baron will have to drop out of this conversation, we don't

71

know enough conversation for rainy days to keep him in it.)

ELIZA COOK:	I love to get wet! I love to get wet!
SOPHIE C. HADIA:	NEVER ASK FOR SOMETHING FROM ANOTHER'S PLATE!
BARON VON SCHLUTENHEIMER:	Achtung! Puddles!

Mrs Agens Foster, when asked for a statement, replied:

This rain makes those trees grow too fast they are in the way the borers will get into the house not that you'd care it wouldn't matter to you if the house collapsed of course you've seen borers the trees are full of them I must cut them down bring me the axe Joe and you can start on the smallest one then you can cut down the others in the week end.

She was presented with an ornamental fruit-bowl by the Ladies Committee.

Just imagine a wet Wednesday in the public service: no sound but the click-clack of a lonely typewriter (mine). A solitary person stands at the counter, vainly looking for someone to assist him. He pulls himself up to his full height, squares his shoulders, and rings the bell. For a moment an eye peeps out from the cover of some files, then a head appears. Somewhere an owl hooted.

Enough of this!

Two men have just come in with a lot of bags and tools to fix my telephone switch. They have taken the back off and revealed a fiendish complexity of wires and gadgets. Something went wrong with the switch (whether I am responsible I don't know) and it started "giving off" sparks and making queer noises and the shutters hopped up and down without reason. The men are digging themselves in for the afternoon, strewing their tools all over the floor. Oh! this is wonderful, they've started a little fire in a metal cylinder and are melting solder on it. They are pulling out hundreds of wires and poking long things like ibis's beaks into the bowels of the switch and making sparks. I wish you were here to see it all.

ELIZA COOK: I love it, I love it, I love to own

> A magical, complex telephone. (Not very good, this line)
> I polish its plugs, and shine them well,
> I gently tinkle its musical bell . . .

Alas, the men have packed up and gone. It is a major fault, and they are coming back in the morning. Someone told me that telephone mechanics try to get as many morning and afternoon teas in their daily rounds as possible. If so, they will find us a most unfruitful field. All visitors to the W.D.C. are gently pushed off around morning tea time. I ring up and ask (at the request of the "tea girls", poor little creatures) "Mr A., will Mr B. have tea with you?" and the answer is almost invariably, "No. Hang on to it for a while", or some other evasive sentence. There are great mysteries connected with tea-pouring which I don't understand. I don't like tea, and so I have bottles of milk sent up for me; but one morning I went in and drank the first cup of tea I saw. While I was drinking two screaming "tea girls" descended upon me and started yelling "You've drunk Mr Weitemeyer's tea." I said, "Well, pour him another cup, can't you?" but they were quite frantic. They preside over an array of cups each morning and make quite sure that everybody gets the "right one".

This paper is getting a bit creased on account of being taken out and put back several times. People have been hanging round me, trying to see what I am doing. When they do that I merely take the paper out of the machine, put a paper clip in it and put it away in one of my "files", which I keep only for show as I don't have any real ones. I also have a number of important looking keys on a key-ring, but only one of them opens anything (the organ). One is the key of the late Flossie's kennel padlock, one is a key I found in the street, and the other I took out of an old tin full of things at home.

I'll continue this letter tomorrow.

APRIL FOOLS' DAY
Feast of St Hippo of Augustine.

73

HIPPO, ST. MART. Patron Saint of Boy Scouts. Noted for obedience to his mother. (Agens the Tree-Cutter.) Suffered lingering illness from borers in the bones of his skull, and was finally killed when the house in which he lived collapsed during the night. His relics are preserved in a marmite-jar at the church of St Hippo-the-Mango.

My dear Tony,

I was delighted to have a letter from you last night. How glad I am to know that you're out of hospital; I hope you'll be quite better soon. About the beard, cut it off if you feel uncomfortable. Perhaps you could get someone to take a picture or draw a picture of you in it; my veneration of you (S. Thomasius a Barba Magnifica) would increase a hundred-fold if you could perhaps send me a couple of beautiful hairs from it. If you cut it off before I see it please keep me a bit, which I shall file under BEARDS, A-M (I mean M-Z).

Joe tells me that last night Mr Coar won at 500 by the following unscrupulous method: in 500 there is a thing called "kitty" when you are playing 5-handed; "Kitty" is three cards left over, and the one who calls can take any card from kitty, or all of them, providing he puts out the relative number from his own hand. Joe says that Mr Coar when he called put out only two cards instead of three, and after a few rounds examined kitty again and made further substitutions. This, together with his usual practice of keeping back trumps, proved most successful. Mr Coar also gathers tricks up and puts them in his own pile very quickly, and if you attempt to argue with him he mixes them all up and turns them over and invites you "to pick out your own cards" and play the trick over again. Either way he wins. If you don't, he keeps the trick, and if you do he simply picks up a large trump from the pile in front of him. He wears a checked eyeshade which he forgets to take off when he is going home, and puts his hat on over it. He goes down the front steps with a large torch in his hand, singing out happily "Goodbye Joe, goodbye Gwen." If Joe and I are in bed and don't answer he shouts more loudly until we do answer him. His wife, who died a year ago, was one of the loveliest old ladies I've ever known. When Joe and I went to visit them Mrs Coar used to sit at the end of the table and push things towards us — have some bread, have some jam, have some cake, have some fruit, have some cheese, and so on, until we were entirely hemmed in by dishes of things to eat. Old Coar used to shoot the neighbours' cats at midnight with a small gun and bury them in his fowlyard. They knew who was responsible when the cats disappeared, but it was quite useless to question Old Coar who used to say "Lost your cat, eh? Well, I haven't seen him lately. Saw him walkin' round my fowlyard the other day. Haven't seen him since." Or if they accused him of shooting the cat he pretended not to hear and would reply "Oh yes, terribly hot. Think we'll have rain, too."

Agens is having a marvellous time with her new acquisition, Daphne. They are "doing out the house". That means that nothing is to be found where it should be, or where it normally lives. The last time Agens "did out" the place I found about a dozen of my books removed to a doomed pile on the side veranda. Agens said, "I thought we'd give all those old books away, or sell them. Nobody ever reads them." "Are there any of mine there?" I asked. "Oh no," said Agens, "I wouldn't touch any of yours." When I "went through" the pile of books I found some of mine, just as I feared. Agens merely said that (a) she didn't know there were any of mine there, (b) she thought I didn't want them, (c) there was far too much rubbish anyway, (d) what did I want to spend money on books for when I had quite enough as it was, and so on . . .

It is quite cold today, and still raining. A city seems to change its character in the rain. Last night I watched the rain falling through the street lights, the drops looking bright against the stone buildings, and I was quite enchanted. I nearly bumped into Zoroaster,[1] but he didn't see me, he was making for H.M. Opera

[1]Zoroaster: Zelman Cowen who, like TR, was from Melbourne and a lieutenant in the RANVR. With Tony, he visited the Foster home in Grimes Street while stationed in Brisbane. He later became Governor-General of Australia after a distinguished legal and academic career.

House in a grim determined sort of way. He looked a bit wet, so I didn't stop the wet prophet. I knew a person who, whenever he wanted to stop one of his friends in the street, would cry out STOP! in a terrible voice so that everyone within earshot stopped. Then he would pick out the person he wanted.

It is (and it generally seems to be at the end of my letters) lunchtime, so good-bye, I must eat. Incidentally your mention of a picnic delighted me, I should imagine that picnics are the best possible things for people who've had dengue. I am with you in spirit; perhaps we'll manage to spend a day up in the hills one day.

With my love,
Ginnie.

P.S. I'm charmed with the name Ginnie; I shall keep it.

(22)

The Holy City,
Crimes Street,
2nd April.

My dear Tony,

. . . *I, Claudius* should have reached you, but there may be some delay. I shall get a little form from the Post Office next week and fill in all the spaces. Don't worry about it, I've got another copy you can read when you come back. I'm so glad I'll be seeing you again soon, with or without a beard. We shall sing "Rule Britannia" and "The Wolf". Did I tell you that Joe admires your shriek in "females shriek"? He tries it himself sometimes, then gives up and remarks "It's harder than it seems."

Last night I lay on the floor of my den reading ghost stories. They never fail to terrify me. I read "Count Magnus", and was reduced to a state of terror. Everyone else was in bed, so that I hardly dared to move.

. . . Joe likes ghost stories too, and frankly admits that they terrify him, but Agens says they have no impression whatever on her. I wonder if she is telling the truth? I can't imagine anyone reading through M. R. James' *Ghost Stories of an Antiquary* and not having a few uneasy moments, at least.

Agens' latest books from the library have been of the "question asking" type. On the inside front wrapper there is a list of questions, like this:

"What was the Vicar of Upper Lipton doing in the vestry at midnight? Who were the three strange men at the village festival? What was young April Dawn, the beautiful heiress of the Bunghole Millions, doing in the company of the notorious 'Bat' Williams? These are questions which . . ."

Daphne has given up Agens' fiction and turned to the *Gorilla hunters.* She is a nice child. I hope Agens' grimness doesn't weigh her down or make her a party to tree-cutting.

Do you like Villon's poetry? I've sent to Melbourne for the *Oxford Book of French Verse,* no one up here had a copy. Villon pleases me immensely; I loved him as a child, though my only source of knowledge was the *Children's Encyclopaedia* which could not be expected to uphold him entirely. I was given the volumes of the Children's E. one at a time, and I was not permitted to have a new volume until I displayed a thorough grasp of the current one. They belonged to Agens originally and were a little out of date, especially in the matter of clothes and inventions. The poetry sections were unspeakable, or rather the little head-notes for each poem were. Did you have the C. E. in your own childhood.

Guess what time it is. Lunch time, of course.

Are you feeling stronger? I hope so.

With my love,
Ginnie.

(23)   Saturday 1943.
                                                     [3 April]

Dear Tony,

You get so used to living in a house that often you don't notice what is happening in it until it's too late. Today I walked into the kitchen and really looked at it. I saw a cupboard LEANING SIDEWAYS, one wall CAVED IN and the ceiling DROOPING

DOWNWARDS. This house is about done for, I think. Even if a cat runs down the side veranda the whole house squeaks and shakes. If my letters stop suddenly you will know that the worst has happened, or you may read in the paper:

Standing among the ruins of her house, which collapsed suddenly during the night, Mrs Foster and her two children examine a wall-vase which miraculously escaped damage. Mrs Foster intends to live with her family in The Opportunity Shop (of which she is the convenor) until such time as a new house is built.

Today is a miserable day. Something has gone wrong with the weather. It is neither wet nor fine, only a poor greyish kind of day with hard light that takes the fine edges and the colour from things and makes them look like unimaginative sketches from children forced to draw what they don't like, all smudged and ragged.

For a while after lunch I was so cold that I sank into an armchair wrapped up in my warmest coat. Then Joe walked into the room with his "usual" clothes on, carrying a "dirty big" crowbar. "Come out," he said, "I'm digging holes." I followed him out and found him putting up the other side of the fence Agens is causing to be built at the corners of the house. "Is there really going to be a Great Dane?" I asked. "No," he replied, "they cost too much. Mr King says they can eat a whole sheep a day." The fence is being put up because Agens has a symmetrical mind, that is, she cannot imagine a useless fence being put up on only one side of the house. It must go up on the other side too.

Joe hit the lime-tree with the crowbar and some ripe fruit fell off. I picked them up and punctured the skin of one with my thumbnail to let its lovely smell escape—how I wish someone would make a "lime" perfume: it would be so much fresher than the eternal flower smells which make picture shows unbearable if the woman next to you has soaked herself in one of them. Have you ever been forced to sit taking in heavy perfume with every breath? I love perfume, but only the faintest hint. It should be mysterious, not oppressive. Cheap scent always smells like flyspray after half-an-hour. Someone (Old Coar's nephew as a matter of fact, who is a "prominent businessman") gave me a bottle of terrible stuff for Christmas last year, and it leaked out powerfully, so I gave the remainder to Daphne, who loves it. Anyway I carried the limes into the kitchen, and saw the leaning cupboard and that prompted me to write to you.

A chicken is cooking slowly in the kitchen surrounded by onions and other vegetables, and a most pleasing steam is being "given off" from the casserole. I know there is ice-cream in the refrigerator. (Poor Tony, I suppose this is like describing gallons of cold beer to a man lost in the Gobi desert. I don't mean to be heartless – I suddenly thought of your awful pudding that you described to me. What a wretch am I.) I cannot see how anyone can fail to be interested in food. When anyone says "What I eat is a matter of indifference to me," I feel like screaming LIAR. Did I ever tell you about the tin of chicken we kept for many years?

There was in the pantry, when I was young, an oval tin of a most interesting shape and a beautiful bronze colour. The label had a marvellous bird on it, something like a pheasant, and this bird was surrounded by smaller birds like glorified hens. The label said: Magnum Brand. One whole bird in jelly. Packed in Java.

I used to hold this tin for minutes in my hands as a child, looking at the picture, reading the label, and carried away by the magic words "one whole bird in jelly". Memories of early days at Mitchelton came back to me as I held the tin, when we used to eat "whole birds in jelly" as a special treat on birthdays or when visitors came. But it was years since we had tasted one. Sometimes Agens would examine the tin, but somehow nobody ever dreamed of opening it. Sometimes we would discuss the question of its "going bad", but that seemed outrageous talk and was soon stopped. So it stayed in the pantry for many years. Occasionally Joe would ask, "When are we going to have that tin of chicken?" and Agens would reply "There'll never be any more of them, you know," or "It seems a pity to open it."

But one day last year Agens was spring-cleaning the pantry, and something snapped in her brain when she came to the tin of

79

chicken; the "whole bird in jelly". She said, "We are going to have this for lunch." Nobody questioned her. It was like hearing a death sentence, or perhaps more like news of a birth – what will it be like? At lunch-time we all knew what the others were feeling. I opened the tin (which had been kept in the refrigerator all morning) and put the "whole bird in jelly" on a glass plate. He was in jelly, all right, the whole bird. The Javanese had performed marvels of concise packing and packed his own limbs around him with great skill. The jelly held him together. There he lay on the glass plate. He was carried into the dining-room, divided up and served. We looked at one another. He smelt peculiar. Agens ate a small piece. "It's no use," she said, putting down her fork. "We'll have to have spaghetti, or something." No one spoke. I carried the plates away and put them on the floor in the kitchen. Diogenes, the grey cat, came and sniffed the bird, then RAN out of the kitchen.

Diogenes' lopsided run broke the tension, and we all started to laugh. The animals came in one by one. Gretchen (as one would expect) ate some, but the cats wouldn't. The Whole Bird (in his jelly) was thrown ingloriously into the rubbish tin.

. . . Did I tell you that every time Mafeking says my name I call out in a fluty treble "Do you want me, Mr Reed?" This has been going on for some weeks, and I wondered how much longer it would pass. Well, Mafeking gave way this morning. He called for me, and I replied as usual, and he lost his temper completely, stood up at his desk and roared, positively roared: "What the devil do you think I'm calling you for, if I don't want you!"

Several people got up to see what was the matter so I smiled at them in turn and they sat down again. Poor Mafeking! . . .

With my love,
Gwen.

(24)

My dear Tony,

This morning from my episcopal stronghold in the W.D.C. I noticed a group at the other end of the office examining something with a puzzled air and then gazing at me. When I looked at them they looked away as if they hadn't been looking at me at all. After a while a girl came down and said, "Do you know anyone on a ship who would write to you?" I at once assumed an air of great concentration and said "Let me think, let me think," and she then handed me your exceedingly delightful envelope of the 8-line address, and retired to a distance . . .

Your letter was so delightful to have on a Monday morning that I felt almost as if you were here yourself. The "border incidents" you suggest are calculated to have the most upsetting effect on any public servants and fill me with joy . . .

About writing, thank you for your kind words, I shall consider it. I have made a study of an English paper (3d or 2d) called Women's Own or something like that. Once I was lying in bed too sick to get out but well enough to read, and the only thing handy was a stack of these papers which Agens buys for knitting patterns. I thought what fun it would be to produce a whole paper like that on one's own. First there is a section on How To Improve Those Last Year's Dresses, written by Janice or Clarice, or someone, in this style:

> That faded old silk will look wonderfully new and bright if you cut out the front panel and insert a contrasting one in bright colours.
>
> Don't throw away that old evening frock! Cut off the skirt and use the surplus material to make sleeves. Puffed sleeves are being worn this season. Or you can make a matching bolero trimmed with gay little flowers.

Then there is a Prose Poem, like this (by a person called Patience Strong). It's hard to be bright when those we love are far away from home; but we must remember that God above is watching

81

them as they roam. He has them safe in his tender care etc.
There is a beauty section:

Send to our office for the new beauty shampoo (3d. per large packet, sufficient for one month) which leaves the hair free and glossy.

Q. My nose is rather too large for my face, what can I do to hide it, or make it appear less big?

A. Use a darker shade of powder on your nose and have simple, soft hair-dos; avoid all angular hats; choose a wide-brimmed straw.

The Q's and A's are always wonderful, especially the ones on intimate problems a la Dorothy Dix.

Q. I have always lived with my mother, who is good to me, but lately she has been chopping down trees, and this has created a breach between us. What can I do?

A. After all, dear, whose trees are they? There's no one like a mother. Mother knows best. Poison her.

Then come the stories. There are always two, sometimes three, all on the same plan. There are certain rules which must never be transgressed. The heroine must have a mouth "too wide for absolute beauty" and must suffer from the jealous plottings of rival females who are exotic, like "hothouse flowers". If they are found bound and gagged by diabolical secret agents or spies they must at least have "a wisp of silk" about their hips. They are permitted one illegitimate child if it is curly-haired and blue-eyed and its father was a "Dashing" army officer who got killed early in the piece, though this permission extends only to 2d. magazines and not 3d. ones . . .

I should love to go to the Cremorne with you. Anything at all may appear on the stage. I remember a team of roller skaters consisting of an absolutely massive woman and a small man who whirled her round about 3 feet above the floor. She was dressed as a Cossack but looked more like a Flying Sealion. The "ballet", poor creatures, will probably distress you—they only know about

5 steps and never do them in time. They rely on leg appeal. We shall probably see the Bridges Trio, a trio (once classically A.B.C.) now reduced to playing "Donkey's Serenade" on a large xylophone; they stand as a living warning of the doom of all who want to play string music on the A.B.C. and make a living out of it. Let us hope for wonders and electric-eyed apes.

Well, Thomas Frederick, I'll continue this tomorrow.

With my love.
Ginnie.

NOTE: between Letters 24 and 25, there was a period of about two weeks during which TR was in Brisbane on leave.

(25)
Monday, 1943
As From 14 Crimes Street, S.W.1.
[19 April]

My dear Tony,

Alas, my state of celestial idleness is, I believe, soon to be shattered for a week or two. MAFEKING ("Most Irregular") Reed has a poor, stupid, tired secretary who dabbles in spiritualism and pelmanism. This nervous creature is going on holidays and I heard from "reliable sources" that I am to take her place. I have already thought out a course of action which will make him unwilling to retain me there for long.

(a) I shall mutter to myself in German or French all day.
(b) I shall prove incapable of finding anything. (The unhappy creature's main job appears to be finding things for Mafeking.)
(c) I shall install a great number of personal belongings in the corner of his sheep-pen if and when I am posted there.
(d) I shall cause small objects such as earrings, brooches etc. to fall under his table and then ask him to pick them up for me.
(e) I shall sing to myself when not muttering.
(f) I shall get as many people as possible to ring me up each day on his telephone.

The greatest blow is that I shall be deprived of my typewriter, and I shall have to find out some way of repairing the loss. Writing to you is my chief joy and I am not going to be deprived of it. Besides, the delight of writing to "callers" right under his nose is something to look forward to!

It is a lovely day, and I hope the air is clear so that you can see the country on your journey.

If I really have to stay with Mafeking during his secretary's absence I shall be glad of suggestions from you. In some ways it will be a golden opportunity. I am in wonderful health and spirits at the moment and feel like some "good clean fun" with the authorities.

. . . I listened to Kipnis last night. It was a fine programme, and I did love the Brahms. I was too tired to listen to Lotte Lehmann so I went to bed and fell asleep almost at once. I listened to the Sibelius too, and it was good—really I don't know very much about his music, and perhaps I am prejudiced. I'm going to borrow his 5th symphony and listen to it.

You have made me so happy that I am still full of joy. How lovely it has been to hear you sing and to walk and sit with you in the bright sunshine.

With my love,
Ginnie.

(26)

Wednesday, 1943.
As From Crimes Street.
[21 April]

My dear Tony,

Agens is becoming a menace. She has developed a craze for "speedy housework" (probably it's part of Daphne's training) and nobody is left in peace. Daphne has not yet been taught how to hover in the background and pick up forks (let them lie there, the servant will bring you another), in fact she never appears in the dining room so we still have to buttle for ourselves . . .

Now, if there is one thing I like (what a commanding phrase that is) it's to eat in peace, and to this end I sometimes go home late so that I can have dinner by myself. But Agens has taken to moving things rapidly off the table before one realises what has happened, and any reproaches are silenced sternly with "You can't sit here eating all night," or "Daphne has to get home," or "Why didn't you say you wanted some"—the last when she has put away something one intended to eat.

Ah, since the last paragraph our address has been changed

CHEZ MAFEKING

And what an annoyed Bishop we are! If you can bear it I am going to tell you something of this part of our diocese.

I have discovered what Mafeking does to keep himself occupied all day—he piles up an enormous number of letters in front of him and then starts lighting his pipe. He makes sucking and wheezing noises for about five minutes with no results and then gives up and smokes a cigarette, blowing clouds of smoke through his mouth up into the air. When the cigarette is finished he starts on the pipe again, with no better results. Sometimes it flares up merrily for a time and then dies out suddenly. He lights another cigarette. Then, picking up the top letter, he howls for his secretary. (Not me, I am for a few days only a "learner".) The poor secretary comes running and sliding into the office, pencil in hand and hand on brow in true style. "Miss H., get me the letters belonging to this correspondence." The nervous creature buries herself in the large files and starts scratching and rooting through pink and white sheets of paper fastened in the corners with very small pins. They become detached and float down to the floor. She scrambles down on her knees picking them up and pinning them (the papers, not her knees) together, holding pins in her mouth as Lear would say, in a vigorous and alarming manner. She stuffs them back crookedly in the file, mixing them up in her haste to serve the master. This never fails to delight me, especially when a whole file collapses on to the floor.

. . . When dear Mafeking has been given the correspondence in question ("correspondence" often runs to amazing lengths over nothing at all) he unpins it and reads it with a look of intense concentration, making little ticks and dots along the margin. Then

85

he has another round with the pipe.

. . . I am so greatly distressed at the thought of someone drawing a large salary for doing work that could be carried out easily by any person who could read up to the standard of *Tiger Tim's Weekly* that I feel like suggesting to the proper authority that I should take over the whole department singlehanded. It would be interesting to see their reaction!

Before I joined the Examining Officer's Dept. I was given a little lecture by the Chief Clerk, which I shall quote as well as I can remember:

> Miss Foster, for some time you have been working for Mr R. (See what delusions they harbour!) and you have gained thereby a fair knowledge of the work of the Examining Officer's Department, which is, I may say, one of great importance, indeed, a most important Department. Now, as you know, Mr R's Secretary is going, or is about to go, on recreational leave, and it is, therefore, necessary that someone should take her place in this very busy department. We have chosen you (fools!) to take over this work. It will, of course, be impossible for you to remain in charge of the telephone switch during this time, but you will return in due course with a much deeper insight into the work of Mr R's department even than you have at present. This will be most valuable to you in the future (liar!), that is to say, in time to come you will find this additional knowledge of great use. The work of the department is, as I have said before, most important, and you will profit indeed etc . . .

This uplifting little speech cheered the Bishop immensely and she resolved to return to the switch (in several weeks' time) tired but happy. A good time will probably be had by all.

Apparently I have taken a step upwards in life, and they have decided to "deal lightly" with the matter of irregularities and "callers".

Last night I found a most delicious green jelly in the refrigerator, and I was just beginning to eat this when I heard a tremendous sliding of earth from the air-raid shelter. Joe, who was with me, went out to see what was the cause of it, and found five cats sitting on top. Two of them ran away – the other three were ours, Diogenes, Svasti and Spondulix. When he came inside a terrible crash was heard in the kitchen, and we found there a strange black cat with a horrible expression on its greedy face eating a plate of prawns from which it had knocked the cover! It was a bold creature and didn't attempt to move until Joe clouted it on the behind.

This isn't much of a letter, but you will understand that affairs in our diocese have been unsettled. When matters are under complete control once more we hope to do better.

With my love,
Ginnie.

(27)   Maundy Thursday, 1943.
                                           [22 April]

My dear Tony,
Last night the moon had a golden ring, as the old sailor remarked. It was really most beautiful. The sky was full of soft white clouds which the wind had rippled like sand, and the moon shining through them looked as if it were lost among flat snowfields.

It was quite cold last night with a dry wind bringing dust into the air. It is so dry that paper crackles and curls up and one's hair flies off the comb. There was a fine coating of dust on the keys of the organ that was most unpleasant to touch and today the whole city looks dusty; there is no sunshine, only a greyish hard light. I woke up though to find the sky ablaze with orange light: the low-hanging clouds caught the light and its reflection made a beautiful glow even over the green trees and grass. It faded very soon and the dusty light crept around everything.

This morning after mass the Blessed Sacrament was moved to the altar of repose where It will remain until tomorrow's mass of the Presanctified. The little altar is set up in a porch in the north side, with lovely altar hangings of white silk and many candles burning all the time. I love the way candle-flames seem to burn in the air by themselves above the wax. A continual watch is kept until tomorrow morning – the clergy watch throughout the night. Tomorrow's mass is the most moving in all the liturgy: it is really a re-enactment of the Passion. I hope that one day I shall see it carried out in full, with the proper music sung by a liturgical choir. But holy week in Brisbane is not holy week in Seville, so I must wait. I have two students from the seminary to sing the reproaches and tracts, that is all. The celebrant has a cold and can hardly sing, the deacon will sing out of tune in the responses, and the sub-deacon will probably not sing at all, though he has very little to do. There are a tremendous number of collects to be sung, all prefaced thus:

Celebrant:	Let us pray.
Deacon:	Let us bow the knee.
Sub-Deacon:	Arise.

You wouldn't think that much could go wrong with that, but it can.

You know, Tony, I really do love being an organist, even if I'm not a good one. Years ago I used to listen to organists and think, How wonderful to walk into a church and open up the organ and fiddle with all the stops and dig music out of the seat, then sit down and look around at everyone before you began to play. By a series of accidents and episodes, not through any merit of my own, I am now an organist and my simple delight has never left me.

The touching little design . . . was not put on quite straight, I'm afraid, but I hope its simple appeal will touch your emotions. It reminds me of the first picture I ever took with a camera — one of Joe at an early age, standing on a rock by the seashore and apparently defying the laws of nature by leaning at a perilous angle towards the sea. I think this masterpiece has been lost, like the photo of great-grandfather Jaggard which Agens speaks of, though nobody else has ever seen it.

They painted the bathroom floor bright red yesterday. It looks most pleasing but it wasn't dry last night. They left a little track to and from the bath for us to walk on. Sometimes Svasti (who likes the bathroom) tries to walk round the edge of the bath, and does so without falling in. The late Flossie also used to spend her days in the bathroom, lying in the corner between the wall and the bath. That was in winter. In summer she chose to dwell behind the stove—the hottest place in the house. On hot days she would pant and wheeze (in her latter years) in a truly pitiful fashion, and in winter she would sit behind the bath and shiver. This shows her to be a dog of very little brain, though she had a great deal of cunning, as I have said before. Father used to wash Flossie in the bath if he thought nobody was around but Agens discouraged that practice—I remember one occasion when Dad gave Flossie a hot bath in the wash-basin, and half-way through someone called him, and he forgot about her. Flossie was too rheumaticky to jump out, and she was discovered half an hour later sitting all stuck together with soap. Joe used to wash Flossie in Lux when he was given the job, and it made her quite soft according to him.

We have more family rows about the bathroom than about anything else, particularly with Dad. You see, he is so large that he says he needs six towels to dry himself with—two for his trunk and one for each limb. He always chooses a new cake of soap in the morning, and before long the bathroom seems to be hidden under quantities of wet towels and a lot of partly used cakes of soap. (Dad uses nearly a whole cake of soap if he decides to do the job thoroughly.) I keep my soap in the late canary's bath, and Dad has been sternly warned not to touch it. (The canary died without reason one day last year after having brutally murdered three wives in succession: we tried to breed canaries but Patrick would wait till his wife had laid some eggs and then peck her to death and sit on the eggs himself. Definitely a case for Freud.) Well, if you can get into the bathroom before Father it's all right, but if he gets there first and shuts the door you can be sure of finding your towel (if you left it there) soaking wet. Sometimes he chooses a towel at random and gives Gretchen (who runs about on the wet grass in the early mornings when Dad lets her out) a "rub down", which means drying her dirty paws on the towel!

Thursday evening.
Crimes Street – really
from Crimes St., not
"as from".

I had some "final rehearsals" with the people who have to to sing tomorrow, and I didn't have time for any dinner tonight. I arived home at about 8.30 to find father sitting rather miserably (he has a cold) listening to some poor fool singing "The Holy City" on the amateur hour. So father and I had bacon and eggs and coffee and I was delighted to hear that he had brought home a whole case of oranges for us. I had some orange juice but father had a lot of rum (for his cold) and then a bit more rum (for himself).

Diogenes is sitting on the table watching me type. He is handsome although he is so fat. When he was a kitten he was silver-grey and at night used to look like the ghost of a cat with big yellow eyes.

One of the joys of winter for me is that I have pockets. In summer I don't and I live in a pocket-less state, very simply. But in winter I fill my pockets with strange and fantastic things and think of winter scenes which I have never seen, because we don't really have winter up here at all. Men are lucky to have pockets all the time. I suppose I could have pockets on my summer dresses, but that is not the same thing, pockets should be deep and mysterious and lined with silk; if I went round in summer with strange bulging pockets people would suspect me of stealing small objects and might even demand to search them and that would delight me, but summer pockets are not made for greatness.

Dad has gone to bed and the house is beginning to take on an air of stillness and awareness that makes chairs and doors and all sorts of things around me seem suddenly alive. This house has been spoilt. When I was about seven years old we came here and I still know places where I can find "Gwen" written by my hand at that age. It was a mysterious house painted dark green and instead of gaps there were beautiful camphorlaurel trees not growing as they grow now, but old with strong branches and moss around the trunks. The doors were of cedar, but some fool painted them, and painted the wooden walls with depressing chalky blue. Agens never understood the character of the house, and her "improvements" are of the nature of eyebrow-plucking, a device which I can't bear.

Don't you love the names of trees? —cedar and cypress and fir enchant me. I don't wonder that our Lord was a carpenter.

Delicate green shoots are breaking out of the stump of the locquat tree, so it is alive. You will be glad to know this.

> With my love,
> Ginnie.

(28)   The Earthly Paradise,
                                    Crimes Street, S.W.1.
                                    Holy Saturday, 1943.
                                    [24 April]

My dear Tony,
I have discovered in an old bookcase a most wonderful book on English History: —

> Outlines of English History,
> including notices of the
> National Manners & Customs, Dress, Arts, etc.,
> of the Various Periods
> Six hundred and fifty-first thousand,
> revised & corrected by

Arthur Hassall, M.A. Sometime examiner in the Oxford Local Examinations.

> Price 10d.

It begins (apart from lengthy introductions, prefaces, forewords, etc.) with a section called PRINCIPAL FACTS, IN RHYME, beginning:

> In 43 a Roman host
> From Gaul assailed our southern coast.
> . . .
> St. Alban suffered in 3, 0, 3,
> And Britain in 4, 1, 0, was free.
>
> THE EARLY ENGLISH PERIOD
>
> In 4, 4, 9 the Jutes arrive;
> Horsa was slain in 4, 5, 5 . . .
> In 5, 9, 7, Augustine brought
> The blessed truths our Saviour taught . . .

Isn't it grand?[1]

. . . Father is playing "Hold the Fort" in a most jovial style, mixed up in a brilliant way with *Rescue the Perishing*. A pleasant occupation for one who was once a subject of the Good Queen.

With my love.
Ginnie.

(29)   Monday, 1943.
                                                              [26 April]

My dear Tony,

This is Easter Monday, and I have a holiday, as I should. Just as I was making for the typewriter Dad appeared and took possession of it—he has to write some "important articles" for the *Brass Band News*. Joe is playing a German beer-hall record over and over again in the dining room; and the man next door is sawing wood in his workroom; Agens is beating things with an egg-beater in the kitchen and children are screaming happily in the street. I'm sitting on the veranda and all these sounds reach me at once. There is one delightful fat small boy in the street on a tricycle who is trying to persuade Spondulix to come out of the

---

[1]The rest of this letter discusses the contents of *Outlines of English History*.

paddock next door; Spondulix distrusts the fat small boy and refuses to move. They just gaze at each other through the fence.

Good Friday dawned most gloomily with black clouds and heavy rain. The two students from the Theological College who sang the Reproaches for me were really splendid; it's the first time we've had the proper plainsong at the Mass of the Presanctified and it was most moving. I was very worried about the music, but everyone who had anything to sing did so beautifully — except the fools who refused to practise "Let us bow the knee" and "Arise" who sang as badly as I feared. Thank God, not one of the Village Choir turned up.

. . . I spent Saturday in celestial idleness, as I intend spending today. I lie in the sun in Dad's swinging chair drinking orange juice and reading fantastic stories from one of Agens' library books about a master magician and his long-lashed, violet-eyed lady friend who is called "Laroo" and has a tame puma or panther in the best style. The master magician disguised himself as a red-haired professor studying moths and got a man out of Dartmoor. He also spent a night in the British Museum in a mummy-case. Agens came out and saw me reading her book. "Is it good?" she asked. "Ah, wonderful!" I replied. Agens was so pleased with my simple words of praise at her choice from the library that she brought me out some more orange juice!

Robin, whose leave was up today, has developed influenza. A military doctor came out and has given him five extra days. Agens is enjoying herself and tears in and out to his bedside rather like the nurse we saw at the Cremorne.

As I am writing the clouds are piling up over the sun. I think it is going to rain this afternoon. I may be going to see *The Man Who Came to Dinner* at H.I.M. Opera House if I feel energetic enough. I read the notices in the paper to see what they said but they hardly mentioned the play — they got mixed up with the social columns and seemed to be about Mrs X's gown and Miss Y's furs . . .

With my love,
Ginnie.

Tuesday, 1943.
                                              [27 April]
My dear Tony,
Yesterday afternoon I went to see *The Man Who Came to Dinner*
and enjoyed it immensely. It is a long time since I've seen a play.
A lot of the audience were disapproving in their attitude to the
dialogue, and several stern matrons round about me refused to
laugh and looked angry with their husbands for doing so. A
dreadful little girl was sitting next to me, done up like Shirley
Temple in her youth, and her mother, decked out in false
jewellery, gave her little treasure constant instructions in a loud
voice:

> <u>Do</u> sit down, darling, or the people behind can't see.
> <u>Please</u>, darling, <u>don't</u> put your icecream over your new dress. Darling,
> <u>don't</u> ask so many questions, look at the stage. <u>Don't</u> fiddle with your
> curls, darling, leave them <u>alone</u>.

Little treasure studied the programme with great care during
the interval, and read the price list of Adams' Rich Cakes upside
down. Considering that she was about 4 years old that's not bad.
A typical Brisbane episode occurred just before the second act.
The little screen they let down in front of the curtain to show
advertisements on got stuck, and when they hauled it up it just
fell right down again with a bump. They got it up halfway, and
it fell down again. This went on for nearly ten minutes, with hoots,
cheering and cat-calls from the audience.
Agens and I went to the pictures in the evening, but after seeing
a play I found the pictures most lifeless. There was a dreadful
picture of Old Virginia (c. 1913) with faithful niggers, southern
girlhood, potatoes etc. in abundance. The other picture, "Ellery
Queen & the Spy Ring", was more in my line; it had plenty of
jaw-socking, people being laid out, "typical" Nazis, stupid police,
sinister foreigners (one of them was found "cold" in a
mummycase) and kidnappings. There was one scene in the finest
tradition where the murderers told X that a car was waiting for

him (they were on a train) at the next crossing, and that he was to jump off when the train slowed down. As they came to a bridge they made him get ready, standing on the foot-board, and when they were in the middle of the bridge one of the murderers planted a foot in his back and pushed him off into the stream below. I liked that!

It turned out that Robin had dengue, not 'flu, as I said yesterday. (This will probably make you envious.) About midday yesterday Robin got delirious and got up out of bed. Joe said, Get back into bed, Robin! Robin promptly screamed in a piercing soprano and knocked Joe down with great force. Joe got up and knocked Robin down, sitting on his stomach. I looked in, thinking they were just fooling, as usual, and found Robin getting up again to attack Joe, who did his best but was obviously losing. Dad came in, and Robin got really violent, and the two of them couldn't hold him down. Agens then came in and seized a jug of water which she poured over all three of them indiscriminately. (That was absolutely beautiful, Tony, I'm terribly sorry you missed it.) I was sent to get Mr King, a very large man who lives at the back, and he came in and sat on Robin's legs, which was a great help to Dad and Joe who were constantly stopping terrific bangs on the face and chest. Agens poured more water over everyone and Robin suddenly collapsed and remained unconscious for a good while. When he "came to" he didn't remember anything about it. The whole performance was magnificent. I'm quite sure Dad had the time of his life and he'll probably add it to Uncle Fred's tombstone with various "improvements" as in his story of Dr Crippen. What Agens will make of it I can't imagine—her powers of exaggeration are fantastic.

WEDNESDAY

I had a marvellous dream on Monday night, about what do you think?—A WOLF. There was a long white road covered with fine dust running across a plain. At the end of the road was a deep gully of red earth cutting it at right angles, and in the gully was a most splendid fiery-eyed WOLF who ate babies' hands off and then left them to die. It was my duty (in the dream) to shoot this

95

wolf with a small pistol. I loaded the weapon beside Agens' refrigerator, fired a shot or two to make sure it was working, and set off from my old school gates down the long road, running at tremendous speed. I came to the gully and found there Joe and a little girl to whom I used to give music lessons. In the corner was the wolf, licking his jaws hideously. I shot at him, and missed. Immediately the wolf and I were back at the beginning of the white road at a sort of garden party, amongst groups of women in white dresses.

The dream is confused after that, I can't remember any more clearly. Wasn't it a fine dream?

Yesterday I got the record of "Oh Sleep, why dost thou leave me" that I have been wanting for so long. It is sung by Dorothy Maynor with an orchestra, Koussevitski conducting. On the other side is "Ach, ich fuhls" by Mozart from The Magic Flute. I had not heard this before, so I was very pleased with the record.

WEDNESDAY EVENING

When Dad is home by himself at night he goes to bed and allows Gretchen to join him there, instead of putting her in her own bed downstairs. This means that people coming in late have to get Gretchen from Dad's bed and carry her downstairs, which is not as easy as it sounds. The little beast knows that she can go to any lengths with Father near and quietly sinks her teeth in the hand that seizes her. If you do succeed in picking her up she moans in a fearful manner and Dad says "Poor little doggie. You're hurting her." Perhaps you wonder why she isn't left upstairs; well, Agens sleeps with Dad and has no desire to spend the night with a dachshund sitting on her stomach, tearing feathers out of the eiderdown or biting the bedclothes to bits. Her greatest fun is with the mosquito net, in which her claws get caught. When we got in on Monday night Dad was addressing Gretchen as "Porky dear". Little Porky Dear was enraged when I took her off to bed and tried to bite me, but I carry her wrapped around my waist (her head and feet nearly touch) so she can't reach anything to bite.

I have just picked up off the floor (I'm typing in the "spare room" which contains the sewing-machine, three tin trunks, a bookcase, a linen press, Joe's drum kit, a "dirty big" picture of George V, five photographs of committees, three war scenes, two oil prints and a watercolour, the ironing basket, a straw hat, a xylophone, two chairs and a table, a big box of tools, two framed certificates, one scene of Brisbane, a shepherdess's crook which I used in a play when I was young, two small "plaques" painted by hand — the work of the youthful Agens — and all the things that there is no room for anywhere else) anyway I've just picked up a guidebook of Melbourne hotels which has in the front a map of Melbourne and suburbs. I have found Surrey Hills station (the railways are all marked in red) and I'm delighted to have found Mont Albert Road.[1] I love looking at maps. Mont Albert Road appears to be a long road, about a mile. I'm afraid Grimes Street is only found on maps of a very large size, and then not always. Grimes Road would have been better, because the natural pronunciation of the former is Grime Street. Enough of this. I like looking at maps of Germany best: the names fill me with longing — Augsburg, München, Nürnberg, Schwarzwald.

This room is full of surprises. I discovered in a drawer a small Certificate which said:

Awarded to . . . Agnes Jaggard . . .
for . . . 1st Prize Senior Exhibition Doubles . . .
in this year of the War, 1915, when prize winners have
chosen to give up their prizes for the benefit of
Patriotic Funds.

I think that possibly explains Agens' present devotion to Patriotic Funds — she is making other people give up things for them as she had to in her own youth. I suppose being a runner you have a collection of "cups" — objects which should be permanently abolished or else given to people over 80 years of age. Don't you like the "prize winners have <u>chosen to</u> . . ." The "chosen to" is wonderful.

[1]TR's home was in Mont Albert Road in Melbourne.

. . . Old Coar has arrived with a bag of amazing lollies. Their colours are unbelievable but they seem to be harmless. I can hear shouts of "You fool, what did you go nine spades for?" – "<u>My</u> trick, Mr Coar" – "<u>No</u>, Mr Coar, <u>spades</u> are trumps." Apparently Old Coar is in his usual form.

I hope to hear from you soon because although I like writing to you I like getting your letters much more than that. I might write some stories, too, I have a few ideas, but whenever I start to write seriously I feel hopelessly inadequate.

Take care of yourself and of your beautiful beard.

With my love,
Ginnie.

(31)   Crimes Street.
                                              Friday Night 1943.
                                                      [30 April]

Dearest Tony,

. . . It is good to have a letter from you; as it was written on Good Friday and continuted (I don't know how that "t" crept into continued) on Saturday it has taken less than a week to reach me . . .

Perhaps you would like to hear how I'm getting on with Mafeking. Let me assure you that life with him is beyond all my expectations. To begin with, I have "gone up in the world". My position is a comparatively exalted one. Nobody knows what I am supposed to be doing, and as Mafeking's secretary I have access to all the files in the place. This means that I can wander in and out pestering everybody at my leisure, and making scenes if "correspondence" is not handed to me immediately. I hope it won't turn my head or send me crazy with joy.

My work could be done with ease by any second-grade child. Miss Harvey, whose place I have taken, has built up a complicated filing system in Mafeking's little sheep-pen, and I have a little desk in there covered with spring-back files, cardboard files, Clarence Rapid Files, Riven Expanding Files, Sym-Plex Files, loose-leaf files and indeed every kind of file anyone could possibly want.

All these files are full of "correspondence", that is, bunches of letters pinned inadequately with "Lills" and secured insecurely with paper clips which keep getting caught in other letters—they swallow each other up.

Because I saw that possibly I might not want to be in there all the time I "demanded" another desk outside, with my typewriter on it. There was a little trouble about this, but after the first morning Mafeking decided that I was right after all, because I kept pushing things off the table under his desk and then crawling in after them. As I stood up I would knock something else down and spill the waste-paper basket. So the office boy was ordered to "find a desk for Miss Foster and put it where she wants it".

You have seen, of course, the BRING UP stickers. These, in their turn, are entered in a large diary (those relevant to Mafeking's dept., that is) which is simply referred to as "The Diary" or, if I am there "Your Diary". So day by day I have to look into the diary and see what names are entered there for "bringing up". Then I have to "locate" the "correspondence" and pin it together if it has come apart. These things are simply called the "Bring Ups" . . .

Mafeking's correspondence runs to enormous lengths, and he is constantly dictating, but not to me. (There is rather a curious arrangment about stenographers. I've never been "used" because I couldn't be "taken away from the switch".) It naturally does not occur to anyone that my shorthand displays more imagination than accuracy—as Peter tells me someone said of his Anglo-Saxon. They seem to imagine that I am a competent but "unused" stenographer. I have already tried your suggested "I beg your pardon" stunt with the "dirty big pie" Weitemeyer, and his enraged self-control was wonderful to watch. However, there are four full-time stenographers who are circulated from office to office under the following system, which causes some "border incidents" that make me rock with laughter. Battersby, of course has "first pick". Watson, the Supt. of Claims, has "second pick". And it's a case of snatch and grab for the other two between the remaining dignitaries of the institution. Suppose, for instance, that the Chief

Clerk and Mafeking both want Miss Banfield at the same moment. There are "scenes".

MAFEKING:	Miss Banfield was just going to take some letters for me.
CHIEF CLERK:	Oh no, I'm afraid Miss Banfield is coming to me now to settle the Thursday Island correspondence.
MAFEKING:	But I have all the bring ups for the 26th to deal with.
CHIEF CLERK:	I arranged yesterday with Miss Banfield to do Thursday Is.
MAFEKING:	The bring ups can't wait. Mr Battersby wants them this morning.
CHIEF CLERK:	Mr Battersby particularly wants to find Thursday Is. finished by midday.
MAFEKING:	I'm afraid I shall have to see Mr Battersby about this.
CHIEF CLERK:	I shall have a word with him myself.

That sort of thing goes on for a quarter of an hour at a time, both of them talking at the top of their voices. It is wonderful to see two grown men leaning across the barrier of a sheep-pen, bundles of "correspondence" in their hands and pens behind their ears. Mafeking is constantly "seeing" Mr Battersby "about" his co-workers. It reminds me of school, and is only another manifestation of the "dirty big pie" spirit.

This afternoon I sat at my desk in Mafeking's room and made a little horse out of cardboard, using my penknife to cut the cardboard. Mafeking watched me for a few minutes without saying anything, then

"Miss Foster."
I took no notice.
"Miss Foster!"
"Yes?"
"Miss Foster, what are you doing?"
I just grinned.
"Miss Foster, I asked you, what are you doing?"
I said nothing.

"Are you making something, Miss Foster?" . . .

"Yes."

"Is it something to hold cards in, Miss Foster?"

"No."

"Is it to put in a file, Miss Foster?"

"No."

(The monosyllabic replies were given without looking at him, but out of the corner of my eye I could see he was cracking up. I just went on cutting out the horse's ears.)

"Miss Foster, haven't you got plenty to do?"

"Yes." . . .

"I don't think you've got any time to waste, Miss Foster."

By this time the horse was finished, so I just took it out to show to Diana. I suppose it is just another nail in the coffin selected for me.

The monosyllabic method is most effective. If I am at my outside table (which is really a self-contained flat) and Mafeking calls me from inside I ignore him, and at about the third call I reply in a high key "Do you want me, Mr Reed?" . . .

They will find it impossible to dismiss me for some time, because I am filing under a system of my own, from memory, so that Bates is in the "Y" file, for instance. When Miss Harvey returns she will be unable to find anything, and will have to ask me.

. . . Mafeking is going to fly to Sydney on Sunday for a week "on conference" so I shall be a sort of Demon King. If you were here you could come and sit in his chair and talk to me. I wonder what arrangements would be made for "ejecting" you, and who would get the job? The amazing thing about all this is that Fate has put a person like me in such a position. As Alfred said, "Someone has blundered."

Have you read *Death of the Heart* by Elizabeth Bowen? It is about a young girl of sixteen whose penetration and innocence have a disturbing effect on the lives of her half-brother and his

101

wife with whom she is sent to live. I think it is a beautiful novel, and I like the way it is written. The girl's unconscious demands fill people with a sense of inadequacy. The scene is partly in London, partly by the sea. If you would like me to send it, tell me.

You were speaking to me of John Nash's paintings. I have seen one called "The Moat". It is most lovely. If I could paint, I should want to paint like that . . .

With my love,
Ginnie.

(32)

Examining Officer's Dept.,
Tuesday 1943.
[4 May]

My dear Tony,

Mafeking has departed for Sydney. I am sitting in his chair, writing to you. I am only hoping that a few phone calls will be put on to me by mistake, but none have been so far. Being at Mafeking's desk gives me a feeling of intense pleasure. I must be careful that the seeds of ambition are not sown in my soul. It would be dreadful to have a secret desire to become an Examining Officer—I could never face you again. Mafeking has two cushions on his chair—one of leather, nicely padded, with a dip in the middle (caused evidently by many months of examining), and another that fits into the dip—a pleasant affair with springs. I have distributed my belongings over his desk, and my clothes hang on his coat and hat rack (some of them, that is). So far I have had only one visitor—Mr Battersby, who came to ask if I had plenty to do. Several people have looked over the sheep-pen at me, and seem to be surprised to see me occupying Mafeking's chair. Nobody has said anything.

. . . Mafeking has on his desk—I mean, I have on my desk, a bunch of dates with little notices on the page for each day . . . There is also a note saying "Dowling's birthday". I don't know who Dowling is, or I'd ring him up and wish him a happy birthday from Mafeking.

. . . When we heard that Darwin had been raided I felt rather worried about you. Joe, who is bloodthirsty, said he was glad, and gave a convincing imitation of various planes taking part in an air engagement. Of course his heart doesn't lie with present day aviation—his heroes are Richthofen, Boelcke, Immelmann, and the fliers of Neuport 28's and Fokker D7's. But when he remembered you were there, he expressed concern, and flew up the hall as a Sopwith Camel. You will not be surprised to hear that he is still wearing the same clothes. The green shirt has several more holes over the stomach. Joe says that after the war he is going to buy a model of a 1914 plane and have it shipped out here. He is going to perform those feats with ease which Richthofen and Immelmann performed, and is going to "check up" on literature concerned with 1914-1918 flying. He built yesterday a little solid model of a "Zerstörer" and painted it grey and blue. He takes infinite trouble with his models, and if they are only slightly imperfect when finished he smashes them up.

Last night All Saints had its "Annual Parish Meeting"—a gathering which never fails to amuse me. I appeared in my capacity as organist. Several votes of thanks were passed to me for the "fine work" I was doing. I enjoyed this immensely . . .

After the meeting was over pious ladies fed us with stale cakes and dry scones. The material arrangements of our Holy Mother the Catholic and Apostolic church must amaze the heathen!

I called in at the Gramophone Society after that and was introduced to one of the "promising" poets of Brisbane, a youth of the most appalling type, with thick lips and a wonderful accent. Most of his words were produced from the back of his nose. I said "Good morning. You look like Dylan Thomas." He was quite overcome, and said "Oh, I say, thank you." He asked me if I had read somebody's commentary on *Finnegan's Wake*, if I thought *Ulysses* was "permanent" and if Wales could possibly produce any good poets. I was glad to abandon him for a cheerful Irishman who had just read *Mr Justice Cocklecarrot* and we spent our time praising Royal Gertrude,[1] to the disgust of the poet. In parting

[1]The singing mouse in the "Beachcomber" sketches.

I recommended Eliza Cook to the poet. I said "She repays close and careful study." He had never heard of her!

Well, Tony, even examining officers must have lunch. I am beginning to feel like an examining officer already; soon my letters will be full of — "as to whethers" and "yrs of 17th ult.". What a pity you're not here! We could bring in some beer and have a little party among the expanding files.

With my love,
Gwen.

(33)

Wednesday, 1943.
[5 May]

My dear Tony,

I am still sitting in glory in Mafeking's chair. The chief clerk came in yesterday and saw me here, and looked absolutely horrified — as a Father Superior would look if he found a novice occupying the abbot's chair in chapel. However he said nothing.

Weitemeyer (the pie man) came in a few moments ago with several sheets of paper and said, "The other day you were talking to me about poetry." I said, "That is so." He went on, "You said that Alice Duer Miller was not much good." I replied, "That is definitely so." He handed me the papers and said, "I have written out a few poems here. Just see if you can identify them. Ha-ha. A test for a highbrow." He departed. I found written on the paper:

(1) Under the greenwood tree.
(2) Crabbed age and youth Cannot live together.
(3) Prologue to the masque in *Midsummer Night's Dream*.
(4) Wordsworth's Daffodils (one verse)
and (5) a strange poem which I couldn't make out at all.

It sounded like one of the very minor Elizabethans at his worst and was full of laments for "the turtle and the phoenix", and yet it had some most un-Elizabethan phrases in it. It referred to "married chastity" and said "Now to earth let those repair, Who were either true or fair." So I took the papers back to the pie man and impressed him with my recognition of the poems above; then

I said, "I cannot identify this at all." Mr Roland Weitemeyer drew himself up proudly and said, "I wrote it!" "Good Lord," I said. "Well," he acknowledged, "not exactly all of it. Mother helped me." . . .

Dear Mafeking is returning tomorrow morning—he comes back, I discovered by reading a telegram not meant for me, on tonight's plane . . .

WEDNESDAY NIGHT

I arrived home and Joe met me in the hall. He invited me into his room, saying, "I have a present for you!" I couldn't guess what it was. When the present was given to me I was very pleased: *Jesus meine Zuversicht* (Johann Cruger) and *Was Gott tut, das ist wohlgetan,* two records that he "picked up" in a second-hand shop, both sung by the Dom Church Choir, Berlin, conducted by Prof. Hugo Rudel.

The other record was made at the XXIXth Eucharistic Congress—a polyphonic (or The Polyphonic) choir singing *Ave Verum Corpus* (Moreno) and *Tu Es Petrus* (Pettorelli), conducted by the composer of the second work, Mario Pettorelli. *Tu Es Petrus* starts off with trumpets, on a theme very like that of "We joined the navy, to see the world" and is very jolly and definite about the Church's rock. I love getting unexpected presents, and Joe's was most pleasing.

On Sunday I heard "The Marriage of Figaro" in the opera hour. Apart from the announcer, one of those infernal women the A.B.C. pays to annoy us, I enjoyed it very much . . .

With my love,
Ginnie.

(34)

Sunshine Home.
Friday, 1943.
[7 May]

My dear Tony,

A "border incident" occurred last night at choir practice. Ethel, the prize soprano, brought along a dreadful song she intends to sing at a wedding tomorrow. Some time ago Clarice, the Demon

Contralto, sang it at a wedding (in a lower key). When Ethel handed me the song before choir practice nobody else was there. I mentioned that Clarice had been singing it, and Ethel at once became most contemptuous of her professional rival and criticized her solidly and viciously, at some length. We began to practise, and no sooner had I played the introduction than the door groaned on its hinges and IN WALKED CLARICE.

Ethel turned round, saw it was Clarice, and missed her entry. Clarice remarked rather absently that it was a cold evening, and not to let her worry Ethel – "You go right on practising, don't mind me." Clarice sat down behind Ethel, arranged her belongings noisily, and rattled her heavy beads.

Ethel nodded to me and we started again. Ethel "came in" on the right beat this time, but she forgot the words after the first few bars. Clarice prompted her, and Ethel turned on Clarice with a look of such intense fury that Clarice "dropped her head". Ethel picked up the words and went on a little further, but before long she noticed that Clarice was humming the tune very loudly. Ethel stopped. I stopped. There was dead silence for a moment and then Clarice said in a most condescending voice: "Never mind, Miss Peters, you'll be all right on Saturday." Ethel "turned on" Clarice and said with rage "I know this perfectly well. Don't take any notice of this – actually I'm only fooling – I just want the organist to run through it with me."

So we started again, and Ethel simply howled to drown Clarice's humming, which still went on, of course. The climax came when Ethel, "mad with fury" wobbled on her top G, and Clarice said audibly "Well!" They did not speak to each other again – indeed if a few people had not arrived for the practice I don't know what would have happened. But Clarice didn't forget her triumph, for she walked out after practice still singing snatches from the song in a joyful manner. "My word," remarked the bass, George, who is a strong supporter of Clarice (they sing duets, sacred and secular, at parish concerts), "that's a beautiful song, that 'Song of Thanksgiving'. A beautiful song." "Yes, isn't it," replied Clarice, and then hummed a few bars. "But," she continued more loudly, "it's not often you get it sung properly."

. . . Daphne is living with us now. Her aged grandmother, with whom she used to live, is moving to Maroochydore—a north coast town—and Daphne wanted to stay with us. I like Daphne very much, she is a nice child and seems to be happy with us. She is certainly better than the domineering Booth and the film-crazed Gloria.

I have been moved to a "dirty big" table a little way from Mafeking's door—or rather where his door used to be . . .

This morning I told him that the people who chose the texts or mottos for each day on desk calendars had "fantastically inadequate minds", and he was horrified, and proceeded to read to me a selection of the appalling things, to prove how true, wise and helpful they really are. I think he has based his morality upon them . . .

Tomorrow afternoon I have a wedding at 2 o'clock; after that I have been "invited" to play at a "musical afternoon" at All Saints held by some Ladies' Guild. There will be a lot of old ladies there, probably, and many pious brass-cleaners. I shall play "Das Schwarzbraune Bier", "Bier, hier", and "Then give me ale" with heavy chords, and possibly "Mad Floss".[1] If I have to accompany singers, God help them. I shall eat enormous quantities of home-made afternoon tea, particularly pikelets, to comfort me for being the only one of my generation in a stuffy gathering. Very often I wish I were a young man, because then I could get gloriously drunk before playing at musical afternoons; it must be wonderful to be drunk in the society of a Christian body devoted to eliminating drunkenness from the community. As a rule, however, such bodies are far from Christian. Wouldn't it be grand, when some pious creature in a feathered hat offered you a cup of tea, to produce a small bottle of violent alcoholic fluid and pour it in while she held the cup out to you! I can't do these things so I generally begin, at afternoon tea-time, by taking hold of the first plate offered to me and keeping it on my knee. Reactions

[1] Mad Floss: a piece GF wrote herself.

107

are always wonderful. Or else I walk over to the "special" plates set out near such dignitaries as the Rector, the other clergy, presidents of the society, etc., and select the choicest food, which I place on my own plate and bear away with me, nodding in a friendly way to the dignitaries . . .

DELUSIONS

Dear Sir,

Yours of 6th inst. to hand and contents noted. It would appear that you harbour a delusion. We have before us your statement

re FOOD

"One's taste no doubt deteriorates if continually vilified."

We beg to state that above statement does not appear to us to be true. Our Miss Foster spent six (6) mths. in a convent from August–January 1941–1942. We have every reason to believe that she related to you the incident of the Mouldy Pears. Do you realise that every morning, for breakfast, she ate some form of chicken-feed, and for lunch had pudding made with DRIPPING? I suppose some puddings are all right made with dripping, but these weren't that kind of pudding. (They were of a sponge-like texture, and had cold fat on the edges.) She also consumed obediently a Yellow Pudding (un-named) which contained lumps of unknown substance THE SIZE OF A FULL-GROWN CANARY'S BODY, floating in stuff which she will not attempt to describe.

And last year she spent five (5) months in a school, and was fed on food which Agens (quite rightly) would have THROWN OUT, including forms of floury paste and soup which she believed to be pig-wash. Like you, she was kept alive by her mother who provided her with tins of edible food and fed her enormously during week-ends. Her taste *did not* deteriorate.

Yrs. faithfully,
Cegar Zamboni.

Poor Tony! I can sympathise with you. Obviously you cannot adapt your views or your taste to those of the "my country right or wrong" person who had certainly gorged all his life on dirty big pies.

SUBJECT: HEADACHES

I'm terribly sorry you are not well; the climate, from what I hear, is awful. Don't bother writing if you don't feel like it. I'm glad my letters please you: I am delighted to have someone like you to write to, because sometimes the thought of the time I'm wasting against my will and the minds, sluggish and infected, of the people round me all day, fills me with heaviness which I cannot shake off. But when I write to you thoughts like that drop away, and I feel as happy as a croquet player whose ball has just gone through five hoops without stopping (if that is possible) . . .

With my love,
Gwen.

(35)   Saturday,
                                                     [8 May][1]

SUBJECT: Rain.

Brisbane had a "dirty big" storm yesterday, with hail and thunder. Actually I didn't see any hail, but the paper said there was some. It is probably a lie, but it's good to think of. I love storms, and I am surprised that God arranges so few in Brisbane. If I were God, I would wash Brisbane out "throughly", as the Prayerbook says, every week or so. I should pelt Weitemeyer with dirty big hailstones, and send thunderbolts through Mafeking's roof, to frighten him. I love rain. It rained on the "musical afternoon" and sent indoors the pious ladies and their home-made potholders, which I refused to buy. I played German folk-songs, but there were no real chances, as nobody at all listened to me, and I didn't feel quite in the mood for Mad Floss, which demands an attentive and silent background. However, I ate loads of delicious small cakes and baked loaves, and when anyone tried to sell me a basket of sweets I picked out some coconut ice—which I love—and said, "Oh, thank you." . . .

It is just evening now; gentle, misty rain is falling around the

---

[1]This letter, of which the first page is typed on WDC Internal Correspondence paper, appears to be a continuation of (34).

109

dark shapes of the trees, making the evening soft and quiet and the lighted windows look most comforting.

I have had a fantastic letter from Robin, who is back at Wallangarra camp. He appears to have retained the inward, if not the outward signs of his delirium. After telling me some of the faults of my character (an easy job) he says "My lectures on your character were only efforts on my part to prevent you from doing anything rash." Can you imagine—he's 18 (eighteen)—a person of that age "lecturing" someone five years older (I'm not quite yet, but I shall be 23 in June)! The dreadful cautiousness of "to prevent you from doing anything rash" strikes horror into me. No wonder he and Agens get on so well. "Don't do anything rash," spoken in earnest, freezes me with rage. Can't you imagine someone saying to our Lord as he took up the cross: "Be careful now, don't do anything rash; you might get hurt." Or the announcing angels to the shepherds: And suddenly there was with the angel a multitude of the Heavenly host praising God and saying "Don't do anything rash." Or St Paul, to the Hebrews: "Therefore leaving the principles of the doctrine of Christ let us go on to perfection—and don't do anything rash." Oh hell, said Tiny Tim.

SUNDAY, 1943. [9 May]
Joe has given me a delightful green flag; on it there is a bright yellow full-bosomed Greek lady with a harp attached to her, behind. I have hung it up over St Francis, who wears his cardboard halo with an air of indifference to haloes.

Last night I was really in a violent rage, so I polished all my furniture with Nobby's Clear Veneer (gives a lasting gloss). I suppose it was rather funny, really, but I put some violence into the polishing, and today I feel rather pleased with the "lasting gloss". I also threw all the contents of several drawers on to the floor and found a lot of clothes which I never wear, so I threw them out. Agens collected them this morning from the heap and "went through" them with a grimness characteristic of those who throw nothing out if it might ever "come in". I love clothes, but I rarely have enough money to buy any, so I let Agens make them for me. She loves making me a skirt for 2/3d. or something like that and it makes her so happy to think of what she has done that she sits down and watches me walk around in it, saying "My word, when I think of how little that cost . . ." or "That was two shillings for the material and a shilling for the buttons and 3d for the cotton, <u>you'd hardly credit it</u> . . ."

I'm glad you are amassing such sums of money, but I feel uneasy about the financial state of the world after the war. I think you should buy diamonds or houses or something that won't collapse. Did I tell you that I saved up £11 since you left, but it got on my nerves a bit. I kept it in two £5 notes and two 10/- notes in a lacquered box, and every time I heard someone say "Money isn't worth what it used to be" I felt uneasy, so I bought some clothes, and a couple of German books.

What a splendid day it is: there is bright sunshine, and everything is washed clean by the rain. I have moved the typewriter out to the back steps, and I am sitting on the second step writing to you, with my legs in the sun. Joe, alarmed at the whiteness of my legs, rubbed them with Vita-Tan, a pink preparation supposed to have much the same effect on legs as Nobby's Veneer on furniture. I see a lot of freckles appearing, that is all. Joe himself is liberally covered with Vita-Tan, and is lying on that ground-sheet stretched out in the sun. I am listening to Berlioz's "Damnation of Faust", which I like. I used to have a score, but I must have lent it to someone or lost it. It would be fine if you were here. Once you had "beat off" Joe and his Vita-Tan, you could lie in peace in the sun eating peanuts. I have sent you some, and hope they arrive uncensored and edible.

. . . Gretchen, for the winter nights has a "dressing gown" made especially for her at Father Foster's request, by Agens. It has three belly-straps underneath and she has eaten two of them off, so she is tied insecurely in it by the remaining one. She looks very strange wandering round in a sort of horse-blanket. It used to be bright green, but long contact with Gretchen has turned it into a uniform "off-green".

Joe, having toasted his chest has turned on to his stomach,

and is singing a gallopy tune from "The Damnation of Faust" with the orchestra. Unable to understand the words of the chorus, he is singing in 6/8 time "The buggers are off, the buggers are off."— The simple pleasures of the poor! Can't you imagine the reactions at a performance of The Damnation if one particularly strong-voiced chorister sang the above words fortissimo!

. . . I found out something yesterday: the day you "took me away from the switch", Battersby got up and looked out of the little side window affair which connects his office with the chief clerk's and gives him a view of the whole department. He watched us go out of the door and exchanged "significant" glances with Weitemeyer at the other end of the room. Also Mafeking, discussing me with another said I was "strange" and "queer", but that he "got on very well" with me. I cannot understand this at all. When he told me yesterday that his assistant was returning from her holidays on Wednesday, I expressed great delight at being about to return to the switch, and learnt that I am to be "attached to" his department "for a while". We shall see. Yesterday morning he told me about his old mother and father and sang me music-hall songs while I "dealt with" his mail. I am obviously a failure, and I hope you can suggest something brilliant which will prevent Mafeking from imagining that he "gets on" with me.

Fred Hackleskinner[2] tried his hand at a story called *The Crazy Mistress,* which was supposed to be related by an insufferable young person, but the person was so insufferable that Fred couldn't finish the story. Maybe he will try it again later from another angle.

I can hear a willie-wagtail somewhere. A few years ago one built a nest in one of our front trees—the one overhanging the little gate. He used to sing at about 3 a.m., and this woke up father Foster, who is not fond of birds singing at 3 a.m. The monotony of the wagtail's early song got on his nerves, so he commissioned Joe to bring up a huge pile of "gibbers" and put them in readiness just outside the front door. At 3 o'clock we would be awakened

[2]One of GF's early pseudonyms.

by the sound of father getting heavily out of bed and throwing stones ferociously into the camphorlaurel tree. After about a minute the wagtail would die down. Father would return to bed, and before very long the bird would start again. If Joe failed to replenish the supply of gibbers father would fling anything over — a small stool, now useless, went over one night. (It's a wonder Agens didn't use the bird as an excuse to cut down the tree.) Father's slippers were flung at the bird one night, too. Fortunately the bird went away before anything really serious happened.

Now I am listening to a Handel organ concerto. It is getting colder and the sunshine has gone. Joe has got "dressed" — three guesses what he is wearing.

With my love,
Gwen.

(36)   Grime Street,
                                                        MONDAY NIGHT 1943
                                                              [10 May]

My dear Tony,

. . . A terrible hammering is going on. Joe is rearranging his room, and is putting up many pictures and photographs of aeroplanes. He has framed and hung a great many photos of himself at various ages and in various activities — as a Young Drummer, as a Wolf Cub, and most of all as a prominent figure in the Scouting World. It is interesting to note that at the age of thirteen or so he was horribly fat — you can almost trace his fanatical muscle-developing course from the photos. High up on the wall, looking rather out of place, are two "wedding groups" of Agens and father, for which there is apparently no place elsewhere in the house and a picture of Agens as a baby. Her face shows no trace of the tree-cutting fury which, alas, has marred her later years.

Daphne has been given the room where the dreadful picture called "The Kiss" hangs — I believe you remarked on the size of the mammoth arm attached to the woman. It is to be hoped that Daphne's immature brain is not permanently warped by contemplation of that picture and father's hand-painted roses (they belong to his early period: the works of his later period are always ludicrous drawings of smiling cows or Gretchen).

I saw the cat that the drunk addressed as "Little Minnie" again in Wharf Street. Little Minnie appears to be a dim-witted cat Dr Dalley-Scarlett had a cat definitely sub-normal called Dora. She went about with her tongue hanging out, and would sit regarding visitors with an uncomprehending stare. Whenever anyone tried to sing or play the piano she would rush at them wildly and claw and scratch them unmercifully until they stopped. I sometimes think she was driven out of her wits by "musical evenings".

MONDAY

Sweet Mafeking has gone out and I am running this important department lone-handed. This morning he confessed to me that he was "worried" about the number of things lost since I had been in charge of his "files". "Do you know," he said, "I was thinking in bed last night, 'How <u>could</u> Miss Foster manage to lose all those things. I <u>know</u> she files carefully.' " I said, "As a matter of fact, I think the pixies took them during the night." He ignored that, and went on, "Every morning I think over the mail while I'm shaving, and often during the night I get up and make notes." Oh hell, said Tiny Tim.

Last night was very cold, with a bright moon. I love to walk round in clear moonlight on a winter's night. I wish we had snow here. I have never seen snow, except in pictures.

TUESDAY [11 May]

Today is Mafeking's birthday. He has worn his best suit and has been in a wonderful mood all morning. He remarked to me that he wished his mother had not been so enthusiastic about the relief of Mafeking: he simply hates having to sign his full name on forms.

Today it is cold and dull, with no sunshine. Last night I dreamt I was in Melbourne, walking through the Fitzroy Gardens; I came out of the gardens to find myself in a long street with tall houses on each side. I walked into one of the houses through a small green archway and found a lighted room with deep carpets and

114

a glowing fire where some people were waiting for me. I cannot
remember any more . . .

With my love,
Gwen.

(37)   TUESDAY NIGHT 1943
                                                [11 May]

Dearest Tony,
Today there is a letter from you; I am always glad when there
is one. The little poem about autumn filled me with sadness. I
have never seen the lines before, and I don't know who wrote
them, but they have brought back to my mind an evening in
Melbourne when my uncle was driving us around in his car; we
went down to the docks and I saw the masts of a ship standing
out against the sunset; afterwards he drove us among avenues of
trees — I cannot remember the names of any places, but as evening
drew on the leaves seemed to crowd in upon me, whispering. I
wish I could show you the picture I have in my mind of that
evening — I remember glimpses of grey water — we must have been
driving round near the sea. Anyway, the little poem has brought
back that evening so clearly to me that at the moment my mind
is full of it. I love the poem, although it makes me sad . . .

I'm quite useless, however, at writing "about" poetry. I cannot
even be bothered reading anything "about" it, except by Jacques
Maritain, the Thomist. I agree with you that most modern poetry
"peters out" — as Eliot says "not with a bang but a whimper". I
prefer the bang. I think W. J. Turner, Madge, and Auden are
tiring. Stephen Spender " 'as zomezing" and so 'as Lewis, don't
you think? While we are on the subject of poetry, I am enclosing
another I wrote. It is raining again. Rain is very comforting.

How I should love to see your stiff burgundy-coloured flowers
in the brown grass. Are there any hills around, or is it flat country.
Are there trees?

. . . An interesting thing happened this morning. A "new girl"
came to work one of our complicated "dissecting" machines (they
very cleverly add up totals of "agricultural fencing", "private

115

chattels", "livestock" etc. which people are foolish enough to insure). At morning tea-time a rather nice young girl called Mary (I believe she stared at you on that memorable day) introduced the new arrival to me, and then said to her "Miss Foster's 'got' a bearded sailor. Do you know what he did, he walked right into the office to see her." I'm sorry the typewriter does not allow me to give you the tone of those words, but "right into the office" was said in a tone which possibly you can imagine. Mary confided to me afterwards that she has a cousin at Moresby who is growing a beard. I said, "You must persuade him to call on you," but Mary replied with anxiety, "Oh no, I think I'd just die if he walked in here." Fancy a person of sixteen dreading a call from a bearded cousin because of office restrictions! In twenty years' time our lunatic asylums will be crowded – no, that is a silly idea; lunatics of that kind always grow up to be public servants . . .

I've never read any of Virginia Woolf's work. Thank you for the promise of the book . . .

With my love,
Gwen.

(38)

CHEZ MAFEKING
THURSDAY 1943
[13 May]

My dear Tony,

I really thought that after this week my address would not be with Mafeking any longer. His secretary has returned, but I am not once more at my favourite post, the switch, oh no! Another is there – Diana. Fortunately she has enough sense to keep well informed of the interior life of the W.D.C., and so indirectly I am more in touch with things; she also "hooks up" people, in fact she seems to have caught the right spirit of switch-attending. But I am retained in Mafeking's department, against my will. His secretary is engaged in a mysterious and secret operation called "Taking Statistics", which appears to be counting up letters and cards and is probably no more than that. I am "in charge of" the correspondence files, and have developed a wonderful system by which anything that puzzles me is at once "eliminated". I kicked up a terrible fuss about not having adequate files to accommodate my "correspondence", and succeeded in getting a "dirty big" filing cabinet installed just outside Mafeking's door. It is a terrible nuisance, and being made of some metal, gives hollow clangs, bangs, crashes and creaks whenever I open one of its four drawers. This morning Battersby came up to see how the "correspondence" was arranged, and found that I had lodged in it only one small cardboard folder. It was wonderful to see him open the drawers one by one and find them empty. I should really have put a pie or an iced cake in it, but I didn't remember until it was too late, and now the arrangement has been "taken out of my hands"; probably the cabinet will remain unused for several weeks while the Great Brains go into a trance over the arrangement.

A typical incident occurred early in the week when Mafeking arrived one morning and found that his light would not switch on. He pulled angrily at the cord six or seven times to make sure, and then, without waiting to take his hat off, strode down the office shouting at the chief clerk: Mr Walter! Mr Walter! My light won't switch on. The chief clerk came over to the wall of his little office and leaned across, pen in mouth. He said something (without taking the pen out of his mouth) that sounded like "Uhrr." "My light won't switch on," repeated Mafeking impatiently. "Brother" (called that because he really is a Plymouth Brother) Walter looked in the direction of Mafeking's light and said again, "Uhrrrr." Mafeking said "What's going to be done about it?" Brother took his pen out of his mouth and said in his slow, considering voice, "Oh, won't your light go on, Mr Reed?" Mafeking danced with impatience and said "No it won't go on, and something must be done about it at once." "Ah," said Brother. "Ah yes. Yes. Ah." "What does one usually do in the circumstances?" asked Mafeking. "Ah," said Brother again, ignoring his question, "do you really need the light, Mr Reed?" Well, Mafeking got absolutely mad. He choked and spluttered "Do I need the light? *Do* I need the light?" "Perhaps," continued Brother, "you could do without it for a time?" "No," shouted

Mafeking, "I could not. You don't seem to realise, Mr Walter, that mine is by far the darkest office in the place. I get absolutely no light over on that side. It's all right for you, you get the light from these windows, but everyone hasn't got an office as light as yours, you must remember that, Mr Walter." Brother put the pen back in his mouth and sat down again at his desk, turning over some papers. Mafeking pushed his way in and stood by Brother, saying in clear tones, very slowly, "Mr . . . Walter . . . something . . . must . . . be . . . done . . . AT . . . ONCE!" Brother took the pen out of his mouth again and said, "Ah, yes. Yes. We must ring up about it. Yes. All right, Mr Reed, I'll see that we ring up about it."

Mafeking returned to his own office, and Brother forgot all about ringing up. In half an hour Mafeking came down to Brother once more and said "Nobody's come to fix the light yet, Mr Walter." (Of course nobody had.) "Ah yes," said Brother. "Yes. Yes. I'll get someone to ring about it right away. Yes." Mafeking, "mad with fury", was trying to dictate letters to someone in his dim office. "Can you imagine," he said to his stenographer in injured tones, "can you imagine, Mr Walter actually asked me if I needed the light in here!"

Brother apparently rang up, for at about ten o'clock a man in overalls arrived and after waiting for a quarter of an hour succeeded in attracting someone's attention. He was shown into Mafeking's sheep-pen and looked at the light. "Can you fix it," asked Mafeking. "I need a ladder," replied the man. "I've got one round in Queen Street. I'll be right back."

That was at 10.15 a.m. The man arrived back with a ladder at 4.30 *p.m.*

There was a bit of trouble getting the ladder (a large step-ladder) in the front doors. One of them is kept permanently bolted. It had to be unbolted by the office-boy because the ladder wouldn't go through one door. After a bit of horse-play in which Norman let the doors swing back on the man before he was through, and after dropping the ladder heavily onto the floor, the man left the ladder standing by the counter and went out again.

118

He came back very soon with two light bulbs in cardboard boxes. He spent some time unwrapping these.

Then . . . (don't miss this) . . . he walked into Mafeking's office, wished Mafeking good-afternoon, and asked "Do you mind if I stand on your table to put this bulb in?" Mafeking said weakly "Go right ahead." The man in overalls moved Mafeking's blotting paper to the edge of the table, stood on it, and put the bulb in the light in about ten seconds. He put the second bulb back in its box, picked up the ladder, and departed, leaving two "dirty big" footprints on Mafeking's blotter.

(39)   FRIDAY MORNING, 1943.[1]
                                                    [14 May]

I have the most fiendish headache. Headaches are rare with me, so that when I have one I become doubly antagonistic to my enemies. Mafeking is finding me extremely "Difficult". Have you read Thomas Mann's *The Magic Mountain*? One of the characters said that when you were sick your personality adapted itself to the disease you had, so that sickness was not as bad as it seemed to those who were well, observing you. When I have a headache my mind becomes perfectly blank except for the actual scenery round me. It is rather interesting. I am looking at a wastepaper basket which looms in my consciousness like van Gogh's cane chair. I suppose that is how animals see, but that is impossible to say. It is strange how meaningless things can become. But then of course I am writing about my impressions, and that is a degree of abstraction. Horrible "infinite series" oppress me at times — the regression to infinity that the schoolmen shrank from bears in upon me. The person I hate most when I have a headache is Martin Luther.[2]

FRIDAY NIGHT

Dear Tony,

I thought of beginning a new letter, but the headache was

---

[1]This letter appears to be a continuation of (38).
[2]Q: Why is Martin Luther the person you hate most when you have a headache?
   A: I've always hated Martin Luther. I hate him most when I have a headache. (GH)

incoherently interesting. At lunchtime it was so bad that I said to myself, "I will go out and spend the money they have given me, I'll have some lunch, I will then come back and tell the chief clerk that I am becoming delirious and must go home immediately."

With this in mind I set off at one o'clock. My head felt like the inside of a boiler, about to blow up at any moment. Hammers knocked on my skull. I was brutal in the street, just bumping people out of my path. On my way to post you some peanuts wrapped up in a hat-bag by Theophilus[3] I passed Thompson's bookstore – the one where you saw "The Master's Violin". I went in to glance at his shelves and found to my delight a copy of *War and Peace,* which I bought. I tried to find out how many pages it had in as I walked to the post office, and rammed head-on into several business men. Twice I said I was sorry, but the third bump jarred my aching head, so I said "Get out of the way, damn you," and a grey-haired director looked at me pretty much as Jeremiah the Prophet looked at the harlots of Babylon. At the post office I wanted stamps, but I did not form a queue as the notice begged me to, I simply pushed in front of a number of office-boys and respectable mothers. Then I thought about lunch, but could not face any food. I went to a music store and bought a record called "Our Village Concert" . . . All through this my head continued to ache. I walked through Woolworths, which was crowded, simply for the brutal joy of pushing people about – it was wonderful to feel brutal. Ordinarily I am afraid of knocking old ladies or treading on tired mothers' feet, but I was a bit light-headed by this time, and had no scruples about injuring my neighbours, though I had to avoid damaging the record. I arrived back a little after two and had a rest. I did not feel hungry but I ate a little preserved pineapple and some biscuits. I talked to a man fixing the telephone switch for a while. He was absolutely fantastic: here are some of his statements.

[3]Theophilus Panbury was an early pseudonym – the name was TR's invention.

Omar the Persian poet liked to drink wine, but the
Church wouldn't let him, so he became fatalistic and
left the Church for good, although he became
reconciled a little to it in his last years.
All civilisation comes from Persia.
Omar Khayyam lived about 5,000 years ago.

I had no idea that such characters existed in the P.M.G.'s
territory! He was a sallow little man with a deeply lined face and
light blue eyes; he had his mouth continually open and his front
teeth were nearly all gold stoppings which glittered as he spoke.

At three o'clock I remembered that I had intended to go home.
I packed up my bag and began searching through the drawers of
my immense table to see that no incriminating documents
remained there, when my head seemed suddenly to lose all its
aching weight. In ten minutes it was nearly better. It felt so good
that I sat down among the filing cabinets simply enjoying the
absence of pain — a wonderful feeling, half mixed with fear that
pain will return: I suppose you know what it is like — a feeling
of empty clear space . . .

Tonight I am feeling fine, but tired. We have some people
staying here; a young soldier and his mother who used to live in
Auchenflower. Since the soldier has been on leave from New
Guinea, Agens invited him and his mother (who now lives in
Bundaberg) to stay here while they are in Brisbane. The boy is
about nineteen or twenty and quite a nice chap. His mother has
a passion for tidying up things, and as she is borrowing my room
to dress in (on account of Daphne's installation in the room with
that mammoth-armed woman) she mistakenly "tidies up" my
books and papers and puts all my shoes in a militaristic row. It's
amazing how Agens installs numbers of people here without any
notice — we seem to have an inexhaustible supply of spare beds
which disappear when the "callers" have gone. For instance, last
year I came home from school once to find an enormous double
bed set up in my room (you can imagine, there wasn't much space
left). "What does this mean?" I asked. "Oh," replied Agens, "X

and her children are arriving from Sydney, so I thought they could stay here." "But why do they have to sleep in a double bed in my room: aren't there beds elsewhere?" "Yes, but Y rang up from Toowoomba and asked could I put her up for a few days." The house was full of strange people for a while and suddenly they disappeared and the next day the double bed had vanished. I have no idea where it is kept; I think it is taken apart and "kept somewhere". I walked into the loungeroom one morning to look for some music and found two Americans asleep on a large mattress on the floor. I had forgotten all about them — Agens had arranged for them in my absence and though she told me about them it was a surprise to see them there. When Mrs Coar was alive, sometimes she and Old Coar would stay with us, because Old Coar on principle never stayed longer than six weeks in a flat or house, and they liked to stay with us in between times. I think Agens could put up any number of people and produce beds for them from some hidden store. Bruce is sleeping in a bed next to Joe's on the veranda, and they talk half the night and keep me awake.

Diana is a very strange person. I am getting to know her better, and find her a queer mixture of contradicting philosophy and practice. She is very eastern in temperament, and longs to go to Tibet. In theory she does not believe in mercy, though she admits that in ordinary life she cannot abandon it. I think I told you that she is interested in Yoga. Even the inadequate knowledge she appears to have of it seems to be deeply rooted in her. Did I tell you that she was once a Catholic, but abandoned the faith because, in her own words "I can't imagine how any thinking person can accept it."

I have never known much about the eastern philosophies, but one thing strikes me again and again: they are devoid of love. I don't mean romantic love, but "caritas". I find the East cruel; its asceticism (what a funny-looking word, have I got the right one?) seems to me to be contemptuous. I can imagine S. Francis undertaking a heroic penance for love, for devotion to the person of Our Lord, but I cannot see that there is anything behind the

Buddhist or Taoist practices, for example, except the exaltation of the individual. St Simeon on his pillar may have been a bit queer, but he was doing it for a person, not for the sake of re-absorption into universal nothingness. Diana loves the east and has an enormous admiration for eastern philosophy, and we often cross swords.

Diana is really very beautiful, or rather, handsome. When she pushes her eyebrows up she looks absolutely Mongoloid with her high cheekbones and contemplative eyes. She has dark, fine hair and dark eyes that seem sometimes green and sometimes more blue.

I'm tired, I shall go to bed.

With my love,
Gwen.

(40)   MONDAY, 1943.
                                                     [17 May]

My dear Tony,

Thank you for your letter of the 2nd May; it arrived on Saturday and I shall answer it tonight (D.V., as they say on the Gospel Hall notices). In the weekend I did not have time to answer it.

On Saturday afternoon I had two weddings to play for. At the first wedding the people behaved abominably; apparently some of them had no idea of what to do. They did not know when to kneel, or when to stand. When the priest said "Let us pray" the first row of people looked round to see what the second row did, the second row turned round to look at the third, and so on, until the back rows had nobody to look at. Some of them stood, a few knelt, and some adopted that meaningless position favoured by protestants—leaning forward sitting down and placing a thumb and forefinger firmly in the corner of the eyes close to the nose. Perhaps the leaning position mortifies the flesh and the shut eyes keep out the world and the devil. It seems to be a compromise between popish kneeling and heathen sitting.

The priest was a visitor who came to me beforehand and said "Are you organist heah?" I nodded absently at him, and he said

"Ai think we will have a hymn." As he said this a fierce-looking girl of about nineteen walked up and said, "I am going to sing." She handed me a copy of "I'll walk beside you", which I tossed aside on to the seat. (I was playing the Young Genius. I have three characters — with variations — which I play at weddings: the Young Genius, the Soulful Maiden and the Embittered and Disillusioned Musician. Circumstances and singers determine which I am to be.) Anyway the singer was alarmed when she heard there was to be a hymn, but we quietened her with the promise that she could sing first. She said to me "Please give me a fairly loud accompaniment. Although I say it myself, I have a strong voice." She asked for it loud, and she got it. She sang

> "I'll walk be-soide you in the world to-doiay
> While somethings and flow-ahs bless your woiay . . ."

It was for her own sake that I drowned her.

After the wedding some shrieking females waited outside the porch with boxes of confetti. They forgot that the verger led the bridal couple out after the ceremony, and when he put his head out of the door a lot of confetti was wasted on him.

Yesterday afternoon I went to Diana Gill's place. Their house is at Holland Park and there are hills around, hardly built on. Because I had never been, they drove up to the Crematorium. Have you ever been there? The atmosphere is deadly. In spite of the cleanness and the lovely little trees I seemed continually to be in a bare room with one window through which hot greyish light streamed; outside were endless plains of grey earth and all around me dust was falling, choking up the corners, falling quietly over me and all around. This picture stayed in my mind while we were there and filled me with weariness of spirit that I could not shake off. Diana's father refused to come out of the car, and when I told him how it made me feel he said that he himself could not bear the place.

Diana's young brother, a delightful child, rolled on the grass. I longed to join him . . . The walls, honeycombed with cells and little brass tablets, made me think of a race of dwarf cave-dwellers.

Some had little wreaths stuck up beside them with sticking-plaster and string.

I was filled with a great longing for the sea; I think I told you, I am afraid of the sea, but I love it in spite of my fear. It was good to be away from the Crematorium. We went home and Diana and I played the piano and Mrs Gill made us an excellent cheese souffle for tea. I was sorry when it was time for me to go back to Evensong.

This morning I saw a hat that I covet. It was like a little top-hat decorated with ribbons and flowers, and was worn by a large fat woman in a new and hideous fur coat. She looked absurd, but the hat was wonderful. Alas, I suppose I shall never get it, or even see it again.

With my love,
Gwen.

(41)   Crimes Street,
                                        MONDAY NIGHT, 1943.
                                                  [17 May]

My dear Tony,

In a way I envy you your wilderness; I could do with a wilderness myself after a day's brawling with Mafeking. You know, it's just like trying to fight a large ball of dough—your hands sink into the dough and there you are! What a mind the man has! He doesn't even know what I'm talking about unless I speak in words of one syllable. He has also that strange habit, that public servants acquire after long years, of reading his mail over to himself in a mumbling voice, with slight inflections at the paragraphs. This makes me laugh so much that he looks up, and because he doesn't know what I'm laughing at he gets frantically annoyed and then goes on reading and mumbling with suppressed rage. Today he asked me why I didn't behave in a normal manner, and I replied "Little Gwendoline was never quite like other girls." The look of blank amazement on his face was worth recording . . .

Agens has not missed her peanuts, and probably never will. I'm glad they pleased you. Don't think I've forgotten my promise to send you peanuts, but I haven't been able to get any. I have asked for peanuts until the shopkeepers know me and leer at me when I enter the shop. I think I had better go over and buy up the stocks of our friend in Toowong who was so overcome with your charm that she gave you incredible quantities of acid drops. Probably she gathers young children round her knee and begins, "Ah, my dears, how well I remember the day when a great Commander walked into my humble shop . . ."

I'm delighted to hear of your vegetable garden. Would you like some seeds for it? At the convent one of my greatest delights was a vegetable garden. I used to muck about in it during the day when I had any free time and after lunch I used to sit on a tree-stump watering it and singing "Salve Regina". Once the Superior tried to grow turnips, but I loathe turnips, and the plants mysteriously withered. Also some things I thought were going to be artichokes grew up to be zinnias, and the artichokes grew in a different place altogether. But I do not mind very much what things are, if they grow. It was pleasant when we had tomatoes and silver beet and lettuce for tea at the convent out of my garden. I hope your plants flourish under your care. If you sit on a tree-stump watering them and singing The Wolf it should have a magical effect!

Your paragraph on Victoria will be inserted in black type in all future editions of Messrs Ince & Gilbert's work. Have you seen her statue in the Treasury Gardens in Brisbane? It is, to use a phrase from Peter's last essay on Thomism, "bird-befouled".[1] Also the metal has turned a bright green in parts. Have you ever thought of Queen Victoria in heaven? Of course she will be glorified, as Stephen remarked of the Dean of Studies. I suppose the Good and Great, whose picture you have, will be there too, singing Hymns A. & M. (No, that is not possible.) Queen Victoria will meet Thomas Aquinas, St Bonaventura, the eccentric Catherine of Siena, and many more people she would probably much rather

---

[1] This adjective is used to describe statues of "staring dryads" in GH's poem "Guardian". *Poems* 1963 (A&R).

not meet. Think, Tony, God made Queen Victoria! He did in one sense, but I suppose we must remember what "that little Numidian ant" says concerning man's use of free-will.

I like your idea of blowing up schools, but it would be useless, as you say. When I remember the days of misery I had in my childhood because of schools I am filled with fury that is quite useless; the only thing that calms me is the thought that I didn't learn anything. The horrible spirit of cut-throat prize grabbing that schools breed in both children and foolish parents is responsible for untold unhappiness. There is one incident belonging to my school days that I have never ceased to regret, and I've never told anyone about it: there was in my class a girl called Ella, who came from Scotland. The children liked her, but used to laugh at her because of her funny accent. Her parents were poor, and she used to be dressed in old-fashioned clothes; I remember she could not run very quickly, though I don't know if she was lame, but she wore buttoned boots. At the end of the year Ella and I were about equal in work (we must have been nine or ten, I think) and I remember a fair-haired girl named Cynthia saying, "I hope poor Ella wins the prize this year," and my own friend said, "Why don't you let Ella get it?" I could easily have let Ella have it, but I didn't, and I can remember how disappointed she was. I've always been sorry about that. But that is what comes of herding a lot of children in the same room day by day and teaching them: "Queen Victoria died after a reign of 63 years. For 63 years she occupied the first place in the hearts of her subjects, being always ready to rejoice with those who rejoiced and weep with those who wept. All knew how fondly she loved her husband, and with what love and skill she guided her Household. . ." . . . (By courtesy of the "Outline of English History" presented to Nessie Jaggard, 1908, for Regular Attendance. As Agens' headmaster at the time was her own father, William N. Jaggard — N for Nathaniel — I think the "regular attendance" is not to be wondered at.) If I have any children who show a morbid desire to win prizes for writing essays on "A Thunderstorm", "Compulsory Vaccination" or "The Place of the

House of Lords in the English Constitution", I shall be ruthless. They will be fit subjects for "Ruthless Rhymes".

(42)

TUESDAY, 1943.[1]
Chez Mafeking.
[18 May]

Today seems like Wednesday, I don't know why. Most of the important events in my life have happened on Wednesdays. The thought of Wednesday in my mind is associated with bright yellow.

The electric-eyed ape at the Cremorne has transformed one common phrase for me: whenever I hear someone say "His eyes lit up with pleasure", I think of the ape and laugh. Even if I say the phrase to myself "lit up with pleasure" amuses me intensely. I think the electric-eyed ape is the most significant character in Tivoli's history, and he shall have a chapter in my next important work, "Apes on the modern stage".

I really did try to get some of K. M.'s[2] work, but there is none to be had from the bookstores up here. I am anxious to read her, so I'll see if I can get anything from the south. I'm glad you liked Theophilus Panbury's "Rose-tree".[3] Theophilus enjoys writing, but thinks you exaggerate his powers.

. . . I comforted myself for the loss of the beribboned top-hat by getting a sort of "Tale of Two Cities" affair, trimmed with velvet. I really need a cloak with little capes to complete the picture. Then, if I travelled about in an open cart, people would take me for a Tivoli advertisement.

WED. EVENING.

I have a letter from you, which I shall answer later.

With my love,
Gwen.

---

[1] This letter appears to be a continuation of (41).
[2] Katherine Mansfield. Tony urged me to "discover" her. (GH)
[3] A short story by GF which has been lost.

(43)   Friday, 1943
                                              [22 May]

My dear Tony,
I heard a piece of news which cheered me immensely. One person here remarked to another, "I think Mr R. appears to be a little scared of Miss Foster." This amused me and pleased me. It is borne out by the fact that the "hat-stand" incidents are changing their nature.

The first morning I was here (chez Mafeking, that is), I produced the green pixie-hat. Before I could hang it up Mafeking said, "You put that on my peg and I'll wipe the table with it."

The next time I had a hat, it was the lady's straw boater, which I hung on his peg. He removed it, and put his own hat there. Mine was put on a lower peg.

But yesterday I put a brown hat decorated with bows of ribbon on his favourite peg, and he put his own on a lower peg.

I told him yesterday that I was quite prepared to take over the whole department, and he lost his temper. Some people are quite impressive when they lose their temper, but Mafeking is quite ridiculous. I think something is likely to blow up before long, and as I enjoy scenes, spectacles and incidents I'm in a mood of pleasant anticipation . . .

FRIDAY NIGHT
I am reading at present *Revelations of Divine Love* by Mother Juliana of Norwich.

   . . . Listen to her marvellous description of the fiend himself:

And in my sleep at the beginning, methought the fiend set him in my throat, putting forth a visage full near my face, like a young man: and it was long and wonder lean, I saw never none such. The colour was red like the tile-stone when it is new brent, with black spots therein, like frackles, fouler than the tile-stone; his hair was red, as rust not scoured; afore with side locks hanging down in flakes; he grinned upon me with a shrowd look, and shewed me white teeth, and so mickle methought it the more ugly; body, ne hands had he none shapely; but with his paws he held me in the throat, and would have stopped my breath, and kild me, but he might not.

That's the real stuff. I think the fiend grins at a lot of things "with a shrowd look", while our Archbishop calmly tells the clergy at his summer school that there ain't no devil. Wouldn't it be grand if the foul fiend appeared to Dr Wand in his study "red like the tile-stone". What would an heretical Abp. do in such a case?

Well, my dear "naval friend", I'm tired tonight and now I'm going to bed.

With my love,
Ginnie

(44)   Tuesday, 1943.
                                        [25 May]
Dear Tony,
Diana has gone out, and I have moved down to my old fortress for a time . . .

I have discovered a delightful new game: there is a wall telephone just outside Mafeking's office, and it is so placed that conversations can be directed right in his ear. So I get Diana to ring the wall phone from the switch, and then I go and answer it as if it were a call for me. Then I hold fantastic conversations.

At least, that is the scheme. I have carried out only three so far. First, I was rung up by an apparently mad German called Karl. I spoke to him in German (not that I know very much, but I wrote down some on a small piece of paper and read it off very quickly). Then, the conversation with the imaginary Karl being finished, I rang up someone called "Henry" and told him (leaving suitable spaces in the conversation, of course, for the answers):

"Is that you, Henry? Listen, Gwen here . . . Gwen. Listen, Henry . . . are you listening? Karl rang up. No, Karl . . . No, I'm not joking . . . it was Karl himself . . . how did he get here? I don't know . . . no, I couldn't make him understand where I am. Listen, Henry, I can't possibly see Karl tonight, but someone will have to see him . . . he's in a most dangerous mood. Yes, I could manage him, but I can't see him. No, you'll have to go yourself, I know where he'll be tonight . . . no, I couldn't hear all he said, he spoke too quickly, and I'm out of practice. Listen, you must go to Bill's at about eight o'clock, and

130

ask him for the key . . . which one . . . oh, tell him I sent you, and it's about Karl, and he'll give it to you. Now, do you understand that? Henry will tell you. Yes, where it used to be . . . the third street. Goodbye, and be careful.

Then I rang up somebody called "Ernest" and gave him mysterious directions for following Henry, and told him to "stay outside" in case he should be wanted. All the time Mafeking was listening intently, apparently reading mail, but really he wasn't, I could see that. I shall develop the situation day by day. I was delighted to hear from Mafeking's stenographer today that he told her: "That Miss Foster's a little devil all right. I can't do a thing with her." Yesterday I staged some wonderful displays of temper, and finally he said "Miss Foster! PLEASE remember, you're in the office!"

I must thank you for the page of hats—they came, I happen to know, from the "Women's Weekly", a magazine patronised by my mother. The text, marked by you, I studied with interest and was envious of the style. The hats themselves reminded me of Andrew Marvell:

These vegetable hats shall grow
Vaster than empires, and more slow.

I read weekly the adventures of Mandrake the Magician and his giant servant Lothar—if only I had Mandrake's hypnotic powers what fun I could have: Weitemeyer would see "dirty big" pies floating before him and Mafeking would suffer all day at the presence of imaginary "callers" around him all asking in loud voices for "Mafeking". If you have not studied Mandrake's style I think you should. He "'as somezing". Lothar is a good example of what Joe will grow up to be if he continues his system of muscular development at the expense of his brain.

Sunshine Home for Cretins.
Tuesday.

Where any person is required by the National Security (War Damage to Property) Regulations to do any act or thing in consequence of amendments made to those Regulations by these Regulations, and the time for doing that act or thing would, if the amendments made by these Regulations had commenced on the date of the commencement of those Regulations, have commenced to run from a date prior to the commencement of these Regulations, that time shall commence to run from the date of the commencement of these Regulations.

The passage quoted above is from an amendment to the Regulations, and I thought you would like to meditate upon the matchless beauty of its style.

NATIONAL SECURITY ACT: AMENDMENT TO REGULATIONS 16 & 17 OF STATUTORY RULES. Price 22/6.

This full-length novel, from which the above paragraph is taken, has created a sensation in the literary world.

MISS GERTRUDE STEIN	(In Rufo-Nanine[1] World Review): "These regulations is those regulations is these regulations is those is these is unintelligible is those regulations."
HUGH WALPOLE:	"The most beautiful Book of Regulations of the year."
MR ANGUS McSLOOTH	(In The Master Plumbers' & Grand Illuminators' Quarterly Review): "Of vital interest to all Plumbers & Illuminators. We suggest that an Illuminated Text from the paragraph quoted would make an ideal gift for a State Controller."
REV. ARCHELOS WOODSER:	"If this does not make the people of our diocese Regulation-conscious, then nothing will."
MR T. S. ELIOT:	"A. . .book. . .of Regulations . . . definitely . . . amended."

[1]Rufo-Nanine: red-bearded, the adjective used to describe the condition of joyful anarchy created by red-bearded dwarfs. See (6), footnote 2.

ELIZA COOK: "I love it, I love it, I love to look
                                     At amended Rules in the Statute
                                     Book."
(Thank you, Miss Cook, that will do.)

. . .

It is time to go home now. I wish you were here to sit on the counter!

                                                        With my love,
                                                        Gwen.

(45)   TUESDAY MORNING 1943
                                                        Creek Strasse
                                                          [1 June]

Dear Tony,
A letter arrived from you this morning which proved that you are still not delirious. It is good to have a letter from you, I have seome (heavens, there we go again) something to answer instead of printing long sections of reminiscences.
    "Either this girl or I are mad. . ."[1]
    Well, Tony, I are certainly mad to 'ave missed that. I are sorry I did, I are now telling you I are sorry to be such a poor recommender. Take no notice of me in future. Anyway I shall post you *Claudius the God and his wife Messalina* very soon. I gave Old Coar, who reads a lot, *Count Belisarius* by Robert Graves for Christmas. Today I'm going to look round the bookstores and see what I can find. *I, Claudius* is magnificent. Wasn't Caligula fantastic!
    You must miss the rain up there. It is raining here now, and rain almost makes me love the city, or parts of it. I do not feel so unhappy when it rains. In Melbourne when it rained I used to put on my coat and go out into the Fitzroy gardens. Were you in Melbourne then? (It was January, 1941.) On Sundays the great

---

[1] "Either this girl or I are mad. . .": a reference to Elizabeth Bowen's *Death of the Heart* which GF had sent TR. Tony's reaction to *Death of the Heart* was unenthusiastic.

hollow sound of St Patrick's bells delighted me, and I loved the long quiet evenings.

Joe and I (who love Laurel and Hardy) went to see "Swiss Miss" and became helpless with laughter at the "piano" scene. Did you see "Fra Diavolo" — there were some wonderful incidents in that, too. L & H are quite on their own in some ways.

The grey light coming through the windows of W.D.C. is so pale that we have the electric lights on, and the strange mixture of light gives the place an unreal air. It always seems a little unreal to me, as if the people here were just playing parts, pretending to be examining officers, state controllers and so on. Sometimes it is hard to believe that they are not acting what they are. How can people ever take a place like this *seriously*? Even their language is artificial — they develop a style that becomes second nature to them, and "Bring-Ups" assume a terrifying position in life. I should like to make them study scholastic philosophy for seven years to restore some sense of proportion.

RECORDED WORDS OF MAFEKING REED

Where's that Miss Foster gone — I never *can* keep track of her.

I really do spoil Ma, you know. (Phone conversation with "Charlie".)

Will you please endeavour to locate that Bring-Up?

Miss Foster, I wish you would stop laughing. There's nothing whatever to laugh at in an office.

At lunchtime I walked around and in my walk I noticed how many hats were on quite the wrong people. I felt like tearing them from their owners' heads and saying, "Look, that is wrong, you should not wear that hat." Theophilus Panbury has drawn up a few rules for hat-buying and hat-wearing:

(a) You must buy hats out of love, not out of necessity. For the sake of necessity you can cover your head with a sugar-bag or a cardboard box.

(b) Hats must "'ave somezing". You have to be a genius before you may wear characterless hats. If you are, wear what you please.

134

If you are not a genius and you wear a characterless hat nobody will love you.

(c) Do not wear a hat on a rainy day and then carry an umbrella to keep it dry. This is ridiculous.

(d) Do not wear a hat unless your occupation permits you to wear it. It is ridiculous to run for a tram with feathers and veils on your hat. You may run for a tram in a straw boater.

Theophilus is very dull today, he is not really interested in anything. There is nothing worse than being dull. I think Theophilus is losing his balance, but it is so good to be able to write to you that Theophilus feels better just by writing. You have the same effect on Theophilus as the sun has on flowers — or perhaps it is more like rain on dry ground. This is a good thing, that you make me happy. Next Tuesday is my birthday, and so I shall be twenty-two only for another week. So far I feel no tremors at the approach of age: I feel more like the psalmist who said: "The folds shall be full of sheep: the valleys also shall be so full of corn that they shall laugh and sing." What a pity that there are so many institutions to cramp the natural flowering of the spirit, so that there are dry places instead of "valleys full of corn".

STILL TUESDAY

I have just arrived home. Dinner is not ready so I shall continue. This evening there has been a most lovely sunset. I saw it first through the trees round the Supreme Court — misty blue and purple through the lacework of leaves. Then it was lost among the buildings until we came out on the hill that leads down to the brewery. Darkness was beginning to fold into the clefts of the hills and lighted windows began to appear in the soft dark blueness. The sky was banded with clouds, and these were coloured dark red and purple and violet, while in between the clouds, laid out like ribbons, were clear spaces of piercingly cold sky. Although it is not six o'clock it is quite dark now and there is no more colour to see. After rain the hills look so clean and fresh that it seems foolish to be unhappy.

I am unhappy, though, because I am dull. There are so many things I want to do — learn German, revive my French, study counterpoint again, practise the organ pedals and do some really hard work at the piano. And when I get home in the evening I'm tired, not so much physically as in spirit. I'd love to play the piano really well once more (I used to) and now I have a much more mature outlook to bring to anything than I had when my technique was better than it is now. (I suppose you are grinning at the self-explanation of a person of 22, but I'm sure you know how I feel or I wouldn't be telling you this.) Also I'd like to cook; there is something about a kitchen that appeals to me tremendously, if it is a nice kitchen; don't you love to see plates of eggs and lemons and tomatoes and green things? But W.D.C. saps my strength and I have to spend the evenings regaining my balance instead of going on to something new. Writing to you is the greatest help of all; millstones simply fall off my neck as I write. What is there I can say to thank you for making me happy?

My thoughts often turn, as I sit among Mafeking's correspondence, to "when the war is over" and I can understand your longing for freedom.

Why don't you write more poetry? If you can write lines like those you sent me you should write more. I'm sorry you didn't find the other poem I promised you, I really will enclose it this time. It hasn't got a name — I wrote it without one and can't find one. It is about the intense loneliness that sometimes takes hold of one's spirit.

With my love,
Ginnie.

P.S. I misquoted the psalm — it should be "The valleys also shall stand so thick with corn that they shall laugh and sing."

Gwen Foster at six months

137

Top: With her father at Michelton, Queensland

Left: ". . . the dress was lavender crochet . . !"

Above: Gwen in 1941

Thomas (Tony) Riddell, *c.* 1945

Top: All Saints' Church, Brisbane
Opposite: Gwen Harwood's parents, Joseph and Agnes Foster, *c.* 1945

Lieutenant F.W. (Bill) Harwood, Gwen's future husband, at the end of the war

Wednesday evening, 1943
                                                    [2 June]

Father gave a most magnificent performance at the piano the other
evening. He wasn't very sober, which probably accounted for its
brilliance. Joe and I were helpless with laughter and admiration;
our only regret was that the incident couldn't be recorded. He
(father) said "I'm going to play the piano."

He sat down at the piano and drew out of his waist-coat pocket
an advertisement for TAUFIK RAAD'S STANDARD WHITE OIL OF
LEBANON, put the sheet of paper on the music-rest, and set the
whole thing to music in the style of Grand Opera. I can't tell you
how good it was, but it had all the virtues of The Wolf. Dad was
simply inspired. He began in a sort of recitative with the
appropriate chords: "This oil is invaluable for the following
complaints:" Then he became dramatic and sang the list of
complaints staccato punctuated with heavy chords: Gout! Cramp!
Bruises! Lumbago! Neuritis!

After that he sang (falsetto) a beautiful aria: "For weeks I
suffered severely with pains in my right knee."

I hope that some day you can witness a similar performance;
the whole work lasted well over twenty minutes, and it was only
towards the very end that father's inspiration gave out, and then
it is interesting to note that he borrowed from The Wolf. You
will be pleased to hear that he sings a version of The Wolf nearly
every morning in the bath and while he is dressing: the culture
of Mont Albert Road has left its mark in Grimy St. By the way,
is the Albert of your road the Good and Great?

Father Foster has brilliant flashes when he is not quite sober.
He gives "one-man" shows with a number of characters and once
sang "The Wreck of The Hesperus" with the most ludicrous
rhymes imaginable. His versions of popular hymns are something
amazing.

Last Sunday evening, as he had Mrs Holmes and Bruce for
an audience, we were treated to the stories of Dr Crippen, Maria
Marten, Jack the Ripper, etc., with new and gruesome details.
We also heard about the policeman who was shot from behind

his Uncle Fred's tombstone, but Uncle Fred has become Uncle Richard!. . .

The bakers in Brisbane have gone on strike, and we have had no bread for days. I suppose the consumption of pies will go up 100%, and the sale of iced cakes and jam tarts, especially dirty big ones, will exceed all previous records. The reaction of the pie and sandwich eating company is well worth study. Their constant cry is "What shall we have for lunch if there's no bread?" Pies, I gather, are good, but they don't fill up the corners, and even the most enthusiastic pie-eaters seem to crack up occasionally. I knew an enormous girl who ate EVERY DAY FOR LUNCH two pies and two ham rolls. I asked, "Don't you ever get sick of them?" "Yes, I do," she replied with a well-fed sigh, "but what else *is* there?"

I have rubber soles on the shoes I'm wearing today, and I find that by a little pressure on the foot as I walk I can produce a horrible squeaking sound on the W.D.C.'s lino. Needless to say I find plenty of occasions to walk up and down. The simple pleasures of the poor!

Tomorrow is Agnes' birthday. I have got her a small owl sitting on a red branch (a brooch) and a brown handbag. Agens is easy to get things for as presents because she tells you what she wants. (I must confess however that she didn't say "I want a small owl sitting on a red branch.") I shan't see much of her because tomorrow is Ascension Day and I have to play for High Mass at 6.30. It is really one of the loveliest masses of the year. I remember one year, before the glass was taken out of the east windows for safety, when just as the priest intoned "Glory be to God on high" the sun came up and flooded the windows with light. It will be dark when I get up tomorrow, and cold. In the evening I have the village choir practice. They were singing so abominably that I had to arrange a weekly practice at night instead of on Sundays after mass. Alas, the practice often turns out to be a free fight between Ethel, the demon soprano and Clarice the contralto. These are both "professional" singers, according to themselves. Ethel has a tremolo that would float a sheet, and Clarice has the idea that if she sings half a bar behind everyone else it adds "weight" to the general tone. George the bass throws his tremendous voice about with no regard for persons. He belongs to the "good old school" and sings

Tu-hurn th-hy face fro-hom my-hy si-hins, and
My soul doth magnify the Lo-hord.

. . .I'll answer your latest letter soon.

With my love,
Gwen.

(47)
Saturday, 1943
Grimes Strasse.
[5 June]

Dear Tony,
Let us consider the simple facts of Frank's[1] visit to the W.D.C.

(1) Frank comes in and stands at the counter.
(2) I run down to meet him, crying Frank! Frank!
(3) We talk for a while.

You can't imagine what a turmoil that simple visit has caused!. . . It appears that all the unrest which you caused has been awakened by Frank — apparently it was not dead, but sleeping. It is as if an ape-man walked down Creek Street. People would say, "How strange. . ." and "How alarming. . ." Then, six weeks later another ape-man is seen in Creek Street. Creek Street is shaken. It does not know how many ape-men there may be hidden in secret places.

One of my contemporaries, a stenographer, said to me: "I wish you wouldn't do that sort of thing. I felt all funny." (She said of your visit, "If any of my friends walked in like that I think I'd die.") They are all waiting for Frank to come back, because you came back the day after and sat on the little counter near the switch!

[1]Frank Kellaway, a friend of TR, also a lieutenant in the RANVR. He later transferred to the Royal Navy.

145

Your serial letter was delightful. I liked very much the description of "terratics"[2] – an excellent word. The narrow limits of Mafeking's intelligence amaze and distress me more and more. "Isn't it a wonderful thing," he said to his poor secretary, "to be in love with one's work!" Work! The work he does could not be taken seriously by any person whose brain was normally developed. As for his secretary, I am sorry for her. She is a woman of about thirty-five and was once, I should think, most attractive. But study of such books as "How to Succeed in Life" and "Succeed by Will-Power", and a morbid dabbling in spiritualism and theosophy have ruined her mental balance. She has developed an "office manner" which consists of tearing into files and boxes of cards like a hungry hen rooting in a lettuce-bed. She always has six jobs on hand at once and walks round with a pencil behind her ear and a bundle of papers in her hand. Her forehead is permanently creased with worry and she mutters to herself continually. . . "Where is that Mt Morgan file, where did I put it, and where is the fixed property return for Johnson's factory . . . oh dear . . . how shall I ever get through all this . . . the figures are wrong and Mr Battersby wants them at once. . .I haven't gone through the taxation file. . ." If I look anywhere for a thing and can't find it she looks for it immediately after I have given up, with a grimness that is not funny, only pathetic. She told me that if her work goes badly during the day she "has a bad night". Her favourite remark to those who say she is looking tired is "But I live so intensely every moment that it wears me out". . .

I think your estimate of Robin is quite right. *Blut und Eisen* might well be his motto. . . His father, who is a German, is not a bit ruthless; he is the "merry peasant" type, the simple beer-drinker. He is teaching himself Latin, although he is nearly sixty. Robin is suspicious of learning and dislikes scholars. . . The Germans seem to mix up the most amazing inconsistencies in their

[2]terratics: TR's word, formed on the analogy of lunatics, who are madmen whose madness is linked to the moon. The madness of terratics on the other hand is linked to the earth and dull and unimaginative things.

nature. I suppose the mixture of opposing characteristics accounts for their fanaticism when they are caught up by an idea. . .

I am glad that the peanuts arrived safely at last. You refer to "an enormous quantity". That was not my intention—I meant them to arrive in small parcels at intervals of a few days, but I see that the postal authorities hoard them and deliver them all at once. You did not report on their conditions. Please tell me if they were edible, or whether I should pack them in tins in future. You will be pleased to know that the little labels are supplied by the W.D.C.; I simply cut out the unprinted part of their package labels. W.D.C. also supplies the string and quite often the brown paper. If there is anything else you think you would like from them, I shall be pleased to steal it for you.

. . . Daphne, far from being the treasure I imagined, is proving difficult. She dropped Agens' porcelain heat-controlled iron and smashed the case to bits. Agens bore this with great calm, and said very little. But Daphne dropped Agens' silver entree dish and damaged the lid and Agens is now alarmed. I don't think Daphne has any care for our things. She is just as film-crazed as the previous Gloria, and reads 2d magazines like Mavis. Agens, who can manage terrifying committees without a tremor, seems incapable of handling servants. I think she could manage a large body of them successfully, but perhaps her technique with individuals lacks somezing.

On Monday I have a holiday. I hope there is plenty of sun. I shall write to you again then.

With my love,
Gwen

(48)   Monday, a holiday 1943
                                    [7 June]

Dear Tony,
Though my birthday is not until tomorrow, today is a holiday and I anticipated the happy feast.

The family have given me beautiful presents.

Joe gave me a pair of brown slippers and two discussions by

147

Eric Linklater, called *The Raft* and *Socrates Asks Why*. Joe says he picked the book because of its title, *The Raft*.[1] That shows a simple and touching faith!

Agens gave me some framed prints: two Cezannes (one is "The Viaduct"); "The Phantom Ballet" and "Above Cadsdean", by Paul Nash; a landscape by a man I don't know, Segondac[2] if I have read the signature correctly.

They are all coloured prints and I have moved some of my other pictures out and hung Agens' prints, which fill me with pleasure when I look at them.

Daddy gave me a lovely Mozart concerto (K453 in G Major) played by Edwin Fischer.

Agens also gave me a blue knitted jumper, but I don't suppose it would interest you.

So you can see what a happy day it has been. I wish very much that you could have been here too, looking at the lovely pictures and listening to the Mozart, and perhaps walking over to buy incredible quantities of acid drops from your admirer in Toowong.

This is the last letter you will have from my 22nd year, and I'm sorry it isn't longer (the letter, not the year), but Theophilus has written you a story.

Please tell me when your own birthday is, and perhaps Theophilus will send you a blue knitted jumper and some brown slippers on a raft.

With my love,
Gwen.

[1] The Raft: the name of a song for which GF had the music.
[2] Segondac: Ségonzac.

148

In Nativitate Gwendolinae[1]
W.D.C.
[8 June]

Dear Tony,

There was a letter from you waiting to bless this happy feast held by anticipation at home yesterday, and again at W.D.C. today. And what a letter it was! I emptied it out on to my desk and read with delight the interview slip and the notice TO TAPE USERS and looked intently at the hat of Mrs Ella Andrews, the land-lady who objected to a <u>bachelor entertaining women friends</u> in his flat.

CONTINUED AT GRIMES STREET. Tuesday evening 1943.

This morning I walked round to the offices of all the dignitaries and said to them in turn: "Today is my birthday."

I said this in a voice that made it clear that the event was one of great importance, and should be recognised. Their reactions were interesting.

Mafeking looked suspicious; he thought a major crisis was upon him, and when he found that nothing of the kind was about to happen he looked relieved and wished me many happy returns.

The accountant, Roland Weitemeyer, turned on a number of fantastic felicitations in his best pseudo-Elizabethan manner — echoes of the phoenix and the turtle — and grinned like a schoolboy.

The assistant accountant, a pleasant but unimportant person, said "Oh, is it? That's nice. I suppose they'll buy some cake for our morning tea." (This refers to the practice of collecting 3d from everyone — except Battersby — when a birthday is known and buying dreadful cake for morning tea. As the cake-buying is left to "the girl" you can imagine what sort of cakes we get.)

The chief clerk was hanging up his coat when I went in. I said loudly at his back "Mr Walter!" He turned round quickly, still struggling with his coat-hanger. "Yes, Miss Foster?" "Mr Walter," I said as magnificently as I could, "it's my birthday."

He looked dreadfully alarmed. He obviously thought I was

[1]In Nativitate Gwendolinae: Gwendoline's birthday.

going to ask for the day off. I felt sorry for him, he looked so apprehensive. "Isn't that nice?" I said, "I love birthdays."

When he found that I was just there for congratulations his face melted into a pleased smile, and he hung up his coat, shook my hand, and spoke pleasantly on birthdays in general.

Old Watson, the superintendent of claims, who loves to play the part of a grandfatherly admirer of young women, talked about himself for five minutes and then wished me a happy birthday as an afterthought.

My contemporaries, of course, couldn't make out what I was doing it for, and couldn't understand why I should walk in to the Big Chiefs and tell them about my birthday. Their concern was magnificent when I said, at morning tea (I had left it till then because he had been interviewing "callers"), "Oh well, I'm going to see Mr Battersby now."

I put down the dreadful piece of cake given to me in honour of my birthday and opened the door of the lunch-room. Someone tugged at my arm. It was the girl who said she'd "die on the spot" if you called to see her without waiting for permission. "There's no need to go in," she said, "they told him it was your birthday." "Yes," I replied, "they may have, but I haven't."

I strolled in to Battersby's office. He was reading a list of External Territories and did not look up, so I said very loudly "Mr Battersby!" He looked up and said, "Yes?" – "It's my birthday." Battersby got up, put down the list, and shook my hand warmly. "Congratulations," he said. I grinned at him. "Are you happy?" he asked. "Yes," I replied, "extremely happy."

Then I went back to my contemporaries, drank my milk, ate the cake and read your letter again.

Mafeking appears to be getting fatter and fatter. . . He has got glasses because of eyestrain, and is most selfconscious about them. If he has to walk the length of the office he takes them off as he leaves his pen and puts them on when he reaches his destination. Unfortunately I can see his face whenever I sit at my desk (my desk is a dirty big table with two drawers in which I keep a great many personal belongings) and the constant sight

150

of his owlish face will unhinge my mind in the long run. The utter blankness of his expression when he is unaware that I am watching him makes me doubt the statement "Man is a rational animal".

There is wonderful fruit in Brisbane at present — great red apples, custard apples, pawpaws and delicious white grapes that look as if they have been frosted over and are ice-cold to eat. I eat fruit mostly for lunch and keep supplies of grapes by me to eat during the afternoon. Last Saturday there was a retreat at All Saints' conducted by the Rector. A notice at the back of the church said, "We will be unable to provide anything but fruit for lunch in the music-room. Those who attend lunch are requested to bring their own." So after I left W.D.C. on Saturday I went up to one of the addresses at the Retreat and then went to lunch with the retreatants. On the table were plates of fruit. Fr Darrell Cassidy said grace and began reading some of Dr Samuel Johnson's arguments about religion — he always picks something strange and reads it in a serious voice with ecclesiastical earnestness that makes it twice as funny. I ate pears, apples, mandarins, bananas and white grapes, and curly fruit skins mounted up on my plate. Retreatants cast stern looks at me. I began to choke with laughter at Fr Cassidy's reading of Dr Johnson's marvellous cracks at the Presbyterians and Scotland in general, and the solemn retreatants (who were probably trying to extract spiritual benefit from the good Doctor and to mortify their desire for lunch) looked at me with anger and sorrow. Most of them had brought sandwiches and buns of their own and regarded my raid on the fruit as un-Christian and self-indulgent. Every now and then Fr Cassidy would give a monkish look round to see if everyone had finished. When everyone had, he said grace once more, and the retreatants took their helpful books back to the grounds and the church. Although the church is in the city streets there is an air of quietness about it: I think it must be the trees; they gather quietness among themselves. Even at a short retreat it is strange how the world takes on a quality of remoteness.

Next Sunday is the feast of Pentecost, the most mysterious feast in the whole year. It always fills me with wonder. When I see High Mass on this day, with the solemn red vestments and the poinsettias through the church I find it easy to think of the descending tongues of flame. (Once up at the mission on the hill a small child was asked to draw a picture of the descent of the Holy Ghost, and she drew the twelve apostles sitting in a row with their heads on fire and clouds of smoke going up to the ceiling!) The words of the introit fill me with joy:

> "The Spirit of the Lord hath filled the whole world, alleluya: and that which containeth all things hath knowledge of the voice, alleluya, alleluya, alleluya."

. . . PLEASE, Tony, go easy on the peanuts, I think the supply has failed. I went round to my usual peanut-supplying shops today, and they didn't have a single peanut. The registered ones are not special, I just had a fit of registering because a sinister postal official, weighing a package for me, said in a gloomy voice "If I were you, I'd register all my parcels." I took this as a warning . . .

With my love
Ginnie.

(50)

W.D.C. Creek Strasse
In Oct.Nativ.Gwen.[1]
Thursday, 1943
[10 June]

Dear Tony,

. . . This morning I bought "The Philosophy of St Bonaventure" by Etienne Gilson, translated by DOM ILLTYD TRETHOWAN Monk of Downside Abbey. St Bonaventure was called "The Seraphic Doctor" and certainly his works disprove the idea that Franciscans cannot be expected to shine in the realm of metaphysics. I have read a translation of his "Itinerarium Mentis in Deum" but it is very difficult, though it has the quality of "radiance". Gilson is,

---

[1]In Oct.Nativ.Gwen.: a reference to the eight day period following a saint's day in the Catholic calendar.

next to Maritain, probably the greatest living writer on mediaeval philosophy. I don't know when I'll have time to read the book. I bought it second-hand at Pelligrini's.

War and Peace, which I'm reading at present, is excellent. Why didn't I read it before, I wonder? . . . The spirit of our red-bearded friends is evident in Russia, especially when Pierre and his comrades tied a policeman to a bear's back and put them both in the river. That was splendid.

Joe is doing the most fantastic exercises in his course of physical development. He now exercises nightly with a CROWBAR which is so heavy that I can hardly lift it. I spoke to him on the subject of mental degeneration brought about by fanatical exercises, but he told me scornfully that his brain was very well developed and added, "For as long as I can remember I have never missed saying my prayers at night." It would be interesting to know what he says. Probably, "Lord, make me the strongest boy in the world, Amen." The useless fence has now been put up on both sides of the house. If only we had something to keep behind it! A large, fierce ape trained to bite anyone at a word of command would be wonderful. An electric-eyed ape for night patrols would be even better. There is some talk of Joe's buying a cocker spaniel. I hope he does, for I love them. It would be fine to have a real dog instead of the greedy and stupid Gretchen. Gretchen is incapable of devotion even to Father. She understands only one thing: food.

Butter is rationed to 1/2lb per person per week. This is rather a blow and will mean the end of various biscuits and cakes made with butter. Agens could not make me a birthday cake this year. In peace time she used to make us great fruit cakes for our birthdays, full of rum and covered with snowy icing thrown over the cake in one piece. One year I went to the tin to have a piece of cake about a week after my birthday and found that there was none left because Joe and Father had been taking immense slices for their lunch and morning tea each day and feeding on the cake for supper late at night!

Mafeking has gone out for a while, and I have been looking

at the book by Gilson. I found in the notes S. Bonaventure's list of the Ecclesiastical Hierarchy, and the interior hierarchy as well . . .

Also of the Celestial Hierarchy:

Angels; Perlustratio
Archangels; Praeelectio
Principalities; Prosecutio
Powers; Castigatio (I like that)
Virtues; Confortatio
Dominations; Convocatio
Thrones; Admissio
Cherubim; Inspectio or Circumspectio
Seraphim; Inductio

Lower than any of these is the War Damage Commission: Regurgitatio (or Bring-up).

THURSDAY EVENING [10 June]

Did I tell you that I have been "demanding" an assistant for nearly a fortnight. I "bring up" the subject daily and surround myself with an elaborate and complicated array of cards and files which I refuse to let anyone else touch. I have trained Mafeking so well that when he brings out mail to me he never throws it down on the table, but asks "Where can I put this Miss Foster?" I indicate a place with my hand and say, "On top of that file," or "Behind the typewriter" or sometimes "You'd better give that to me." Several times he had put things down without asking me, in which case I made him sort them out again so that I could get on with my "entering", and now he always tells me exactly what everything is. The whole affair is fantastic. He is simply a bully who knows he can't bully me. It is ridiculous. I took three (3) days to do an elementary job—"eliminating" names from a file—which I could have done in three hours. When I had finished I took two "dirty big" sheets of paper, with names all over them ticked and cross-ticked in blue and red pencil and red ink and put them on Mafeking's desk. He studied them for about ten minutes and then the following conversation took place:

"Miss Foster, have you <u>got</u> the statistics of these <u>out</u>?"

—Yes.

"How many names were on the original list, Miss Foster?"

—Ninety-six, or perhaps more or less. I can't count very well.

"Oh well, you needn't be too exact, I'll look after the actual numbers." (In M's mind, counting names is "statistics".)

—No.

"What do you mean, 'No'?"

—No, I can't count very well.

"And how many names are on your present list?"

—Forty.

Mafeking then took out a little pad and wrote on it

$$\begin{array}{r} 96 \\ \underline{40} \\ \underline{56} \end{array}$$

He stared at this little sum for a time, and then said (as if he were announcing a scientific discovery): "Miss Foster, do you realise that actually less than 50% of the original names remain?" He fell into a sort of trance for a time and then announced, "Miss Foster, you've done a good job with this."

Then he turned to his poor secretary and said, "Miss Harvey, come here, I want to show you what Miss Foster's done with the Sydney list. Come here and look at the statistics." (The "statistics" being the little sum on his pad.)

Can you imagine it!!!. . .

FRIDAY NIGHT [11 June]

Dearest Tony,

There is an airmail letter card from you tonight. I've never had one of these before, so I read the notices on the front with great interest, especially the dreadful warning IF ANYTHING IS ENCLOSED THIS CARD WILL BE SENT BY ORDINARY MAIL.

The letter itself made me sad because you are so unhappy there. But if the theatre is your mistress, you won't ever be happy in separation. But remember, when you do get back to the theatre, all your unhappiness will melt away, and your present sorrows

155

will be enrichment to you, and not a burden. You will be like the knights of the cross who finally saw the Holy City:

> E l'uno all' altro il mostra, e intanto oblia
> La noia e 'l mal della passata via.[2]

Your letter told me some things about you that I didn't know, I mean about your earlier years, but you are such a mysterious person that I don't think I really know very much about you. I can remember the first night I saw you: I was filled with a sense of wonder which unsettled me: Theophilus did some metaphysical handsprings and still you are a mystery. And I'm not using "mystery" in the sense of "problem" — a "problem" personality is no more than a personified crossword puzzle: once solved, there is nothing beyond. I am using "mystery" in the sense of "ens absconditum".[3] The mind leaves a problem, moves away from it. But in a mystery, the mind, as Maritain says, "pierces further and further into the same depth. The Mystery is its food."

Theophilus is glad you liked his story "Another Country".[4] Tony, will you please send down "The Rose-Tree" and "Another Country" (if you have kept them — don't worry if you haven't). I will send them back to you, but I don't keep copies of anything and I want to take copies of them. Theophilus would be grateful for any suggestions, blue-pencillings or drastic criticisms from you.

You don't seem to be at all well. Please take care of yourself as much as pobbisle (good God, what a word, it was meant to be "possible" but went Learish. Words on typewriters do funny things if you don't watch them.)

When I was very young I was most unhappy because I was the youngest and smallest person in my class at the state school: there were under the school some wooden beams on which the children used to swing. The ground sloped so that only the tallest

---

[2]"E l'uno all' altro . . . via": from *Gerusalemme liberata (Jerusalem Delivered)* by Tarquato Tasso. ("And one shows it to the other and in doing so forgets the weariness and the suffering of the past journey.")
[3]ens absconditum: a hidden being.
[4]"Another Country", "The Rose-Tree": two short stories written by GF. Theophilus Panbury was an early pseudonym invented by TR.

children could reach the end beams, but at the other end of the building were low beams which I could reach easily. My contemporaries used to laugh at me because I couldn't jump up to the beams they could reach, and I couldn't bear that, but pride prevented me from joining lower classes on the low beams. Now one day our teacher read us the story "The Tar-Baby" from the Uncle Remus book. When she had finished she said, "Write down what you can remember of the story, in your own words." So we all did, but it was delightfully easy for me because Old Coar had read me the story so many times in childhood that I knew it by heart. The teacher was pleased and said, "You can go out and play now, till lunch-time." So I went out of the classroom, and down into the playground. All the other children were in school; the lunch bell would not ring for twenty minutes: so, all by myself, I had a glorious time swinging and turning somersaults and hanging upside down with my hands brushing the hard ground. I thought of this the other night when Old Coar came to play cards, and felt very grateful to him. His books were the delight of my childhood when we lived at Mitchelton; he had most of Shakespeare's plays illustrated with dozens of bright pictures, and I knew all the pictures by heart long before I could read. His wife gave me a beautiful bracelet of cameos. They were very good to me.

It is getting late, so I will stop soon. . .

I'm sorry that your chances of returning to Brisbane are "very slight indeed". In the last war my father was in the Army Medical Corps, in the 2nd Field Ambulance. There is a pathetic framed certificate on the wall here which begins "On behalf of the Residents of Rockhampton and District, we desire to express to you our high appreciation of the services . . . we wish for you the peace and prosperity you have so amply earned . . ." and so on, with ludicrous illustrations of cannons and laurel-wreaths, signed by the Mayor of Rockhampton and other dignitaries. There are pictures of Daddy as a sergeant, very slim and smiling, looking rather like Joe does now.

It will be a fine day when I sit in a box in a great London

theatre, attired as a Russian Spy, and watch your acting. At the end of your performance I shall cry (through a concealed microphone) "AH! ZAT 'AS SOMEZING."

With my love,
Gwen.

(51)   Friday 1943
[11 June]

My dear Tony,

I shall not lie to you, as I was tempted first to do when I read your letter this morning, but I shall tell you a very sad story; that is, it concerns a prophecy which arrived too late.

Last night I put on a new dress and arrived to find the family seated eating their dinner. Father Foster looked at me and said, "My word, that is a nice dress." I replied, "I'm glad you like it, it is a new one." "How much did it cost," asked father. I told him. "Well," he said, taking some money out of his pocket, "I'll contribute this towards it, because I like it."

I thanked him very much, and put the money in an envelope in my bag.

Now this morning, because it was bright and fine, I got up very early and found myself in town soon after eight. I walked around looking at people and shops, and thought how nice it was to have some money which I didn't deserve.

Alas! My idle walk led me past the windows of a shop called Paul's which specialises in feminine clothes. In one window I saw a dear little brown hat. It had feathers and a veil, and was built up in a Tower of Babel effect, like this:

with feathers sticking out of the top story and the veil floating round.

What do you think I did? Of course I did; I went in and bought it. I carried it in a bag to the W.D.C. and arrived (late, as usual) to find a letter from you.

I opened your letter, and what did I read. . .

"In your remarkable taste re hats, I detect incipient 'Queerness'."

Can you imagine my feeling of guilt? Can you possibly conceive what dreadful visions your description of a pineapple-crowned old age brought to my mind? Fear came there upon me,

The Target Hat
(for lady archers)

The Nelson's Column Hat

The Clock-tower Hat

The Pagoda Hat
(for oriental types)

The Pineapple Hat

and sorrow, as the psalmist says, when I read the warning: "You would <u>do well</u> not to indulge this taste."

> With guilty fear she sees th'approaching fate:
> Too late! she cries, and Echo moans, Too late!

And yet why should the prospect of a pineapple-crowned old age deter me from wearing what you call "outre" hats <u>now</u>? If I don't wear them now, when shall I be able to wear them? Never. After all, I am but human; it delights me to wear strange hats and carry them off. Do you want me to go round in 3/6d bargains pulled well down over the ears? If I did, you would probably never take me out again.

But still a warning voice whispers in my unwilling ear: Tony is wise; Tony has probably seen the young maiden turn into the bird-bedecked hag; Tony has seen the aged organist in the beribboned top-hat . . . enough . . . take heed.

Your warning has shaken but not cured me: if I am to be cured there must be repeated warnings of a like nature. I think anecdotes or reminiscences of actual characters would help. I shall wear the hats, but the pineapple and the stuffed bird are ever before me.

SUBJECT.[1] LUNACY
Perhaps you have noticed a drawing on this page. It was suggested by the local shopkeeper's daughter, who called to take our Daphne to the pictures. The girl, while she was waiting for Daphne to get dressed, related some anecdote to Agens, and it concluded with the words, "Gee, Mum went mad. Gee, she did tear up the turf."

SUBJECT. JERRY'S DANCING
SATURDAY. This morning I was in Penneys to buy some buttered rolls. I went into one of the little shops in their arcade; there were five girls There, all cutting up things and talking to one another. I thought the scene would please you: here it is.

I stood unattended for about five minutes while the following dialogue (at much greater length) went on.

GIRL:	Cripes, were you at the dance last night?
2ND GIRL:	Yeah.
GIRL:	Cripes, did you see Jerry!
2ND GIRL:	Yeah.
3RD GIRL:	Did you go with Jerry.
GIRL:	Yeah.
2ND GIRL:	You wouldn't get me going with Jerry.
GIRL:	Cripes, he's all right. It's only his dancing.
2ND GIRL:	You should see it, all right.
GIRL:	Well, if you saw him you can imagine what it was like in the progressive barn dance!
3RD GIRL:	You wouldn't catch me in the barn dance with Jerry.
4TH GIRL:	(seeing me, and waving a breadknife vaguely in my direction): Hey, Phyllis, there's someone waiting. (They all ignored her, and went on.)

[1]The rest of this letter is typed on WDC Internal Correspondence paper.

161

5TH GIRL:	(Appearing suddenly from under the counter with a big sausage): Jerry! Huh!
GIRL:	Cripes, in the barn dance he was like a bloomin' kangaroo.
2ND GIRL:	I dunno what you go with him for.
5TH GIRL:	(She appears to be malicious): Huh! Can't get anyone else.
4TH GIRL:	Hey Phyllis, there's someone at the counter.
GIRL:	(Coming over in my direction): Yeah?
ME:	Two buttered rolls, please.
GIRL:	We got none.
ME:	I saw the baker bring them in. (GIRL glares at me.)
GIRL:	Hey Phyllis, we got any bread rolls?
3RD GIRL:	(Phyllis, it appears): Yeah, in the basket. (GIRL takes two from the basket and starts to put them in a bag.)
GIRL:	Tuppence.
ME:	I want butter on them. (GIRL glares at me.)
PHYLLIS:	The boys don't like Jerry, neither.
GIRL:	(She has got some butter out of the refrigerator and has cut open the rolls.) It's only his dancing.
PHYLLIS:	You wouldn't strike me dancing with Jerry.
GIRL:	(Leaning on handle of breadknife): He certainly walks over you.
5TH GIRL:	Huh!
GIRL:	Tom don't like me going out with Jerry.
5TH GIRL:	Huh! Tom!
GIRL:	(Buttering rolls): Tom says, You go out with Jerry and you needn't go out with me.
2ND GIRL:	You wouldn't find me taking talk like that.
4TH GIRL:	(Evidently more or less "in charge"): The lady's waiting. (GIRL just turned round, glared at me, and made no attempt to hurry.)

I got the rolls in the end and departed in the middle of a further discussion on the kangaroo-like Jerry.

SUBJECT. BRIDAL MARCH

There was a wedding this afternoon, and two beautiful "incidents" occurred. The first was at the moment when the bride, who had on a satin dress with a train about four yards long, was ready to set off down the aisle. A little flower-girl was in attendance to carry the train. The bride, a grim-looking woman, stood impatiently for a moment, then turned round to the little girl and said in a fiendish whisper "Pick it up, for God's sake."

The second incident featured the verger's little boy, who always sits in the back seat during weddings. He stood in the shadow of the door as the procession went out and said to his father in a penetrating voice "Hasn't the lady got a big dress on, Daddy!"

Daphne, it appears, is just as film-crazed as the late Gloria. She remarked to the washerwoman this morning (who told us) "Oh, Mrs O'Driscoll, I do wish I was Tyrone Power's wife!"

You will be sorry to hear that the Tower of Babel hat has been launched successfully on its career. I wore it to the wedding and on the way home I sat opposite a girl in an immense fur coat and a violet knitted dress. She was with a soldier. I was having a little trouble with the veil in the wind, so to keep it down I planted my hand firmly on it, leant my face against my hand, and appeared to be gazing pensively out at the sunset. The girl leant towards her companion, the young soldier, and whispered in his ear (a little too loudly) "Get a load of that hat. It's a corker."

SUBJECT. W.D.C.

It is interesting to note that the W.D.C. has "dispensed with" the services of its brightest office-girl. She was a pretty young wench called Marie and showed a fine spirit of resentment when those in authority tried to squash her. For example, one night the men were working back and "Brother" decided that if they "had their tea in" instead of "out" it would save time. Marie was sent round with a pad to write down the orders for dirty big pies, jam rolls, napoleons, iced cakes etc. She came in to Mafeking and said "Mr Reed, may I have your order please, for tea tonight?" Mafeking said crossly "Go away, Miss Duncan, I'm busy." (He was filling his pipe.) Marie said "I have to get the orders now, Mr Reed,

163

because I have to buy the tea before five o'clock." Mafeking put on a fine display of bad temper and said "Don't you try to hurry me, Miss Duncan. I don't like your attitude at all. I'll give my order in good time, and I won't be rushed by you." Marie replied with equal irritability "All right then, you won't get any." I was there at the time, and thought how good it was to get someone of sixteen replying to Mafeking like that. Of course she didn't have a chance, really. I don't know exactly why they "dispensed with her services"—one minute she was there, and the next she wasn't. It's a pity she missed such a chance: how grand it would be to empty a large bottle of bright red ink over Mafeking, to wreck the ice-water machine, to cut all the wires of the switch, to set fire to the papers in a steel filing cabinet, lock the cabinet and then remove the key; to do, in fact, what the dwarfs[2] did. Anyway, the only child who showed some spirit has departed; it is probably a good thing for her. I only wish I could have heard the "fatherly" talks the authorities gave her before she left; they were probably masterly examples of their kind.

Since it seems I am not to return to my outpost at the switch for some time I beg you to send me some suitable schemes I can carry out: my own ingenuity is failing. Mafeking has still the idea that he "gets on very well with" me, although he told someone I was "difficult". I hope to have the pleasure one day of telling him he has the brain of a beetle. I have never met anyone with a brain quite like his—things are simply divided into two classes: regular and irregular. Of course there are degrees; your conduct, for example, came under the heading "most irregular". God loves Mafeking, but I find it impossible. I remember one morning when I was walking idly round the gardens and met Peter near the monkey-cages. We stopped to look at the baboon, and Peter said, "Wouldn't it be awful if it turned out that the world had been designed by something like that, laughing at us all!" What do people like Mafeking think when they are dying? What do they remember? How will the members of the Rotary Club fare, "Cum

[2] Red-bearded ones.

164

vix justus sit securus?"[3]—don't know.

Gretchen is slowly undermining the air-raid shelter and causing it to collapse. She digs there daily, and there have been several "falls of earth". There are holes under the bricks at the sides, and stones are beginning to protrude from their covering of earth. One day it will collapse entirely, and Gretchen with it will descend into a grave of her own making.

I am tired in spirit. I think I'll go and read about our little friends[4]. . .

With my love,
Gwen.

(52)   Saturday 1943.
                                                        [12 June]

Dear Tony,

I have just arrived at W.D.C. and I'm enormously pleased because I have saved a terrific amount of money through the foolishness of a young girl in King & King's music store.

I went in to buy Book 1 of Czerny's Art of Finger-Dexterity. The stupid girl looked up the card index and said, "We have only a bound edition of all the books together, six in all." I was prepared to pay 10/- but no more for the complete work (knowing what thieves and robbers they are), so I asked cautiously "How much is this?" (There was no price marked on the book.) The silly girl looked up the card again, scratched her head, and saw that Books 1, 2, etc. were 2/-. It didn't register in her brain that 2/- meant 2/- each. "That is 2/-," she said. My heart jumped for joy. I paid for the book and departed quickly. So instead of one book I have six books for 2/-. Isn't it fine?

SATURDAY NIGHT. FOSTERS' MADHOUSE.

This afternoon I had three weddings. I dashed home for lungh (lunch: this infernal macbine—machine—is up to its tricks again) to find that the troublesome Daphne hadn't turned up this

---

[3]Cum vix justus sit securus: when the just man himself is hardly secure.
[4]Our little friends: those dwarfs again.

morning (she is living with her grandmother again) and as I arrived Agens and Joe departed for the pictures, leaving me with an immense washing-up. I jumped in and out of a bath, put on the Tower of Babel and arrived at the first wedding feeling like a spy who has just been chased across Europe. I had no sooner settled down at the organ than a shadow fell across the aisle and a "well-known" singer arrived and pushed on to the music stand "Just for Today", in 5 flats. I think she is hired out to weddings by some agency that makes money out of people who want "Just for Today" sugn at (sung at) weddings. I'm getting to know the places where she is likely to go wrong because of the extra flats I put in, and where she misses her entries and I have to go back and give her the note. We take each other for granted. . . A second weeding (wedding) – I swear this typewriter's bewitched – followed immediately. It was the wedding of one of the congregation, so a Sunday audience turned up and made themselves at home in their favourite seats. The third wedding featured an enormously fat bride who wore a hat with a heavy veil, a wonderful "spy" hat, but not for her. I am rich at present: I have 2 (two) £5 notes; 4 (four) £1 notes; 2 (two) 10/- notes; 14 (fourteen) two-shilling pieces; 2 (two) shillings; some small change amounting to 1/9½d.

I'm so overcome by this wealth that I simply have to tell someone about it, and it is not a safe policy to reveal wealth to one's own family. I don't think I have ever had so much money at once in my life before, and I'm terrified that my brain will give way under the strain: you see, I have always lived more or less on the verge of insolvency. Of course the Government will take most of it in tax eventaully (eventually) but that does not concern me at the moment. As you are collecting riches on a large scale perhaps you will be good enough to advise me on the matter. I should like to change it all into two-shilling pieces and put them in a bag. You had better advise me quickly, or I shall BUY HATS. You can see the danger.

Tonight I have been running my fingers over the Czerny Art of Finger Dexterity. It was good to feel the piano under my hands again, but I'm in bad form: I notice an unwillingness of my fingers to do what I direct them to do. One of my teachers used to make me practise long passages of finger-work with the hand quiet by balancing a penny on the back of my hand. If I jerked the hand and the penny fell off I got whacked, but if it didn't I got the penny. I can't remember making much money that way. Robin broke my metronome some time ago, and I am extemely angry about that because it wasn't accidental, he was fooling very stupidly with it. Joe is trying to mend it, but I don't think he can, and new ones can't be got. Though some people think it's too mechanical, I am in favour of practice with a metronome. I'm so tired in spirit these days that I feel about a hundred years old and sometimes I think despair will swallow me up, though I know that is wrong, and anyway I do know that it's only because I'm living in a world that has no meaning for me. You know how unreal a place like W.D.C. is, and yet it robs people of life and spirit. Thank God I can laugh at it sometimes, or I should go mad.

I had a letter from the Mother Superior of my convent the other day, and its gentle calmness made me feel ashamed of myself. She is a wonderful woman, almost broken by illness and pain at times and yet full of joy. I can remember one night when I took her arm to help her up the convent steps, and under the long sleeve of her habit it was as thin as a child's arm. I could carry her easily, and yet she makes me feel like a helpless baby. After all, there's nothing more lovely in a woman than that calm graciousness she has.

Tomorrow is the feast of Pentecost. We are singing the Sequence in procession and Thomas Attwood's lovely hymn at Evensong.

I shall write some more tomorrow afternoon.

I'm still quite unrepentant about cheating King & Kings. They've been robbing me for years, and anyway if they don't know the prices of their own music they deserve to lose money.

DOMINICA PENTECOSTES [13 June]

They told me this morning that Baby Bennie has arrived — a son! I suppose the infant will be given a good scholastic name: Jacques Maritain Thomas Aquinas Bennie. I wonder how much

167

philosophy will be applied to its upbringing? Tomorrow I shall send Peter a telegram.

This morning there was bright sunshine but now the sky is clouding over and I think there will be rain.

Last night Joe reaped the just reward of his crowbar exercises. He sat on the floor and held the crowbar with outstretched arms over his legs. "Now," he said, "a good exercise is to drop the crowbar until it's about an inch from your ankles, then lift it up. Good for the shoulder muscles. Like this. Watch." He had overestimated his strength, however, and instead of stopping "about an inch" from his ankles it crashed on to his shins. Today he has a dirty big bruise on each leg.

Father and Gretchen have nothing to do this afternoon and are a bit of a nuisance. Father walks around with Gretchen, jingling his money. They stop, and a foolish conversation follows, such as:

Doozy dogger, the little dogger
(Squeak from Gretchen)
Little Dill, ruthless dogger, etc.

Then father takes a whistle out of his pocket, blows it, and they move on again to annoy someone else. I think he wants some afternoon tea, so I shall get him some.

Between these paragraphs, I have been in the kitchen making Father some tea. Of course he (and Gretchen) smelt or heard the preparation of food and drink, and both arrived in the kitchen; I put a plate of biscuits and cheese on the table and Gretchen's eyes turned to father with an expression of extreme greed which he took for devotion, and if Joe hadn't arrived father and Gretchen would have eaten the lot. Gretchen has the mentality of a parasite under the "protection" of a bit-time gangster. She simply leers at people who give her orders when father is around, but when father is out she crawls on her stomach.

The grapefruit on the severed tree are nearly ripe. Not one has been lost and the tree is growing little shoots out of the cut limb.

I don't feel like writing any more now. I'm going to listen to some Mozart.

With my love,
Gwen.

WAR DAMAGE COMMISSION	PARTICULARS OF ADJUSTMENT.		
FIXED PROPERTY: reduced to	VALUE £	RATE %	CONTRIBUTION £ s. d.
DATE	AUTHORISED BY	FILE No. R/	

(53)　　　　　　　　　　　MONDAY, in oct. Nativ.Gwen.
　　　　　　　　　　　　　　　　　　　　　[14 June]
Dear Friend,
The charming Device which no doubt you have perceiv'd at the top of this page is but one of many which the inestimable institution for which I work provides to charm the sight and illumine the spirit of its members.

Though you may pass away many happy hours filling in the blank spaces (I recommend this as a Pastime both chaste and godly) you will be griev'd to hear that the Examining Office has been forced to invoke the penalty provisions of the National Security (War Damage to Property) Regulations Act against certain wicked Persons who refuse to take out War Damage Insurance. Let this be a warning to you, dear Friend, never to violate such Regulations, and, indeed, never to Trifle with the Commission at all.

You will be pleas'd to hear that Papa and Mamma are both in good health, and that the bruise on my dear Brother's shin is not as large as it was, though it is yet somewhat Painful.

MONDAY NIGHT
. . . Tonight I read for the first time Synge's *Playboy of the Western World*. At first I was annoyed by the folk-speech, which seemed strained, but I got used to it after a while. I love the

169

richness of Irish curses – spectacular cursing seems to belong to Catholic races, or Catholic times in a nation's history.

Protestants are feeble in many ways. The wretched *Pilgrim's Progress* disgusted me as a child, and it still does. I can't understand why people (who have probably never read it) give the book to small children for a prize or present. The *Children's Encyclopaedia* is also feeble in its attitude to religion: I must say that anyone reading an account of Our Lord would get the idea that he was a well-meaning and rather inspired carpenter who got on the wrong side of the Roman authorities, annoyed the Jews, was crucified, dead and buried and retains a vague but friendly attitude to those who live on their own side of the fence. (I remember an amusing story told by Dorothy Sayers: a young man was asking her questions and she mentioned the seven deadly sins. "Oh," he said, "what are the other six?")

Don't get the idea that I'm about to run into the street with a hair-shirt and pictures of the yawning mouth of Hell. These are merely speculations on the state of affairs in general. But I love the Athanasian Creed, especially "Which Faith except every one do keep whole and undefiled: without doubt he shall perish everlastingly." That seems to me to be the only possible attitude. It makes me want to shout "Hurrah!" I remember one night Peter preached a sermon on that clause, and spoke so convincingly of everlasting fire that letters were written to the Archbishop telling him that Fr Bennie ought to be stopped. Peter enjoyed this immensely, especially as the Archbishop wrote back to one violent objector (I saw the letter) and said that since the Athanasian Creed was in the Prayer Book and members of the C. of E. were bound to believe it, he didn't see what could be done about Fr B. Of course the A'bp (in spite of Peter's admiration for him) writes terrible rubbish as a rule and has his nose too far down in the Episcopal feed-bag to see to the welfare of his flock.

Could anything be worse than the feebleness of our days? Most people carefully shut all doors leading into what S. Teresa of Avila calls The Interior Castle and live on the surface of life, afraid of sorrow and joy. Possibly the war will bring about by suffering

170

a rebirth of true values, but I don't think so.

Baby Bennie is called Francis Peter, so he has two powerful saints to protect him. He will probably be Chaplain General of the Franciscan Order, or a Pope. Peter is probably wild with joy.

. . . Last night was a most lovely night — there was a wind blowing packed clouds over the sky, so that the moon and stars seemed to be sailing through deep black gulfs between the clouds. This morning it was so cold that when I woke up I found myself breathing little clouds of steam into the air. The sun shines right on to my bed now and warms me before I get up. . . As well as writing "bring-ups" in the diary I write little notes in German script such as "Have you remembered to ring the dentist", "This is my birthday", "Buy a present for Agens". These little notes annoy Mafeking's secretary but she never says anything to me, she tells all her troubles in secret to Mafeking. Nothing has happened re the spy episode; no bowler-hatted little men have watched me. I am an international failure.

Mr Battersby, who shows some sense, refuses to let me have an assistant, but Mafeking is trying his hardest to get me one, as I have convinced him that I have too much work to do alone. The subject is to be brought up again tomorrow. . .

Did I tell you that Mafeking calls his men friends "my dear" over the phone? I have not invented this, it is true. Typical conversation:

"Helloooooo, Reed speaking, Wardamage . . . oh, hello, Bob (Charlie Tom Joe professor doctor) so glad you rang up my dear, I can't possibly come on Sunday, I've got Ma on my hands now and I promised to take her out. Not that I don't get quite a kick out of looking after the old lady, mind you . . . sometimes I think I <u>spoil</u> Ma. . ."

I have decided that Mafeking wears a belly-band of some kind, but the only way I could find out is by prodding him, which is

171

too repulsive to think of. The rolling fat of his hanging cheeks, his many chins and the evidence of fat on his chest; all this fat makes me suspect the neatness of his waistline under his double-breasted suits. Father's fatness is jovial and makes one think of barrels of beer, but Mafeking's fatness is repulsive and seems to reflect his pallid and suety mind. Ugh.

Mafeking showed me one of the most wonderful pictures of its kind I've every seen: a photograph of the directors of the Rotary Club for 1942, Mafeking among them. There they were, standing and sitting as the photographer had arranged them, Mafeking in one corner staring blankly at the beholder. If only I could steal it! Neo-Welt-krieg men, the product of our civilisation: on their lips, HONESTY IS THE BEST POLICY; in their minds, emptiness. I know some of them by sight and that is cnough.

This morning after a little "border incident" over a lost file Mafeking actually stamped his feet at his secretary! He was sitting on his two dirty big cushions at his desk, and she failed to grasp something he was explaining to her, so he stamped his feet like a child who can't make its parents understand that it wants a lollie. God, it is said, created man after his own image. Oh, Mafeking!

WEDNESDAY NIGHT:
I have been to the dentist this evening, and he found two small holes in the upper molars which have to be filled next week. My wisdom teeth are coming through—I have mentioned this before—and they ache horribl5. You see, this machine has started substituting numbers for figures: I can't imagine what it will do next. It would be fine to type some fo (of) Mafeking's letters like that:—

Dea4 Si4,

We d9 n95 a&&ea4 t9 have receiv3d a c9n5r&bution f4om 6ou. Are my letters to you censored? OH YJRU STR YJOD DJPIYF HOBR YJR BRMDPY DP?RYJOMH YP YJOML PBRT@[1] (Hippo language). Joe

---

[1] Code: Transpose the letters one space to the left and you get, "If they are, this will give the ? something to think over." (approx.)

has a book called One Hundred Problems in Cipher, but so far we haven't worked out any but the simple substitution ones, even though the answers are given in the back, and we looked them up first in any case.

Because I got roped in for a game of 500 with "Juggernaut" Coar, the Demon 500 Player, it is really too late to write an6 (there you are, this machine is uncontrollable) more tonight. Father is out, so I took his place and carried on ludicrous conversations with Old Coar, such as

"Would you like a rug for your legs, Mr Coar?"

—"Oh yes, ridiculous. Read all about it in the paper."

"No, are you cold Mr Coar? Would you like a rug?"

—"My word! They get so many they won't know what to do with them."

I'm going to take my wisdom teeth off to bed. I wish I didn't have to.

With my love,
Gwen.

(54)   Wardamagecommissioncreekstreetthursday 1942
(an error for 1943)
[17 June]

Dear Tony,

What a lovely day it is! I should like to be flying round the city on a magic carpet that played Mozart as it flew. I am thinking this afternoon that if there is a fault in creation it is the omission of magic carpets from the scheme of things. Still, I suppose if God had allowed everyone a magic carpet by now there would be twenty-five National Security (War Damage to Carpets) Acts and The Commonwealth Carpet-Travelling Board to spoil our fun. The city authorities would forbid travel except under circumstances that would rob it of delight, and the state government would tax carpets so heavily that nobody could afford them.

. . . Perhaps it is just as well that everyone has not a magic carpet—after all the greatest pleasure would be the solitude it

173

afforded one. It would be dreadful to see one's relations following grimly behind on their own carpets.

W.D.C. FRIDAY [18 June]

Last night I was delighted to find a letter from you, and some books of mine with the Woolf[1] which I have started to read. It is certainly "rich and strange", I love it. What an interesting-looking woman V.W. is, with those heavy eyes. She reminds me of some of Agens' people, the Jaggards. I wish my name had been Jaggard — Agens, in her youth, was Nessie Jaggard, and the bearded great-grandfather, who causes the family rows about beards, was Joshua Jeremiah Jaggard. It is a pity in some ways that Nessie Jaggard ended up as Agnes M. Foster, Hon.Sec. of Limbless Soldiers Ladies' committee, Convenor of The Opportunity Shop etc.etc. Nessie has a sound like the rustling of silk that redeems the ruggedness of Jaggard. And think of Joe — Joseph (Jawbreaker) Jaggard, voted the strongest boy in Auchenflower, said last night . . . or — Joseph "Jitterbug" Jaggard, Auchenflower's drumming Scoutmaster. . .

The fools who were hanging round have gone, so I shall continue on the typewriter. (The interruption was caused by the arrival of some dirty big cardboard files, which were put down near me. The chief clerk, Bro. Walter, came up and saw the files. He stood looking at them for some time. After moments of profound thought he said:

—Er, Mr Reed!

"Yes?"

—Do you mind coming here a moment?

(Mafeking came out and stood beside him.)

—Mr Reed, are these for your department?

"No, they're not, I know nothing about them."

—Well, they can't stay here, they will be in the way.

"Why not get Norman to move them?"

—Norman, I'm afraid, is out.

"Oh."

[1]Virginia Woolf, probably *Orlando*. See (58), footnote 1.

As neither had any other scheme to offer, they returned to their offices. Norman is still out, and the files are still in the way.) . . .

"As you correctly surmise, your blue knitted jumper[2] doesn't interest me." The trouble, said Theophilus Panbury, lies in the method of presentation. My friend Fred Hackleskinner interviewed Eliza Cook on the subject, and she penned the following lines:

I love it, I love it, that garment blue,
I wear it in summer, and winter too:

Thank you Miss Cook, that will be all.
Mr Dante G. Rossetti said:

The seven maidens sit at night
Knitting the blue wool;
They hold the needles in their mouths
Because their hands are full,
And sew the seams with mystic wire
In case the stitches pull.

. . . Mr Walt Whitman remarked:

Two-ply or three-ply (O reckless knitters!)
O solitary me knitting (here I am, here!)
Is it indeed wool I am knitting, or string?
O give me that stitch, needles, recall that stitch,
Click click click click click
Is this a jumper I am knitting or only a fishnet?
Damn! There goes another one.

Mr Eliot asked:

And would it have been worth it, after all,
Would it have been worth while,
If one, settling a pillow or throwing off a shawl
and trying on the jumper, should say:

[2]One of GF's birthday presents. See (48).

175

This does not fit at all,
This is not what I want, at all?

Your description of the insects delighted me exceedingly. I love small things and I read the beetle paragraph many times. Did you know that I have a microscope? Sometimes I spend hours looking at the lacy patterns of grass stalks and flowers. The perfection of small things never ceases to fill me with wonder. It has a polariser that shows thin sections of rock in lovely colour – but I don't know how to use it. I believe that snow-flakes magnified show beautiful patterns, never alike; I hope this is true.

. . . I don't know Ernest Lough's record of "I know that my Redeemer liveth", but I have heard him singing "Oh for the wings of a dove". His voice is crystalline. Mr Coar heard him singing in England and has told me about him many times.

I'll write some more in the week-end. With my love,

Gwen.

(55)   In Festo S'smae Trinitatis.
                        (The Feast of the Most Blessed Trinity)
                                                    [20 June]

Dear Tony,

I am amazed at the amount of luggage women with babies carry around. It appears to be baby's luggage, too, though why an infant should need six or seven times its own size and weight in luggage I don't know. Two young women were at the tram stop this morning. One had an infant in arms and the other a small child of two or three; they were evidently out for the day, but their luggage amounted to a large suitcase and two of those dreadful leather bags that bulge out and look as if they contain a baby's body. When they had settled themselves on the tram-seat the mother of the two-year-old put down a paper bag which the small child attempted to seize. "Oh," shrieked the other woman, whose arms were full, "don't let 'er get at them cakes." The child screamed horribly and the mother put the bag on the other side of her. The child toddled round and the same performance went on until the tram came. Theophilus Panbury says that if ever he has to carry any infants he will carry them in a bag on his back. I think he is wise. But I wish you could have heard the cry: "Don't let 'er get at them cakes."

You say I "lose sumzing" when reproduced in sepia: but I'm afraid of letting a Brisbane photographer's dim-witted assistants "tint" my photograph; they would probably make me look like Flossie the barmaid or Clara Bow, whom you probably remember in circus pictures of passion and heart-rending drama, when elephants break loose, the lion gets out of his wire cage and a dirty big fire breaks out in the main tent. Of course Clara Bow never appealed to me, but she evidently "ad zumzing" because the lion-tamer and the tight-rope walker, not to speak of the circus knife-thrower, were crazy about her. In one picture I saw the knife-thrower accused her of being unfaithful and outlined her with knives as she leaned against the wall in her pink spangled tights; unfortunately just as he was about to stick a knife into her faithless heart the lion-tamer entered the tent and caught his wrist.

Joe and Agens and I went to the pictures last night and saw an entertaining mystery with a blind detective and a dog that opened doors and bit criminals in a satisfying manner. The other picture, "Seven Sweethearts" was Hollywood's treacly idea of a Dutch colony in America with paper tulips and shrieking singers. Oh hell, said Tiny Tim. "Fantasia" is to be shown here this week. Father is taking us on Friday; I'm sorry you are not here to come too. I can't remember whether you have seen it or not. I wonder what the intellectuals of the gramophone society will have to say about it! They make me sick, with their "theories" about the ideology of this, that and the other. One young lady asked me if I thought drama ought to be "sociological", so I said "I have devoted the whole of my life to a study of the eidetic visualisation of St Bonaventure, and do not feel competent to speak upon any other subject." The last time I went to the gramophone society (many months ago) a young man in front of me had a score of the 9th symphony. In the scherzo he turned over the pages at regular intervals, nodding his head and smiling to himself, but at the end he still had eight or nine pages to spare, which he hastily turned over!

This morning we sang the creed of S. Athanasius in procession. It filled me with joy to see the priests walking round solemnly vested in white, and the servers with lights and incense going before; I wish Peter had been there—he was always at home with Athanasius. I suppose he is pointing out the everlasting fire to the farmers of Imbil.

It is always strange to see the moon in daylight; yesterday morning I was on my way to mass just after sunrise and as the tram reached the top of the hill leading to town I looked at Mt Coot-tha, and there was the full moon, looking ridiculously large and yellow over the rim of the hill. It didn't look beautiful at all; it seemed as if someone had put it there for a joke.

Today it is very cold and there is a damp feeling in the air. There has been no sun at all and nothing seems awake although it is afternoon. I do not feel very much alive on a day like this— if it would only rain the fingers of cold that are holding everything would be released. I should like a storm, with plenty of thunder and lightning.

Our poinsettias are in flower and dozens of little birds with long curved beaks are taking honey from the centres of the flowers. They must be very light, for they can stand on one of the red leaves.

You gave me an unhappy surprise when you pointed out that I have just completed my 23rd year. At first I didn't believe you, and thought that you'd counted wrongly. So I set out to count for myself, saying "when I was 1, I completed my first year", when I was 2, I completed my second". And of course the horrible truth became apparent: when I am 23 I have completed my 23rd year. This has disturbed me, for it appears that all my life I have imagined myself to be a year younger that my actual age, and now I am in my 24th year without having realised that I was living in my 23rd. Dreadful! When I think of what I could have done with that year I didn't know about I feel "mad with fury". Ah, that lost year! I might have been Queen of Persia, a famous tightrope-walker, a Chinese missionary, the owner of thirty-four giant pandas or the first person to recite Psalm 119 hanging by one ear from a 1,000 ft. cliff. But really I don't want to be any of those things, so it doesn't matter. Still, I wish you hadn't mentioned it. And in any case, even if I had known the truth, I'd have done nothing at all about it.

THEOPHILUS PANBURY'S UNIVERSAL SCHOOL FOR WRITERS, ASSOCIATED WITH THE RUFO-NANINE[1] WRITING TUITION COURSE. Would you like to be a famous writer? Call and see our Mr Hackleskinner, or send for Rufo-Nanine Booklet No. 26574635462435, price 19/-.

Extract from Mr Battlebottom's course on novel-writing (simplified).

(a) Pick your type e.g.
   1. Modern realism
   2. Stark modern realism
   3. Vital & youthful realism.
(b) Decide on the number of pages.
(c) Choose the characters.

A good novelist, that is a novelist trained by the Rufo-Nanine Tuition Scheme, is never without his Rufo-Nanine Phrase Book (18/6). This little phrase book has a complete index of starkly realistic subjects (tabular form for subheadings) and 1,375,782,463 vital phrases. An exhaustive method of cross-numbering will give you the right phrase on any subject in a moment. Read what one of our pupils wrote after only three lessons with the help of the Rufo-Nanine Phrase Book (18/6):

"Old Zog droiled his fribbling feet across the pandiculating infinity of the hexagonal cow-yard. 'Januis clausis,' he mumped behind his tremulous beard . . . ponderous hail battered his grotesque ears; the aphonous cow-sheds twanged."

[1]Rufo-Nanine: red-bearded. See (6), footnote 2.

... There is a beautiful sunset to comfort us after this miserable day. The sun has lit up the edges of the dark clouds in a fan-shaped path, so that there seems to be a grey sea with fiery wave-tops held motionless in the sky. The sky is so full of its warmth that the street-lights seem cold although they are shining brightly. It has made me happy to see the splendid colour.

SUNDAY NIGHT. After Evensong.

This morning father and I were getting our breakfast in the kitchen and father began to cut bread and sing a wonderful song, which ended:

> I asked her if she'd marry me
> But all that she would say was
> "Ting-a-ling-a-ling
> Put your nose in a sling
> Ta-ra-ra-boom-de-ay."

Isn't it the perfect answer! It's wonderful! In future when any fools ask me questions I shall answer

> "Ting-a-ling-a-ling
> Put your nose in a sling
> Ta-ra-ra-boom-de-ay."
> "Miss Foster, do you think that Finnegan's Wake will have a lasting effect on our generation?"
> "-Ting-a-ling-a-ling," etc.
> "Miss Foster, are the bring-ups ready?"
> "Ting-a-ling-a-ling" etc. — I wish I dared.
> "Miss Foster, I am going to sing at a wedding on Saturday. What do you think I should sing?"
> "Ting-a-ling-a-ling," etc.

I don't know who the young lady was who first said — or rather, sang, those excellent words, but she "ad zumzing". That little refrain has lifted a weight from my mind: whenever I'm asked questions I'm not clever enough to answer — and this happens frequently — I shall reply

> Ting-a-ling-a-ling, etc.

180

This is a bit mad; I think the song has gone to my head. But don't forget to tell me what you think of the chorus as a reply to foolish questions.

With my love,
Gwen.

(56)

CHEZ MAFEKING
Monday
[21 June]

My dear Tony,

. . . MONDAY AFTERNOON: This afternoon another letter arrived from you: it has evidently been "held up" by the wicked authorities. Today is June 21st, and the letter is dated on the outside June 8th, that was my birthday! It is the loveliest letter I've had from you and has set my head spinning with thoughts — that always happens when I read your letters: new and exciting thoughts rush through my brain and I want to write about them immediately. It is a pity I can't always do so, for often I "lose" things that I mean to write about, or become dull and uninspired in the meantime. I haven't really absorbed the letter yet, I have just read it through once. After work I have — see, the system is creeping into my vocabulary: "after work", indeed! This evening I have to go to the dentist and have a tooth filled, and then (if I don't have toothache to make me savage) I'll write to you. When I have a letter from you I feel some life flowing into me — my heart, in spite of W.D.C., makes "healthful music".[1] (Was it "heart" or "pulse"? I can't remember.)

MONDAY EVENING

It was pulse, not heart.

I cannot imagine why your letter of the 8th was delayed: I suspect that I am the victim of a conspiracy among the postal authorities. They are trying to frighten me again, so that I will register things once more. Thank you for warning me against their cunning schemes; I have no faith in any branch of the public

[1]*Hamlet,* Act 3, Scene IV.

service and I hope that one day I shall be in a position to repay them justly for the crimes they have committed against me.

I am listening to Gluck's Ballet of the Elysian Fields on the wireless. How lovely it is!

How you must have rejoiced to hear a discussion on Bring-Ups in N.T. It is good to know that civilisation has travelled so far! I have found out that another curious attitude of mind is fostered by the Bring-Up system—forward, in time, means backward, to Mafeking. If I am to bring up something in August, for instance, he says "Put that back to August," or if something is to come up in a week's time, "Put that back a week." I pointed out to him that this was against nature, but he couldn't see my point. This afternoon I heard Mafeking say to the chief clerk, Bro. Walter, "I'll get Miss Foster to re-date that back a month." Can't you imagine a serious discussion between two rival branches of the P.S. on the relative merits of Bring-Ups and Bring Forwards—at least the latter moves in the right direction of time.

As for the fight with Mafeking, I think that there will be no more, for his efforts to avoid such incidents are evident nowadays. When he sees me getting annoyed and fierce he "soothes me down". For instance a trivial incident that occurred this morning will illustrate this:

Mafeking: "Miss Foster, where is Collins' file?"
—I don't know.
"But you must know, you're in charge of the files."
—I don't know where it is.
"Miss Foster, you must know."
(I began kicking the wall gently with my heel.)
—It's not in my filing cabinet, and it's not listed. Therefore I'm not responsible.
"Miss Foster, if you don't know where it is, there must be a weakness in your system."
—Yes, the weakness is that you take things away without telling me.

(Here I began pushing my hair up and letting if fall down again, and Mafeking thought a row was coming, so he changed his tone

182

entirely and made a little speech something like this): "Miss Foster, I'm afraid you misunderstand me, I don't mean anything personal for a moment. Probably I did take the correspondence. I'm not blaming you at all. You mustn't imagine that for a moment."

Poor fool!

I was most amused at the "La Boheme" incident in the picture you saw. Did I tell you that I saw a "musical" film which featured the aged Schumann, playing on a grand piano of a type not made anywhere until about 1890? The sight of orchestras playing from non-existent scores is common; I remember one picture in which a composer composed a waltz at the piano and walked back to his stand, waved his baton and led his orchestra magnificently through the unwritten and unorchestrated music.[2] (Do you remember that evening at the Elite when the Hallelujah Chorus burst forth as the cathedral flashed on to the screen?)

. . . You say, "Christian love can be as arrogant as any other attitude." But if it is arrogant, it is not love – not Christian love anyway. It is the spirit of the Rotary clubs – rotten underneath. Unhappily Protestantism has brought with it a terrible emphasis on good works at the expense of the interior life, which is all that matters. I had a letter from Peter today and he mentioned this very thing – it is the interior life that matters, nothing else. That is why I am against church "societies" – they lose their interior spirit in no time and reach the stage finally where they get the idea that God needs them. It is all very sad. It is saddest of all to see the spirit of children being crippled – they are taught to "get on in life", with horrible results.

It is too late to write any more. I have selected some gems from the Church Times, and finally dipped the glue-brush in the red-ink bottle, so I had better go to bed.

With my love,
Gwen.

[2]Compare the dream in the poem "To A. D. Hope". (*Selected Poems,* p.70.)

My dear Tony,

Queensland has demon winds called Westerlies. Have you struck
them? They are destructive winds and tear flowers and living
plants to pieces: yesterday they destroyed the poinsettias and
heaped green leaves in the gutters; windows were broken, and the
person who writes "Foo" notices over the city walls wrote FOO
HAS BEEN BLOWN AWAY. (Did you read a ludicrous article by a
Sydney dignitary who said that Foo notices were being used to
convey messages to the enemy?) I love clean winds, but the
Westerlies in the city pick up fine dust and carry it everywhere,
making things unpleasant to touch. They take all the life out of
one's hair, too, and make it dry and unpleasant to feel. Although
the organ at All Ss. is covered with a cloth garment made especially
for it by the good ladies of the Sewing Guild, deust (good heavens,
I mean dust) creeps in and I have to keep a little brush to clean
the keys with.

To return to our discussion on Eastern philosophy: you say
that the Eastern philosopher seeks to be absorbed in Truth by
way of self-abnegation. This is true, but in the East it seems that
withdrawal from exterior things is based on contempt of them,
that is they are considered as evil in themselves – which nothing
is. I agree, too, that Western philosophy is "permeated by the
poisonous desire to possess", but the greatest philosophers of the
West have no part in this: Aristotle, S. Thomas Aquinas,
Berdijaev, for example. The fact that the west excels in science
has caused many people to deify science or at any rate to imagine
that it is independent of philosophy which is not true as philosophy
is of a higher degree of abstraction than science and therefore
is in a position to examine scientific truth in the light of its own
truth. Many people imagine that mediaeval philosophy is false
because mediaeval science was inexact and often absurd, forgetting
that philosophy is not based upon scientific data but upon the
principles of truth that are known to man's reason. The statement

"a unicorn cannot be and not be at the same time and in the same respect" remains true whether there are unicorns in existence or not. But I seem to have digressed. Eastern philosophy (about which I know really very little) seems to me to return to the idea that evil is a positive thing and not a negation—that evil has existence in itself. But I don't think I'll write any more because it is useless to speak of problems so subtle that even Maritain admits that the west has little knowledge of them. It is a pity that most people who think of Christianity at all should think of it as a sort of C. of E. spread all over the globe. They do not seem to realise that Catholicism in the East cannot be a sort of second-hand latin christianity. Have you ever seen any of the paintings of the Indian, Angelo da Fonsera, or the little book of Chinese Christian art published a couple of years ago? The paintings are Christian and yet how different they are from Western pictures! I remember one of our Lord as the Good Shepherd with a flock of fat-tailed mongolian sheep! The Catholic church, I believe, should reflect naturally the characteristics of a people and people who imagine that Christianity in China should wed Gothic churches and the Book of Common Prayer should be knocked (very hard) on the head with Hymns A & M.

When I said that Western philosophy had no knowledge of the problems I meant really of the Eastern attitude to those problems. The Eastern mind is not at all like the Western, and I don't think any great Western philosopher has made an adequate study of Eastern religions and philosophy. The knowledge we have of them seems to be reduced to a few Western classifications that are quite foreign to the complex and sometimes inconsistent systems of the East. The doctrine of transmigration of souls, for instance, cannot possibly be as simple as the average western conception of it, and possibly has been given an "artificial" classification to make it fit in with western modes of thought. It seems to me that a philosopher who set out to study Eastern thought would have, first of all, to make a study of its different modes. The East seems to be naturally pantheistic, but in so subtle a way that it can outwardly deny pantheism.

It is strange that the Egyptians, who thought continually of death, and the Jews, who managed to preserve a great body of truth in spite of their lapses, had no body of traditional philosophy, and no great philosophers.

I am very happy to hear your praise of "Another Country". Yes, I do know John's dilemma at first hand. In 1941, when I told my people that I was going to the Franciscan convent there followed scenes of a terrible nature, and for six months – you see, I wasn't twenty-one at the time – the whole of 14 Grimes St. was simply strewn with wreckage. Peace departed from us – at least the outward absence of storms that had previously been accepted as peace. Of course the family hadn't the faintest idea of the interior nature of life in a religious order, and one's family is hardest of all to explain such things to. Looking back on it now it doesn't seem so bad because it has slipped into its proper place in life, but at the time it was agonising. The worst time was when they started loading me with presents – they would say "Why aren't you happy at home?" "What can we give you to make you happy?" How could I explain to my father, who is always so good and generous, that it wasn't a question of being "happy at home"? Books, clothes, records, pictures, tickets for concerts – everything they could think of, they gave me to try to "make me happy", and drive away my thoughts of leaving. One Saturday I packed up my books in some of father's beer-bags and departed. On Sunday morning I woke to hear the nuns singing the office hymn in the little chapel

Now that the daylight fills the sky
We lift our hearts to God on high.

Even at the convent Agens used to ring me up, in tears, and tell me how I was "breaking father's heart" etc. One day a woman I hardly knew stopped me and said "Why don't you go home, you're killing your father." I stayed at the Convent, and father didn't die, Joe didn't collapse, Agens recovered and presently they left me alone. When I found that I had no vocation I returned home with the books in beer-bags (they had been stored – the beer-bags—under the convent). Once again I was showered with books, clothes, records etc, but the danger was over.

WEDNESDAY, 1943 [23 June]

The terrible spirit of the public service was made manifest to me this morning in an "incident"—very much a "border incident" which occurred. As you know, I have been "demanding" an assistant, and so far none has arrived from the outside world. However this morning a fairly large job was given to me in connection with some taxation reports, and though I could have done it myself I staged a little speech in my grand manner and Mafeking APPOINTED ME TWO ASSISTANTS FROM THE OFFICE STAFF. They were simply taken from their other jobs and handed over to me. Needless to say, they were furious at the thought of my having assistants, and took little trouble to conceal their resentment. They went straight off to the rest of our contemporaries and told them the news: "Fancy that Miss Foster having someone to do her work for her. . ." "We don't get people to help us. . ." "She just does it to show off. . ." etc. etc. I divided the work into two parts and gave them half each. I started to write a letter to Peter, but before I had got very far Miss Harvey, M.'s neurotic secretary, came out and said, "What are you doing, Miss Foster?" I replied, "I'm writing a letter." (She had evidently been working up a speech proving that I was writing a letter, but when I admitted it she didn't quite know what to say.) She said, "You know I don't want to tell 'Robbie'—Robert Mafeking—but I'm afraid. . ." I simply leaned back in my chair and said "Go ahead, tell him, and just see what happens. I'll slit your throat." Immediately she changed her tone and said, "Oh, I don't really want to make a row, but everyone is complaining about you." "Who is," I asked. "Everyone," she repeated. "Very well," I answered, "I'll go and find out for myself." I added, in as sinister a voice as possible, "and God help them." So I went to my contemporaries one by one and asked them, "Have you been complaining about me?" The answer invariably was "Oh no," (in a most surprised tone of voice) "I haven't said a thing about you," or "What? Complaining? No-o-o-o!" So I dragged the unwilling

Harvey from her den and confronted her with the witnesses one by one (the fools didn't have the sense to get out of my way) and requested them to repeat their denial. They didn't. They caved in weakly and admitted that they might have said that it really was a bit tall getting assistants, and that perhaps it was hard on other people being dragged from their own work (work, indeed!!) to do mine, etc. There was a little group by the filing cabinets so I took the opportunity that presented itself and made Harvey ask them if they had complained about my having assistants, and so I got a "mass confession". (They had previously denied speaking about me.) Really, I haven't enjoyed myself so much since I've been there. It appears that there was an "indignation meeting" at my outrageous behaviour in general—callers, assistants, strolling about the place, talking in German, and so on—and things were beyond endurance when I actually got the assistants. I suppose that complaints will be made in secret, and I am sure that never again will diplomatic relations exist between myself and the rest of them—except with the accountant's secretary, who has not been crushed by the system, and of course Diana who is still on holidays. I do wish you could have been there, Tony, during the "inquisition". They'll never forgive me. . .

Your poem "In the Night" is fine. I am envious to think that you can write, sing, look like Lenin, translate the Aeneid, ski and do so many things and be an actor. You are very good to me. I am happy to think that you will read my stories if you can. . .

Tomorrow is the feast of Corpus Christi. Mass begins "He fed them with the finest wheat-flour, and with honey out of the stony rock hath he satisfied them, alleluia, alleluia". Do you know St Thomas's lovely hymn for the feast beginning "Pange lingua gloriosi Corporis mysterium"?[1]

IN FESTO SSMI CORPORIS CHRISTI[2] [24 June]

How cold it has been all day! But it has been a bright clear day: I woke to find a delicate yellow sky in the east, and the trees quite

[1]Tell, tongue, the mystery of the glorious body.
[2]The feast of the Most Blessed Corpus Christi.

still. The wind had gone. It was so cold that I didn't like getting up, but once I was out on my way to Mass I felt glad to see the clear thin sunlight over everything. Is it too strange to say that the whiteness of the little clouds, and the honey-coloured light remind me of the introit of today's mass?

I tried to read some more Synge, but sure it is I am that I'd sooner be reading James Joyce. That Irish peasant stuff may be all right for fanatical lovers of peat smoke or homesick Christian Brothers (Peter called the Xtian Bros "ignorant Irish anarchists") but I find it hard to believe that it's genuine "folk speech" and would keep me entertained in a theatre for long. Yes, be Jaysus, said Tiny Tim.

There are a number of people I know who profess unlimited admiration for the Irish; when they start on their pedigrees I claim to be descended from Red Hugh O'Donnell, and sometimes get away with it, if they don't know Agens. Maybe I'm wrong about Synge. If I am, tell me why. I like his poetry, but I don't think his plays are the real stuff.

This evening Dad brought home an Air Force man to dinner. He was just beginning to tell us about Japanese planes when the fanatical Joe woke up and pitched into him full force— . . . Joe's eyes gleamed with maniacal light: he produced rare aeroplanes for "identification" and asked trick questions at great speed. "Non-retractable undercarriage" and such terms were flung about faster than the ear could follow. Before dinner was over the man—who was a pilot in the last war—wished he had never spoken of aeroplanes! Joe will probably be found in the spacious grounds of Goodna in a few years, trying vainly to "take off" as a Fockewulf or a Sopwith Camel.

With my love,
Gwen.

Foster's Madhouse
Saturday, 1943
[26 June]

My dear Tony,

Yesterday Father, Agens and I set off to see "Fantasia". Agens and I got in the back cabin of the tram with Father, who was wearing his greatcoat and looked like the tenor in an Italian Opera Company. Agens and I sat together and Father sat next to a magnificent old man who had a stern expression, as if he were considering the decay of morals, or jazz bands. Now Father needs a whole seat to himself in the tram, and so he gently leaned on the old man, who moved a little nearer to the window and looked very stern indeed. Still only half of Father was on the seat, so he gently squashed the old man a bit closer to the wall. At the next tram stop the old man got up and went outside to another seat, glaring at Father as he went. (I don't blame him.) Father moved happily into the space. Nobody else tried to sit next to him.

When we reached the Regent we saw a notice

FANTASIA
MUSIC BY STOWKOWSKI

Why can't they do anything properly here? The whole thing was cut, and some of the cuts in the music were as clumsy as those we're accustomed to hear from the A.B.C. The Bach Toccata and Fugue was omitted. The Nut Cracker Suite began very prettily but before long some damned FAIRIES appeared, with no clothes and cretinous faces and dirty big wands. If there is one thing I can't stand it's damned fairies — gnomes, pixies, imps, elves, dwarfs, sprites, hobgoblins, banshees, ginns, bogies, kobolds, leprechauns, brownies, pigwidgeons, trolls: all these 'ave zumzing. But fairies, NO. I hate them. But there were some wonderful snowflakes in lovely patterns and beautiful scenes of autumn which filled me with longing: I have never seen autumn; we do not have such a season here. The Rite of Spring began with sulphurous fire and erupting volcanoes and showed the growth of life on the earth from amoebae to pterodactyls with the simple faith of the Children's Encyclopaedia. There were very satisfying scenes of lava pouring into the sea, mountains turning upside down and cracks splitting open in vast cliffs. Large armour-plated animals fought each other and finally died of thirst. Aha! said Tiny Tim, this cannot keep up for long. He was right; before long there appeared Mickey Mouse as the sorcerer's apprentice. Tiny Tim likes Mickey Mouse better than fairies, anyhow.

The best was Beethoven's Symphony VII. It was lovely, the colours, bright and clear, filled me with joy. Winged horses and centaurs appeared, little cherubs and Jupiter himself hurling lightning and thunderbolts. The pastoral scenes were calm and full of sunshine.

The Dance of the Hours featured a ludicrous ballet of ostriches, splendidly done—they aped the mannerisms of ballerinas to perfection. Next elephants danced among airy bubbles, and a giant hippo in an elegant lace frill for a skirt reclined on a couch. I was quite helpless with laughter; crocodiles came and danced with the elephants, and a crocodile carried his elephant partner through two immense stone columns, where the elephant got firmly wedged! Another fantastic scene showed an elephant imprisoned in a bubble!

Night on a Bare Mountain terrified me—there was the devil on a great mountain, and innumerable smaller devils, demons, fiends and evil spirits, all with wonderful electric eyes, flew around under his immense wings. Skeleton horsemen rode in apocalyptic fury on the winds of hell. I am terrified of evil spirits, and "fear came upon me".

And then, for an ending, we had as feeble a slice of Hollywood iced-cake-for-nitwits as I've ever encountered: Schubert's Ave Maria with chocolate-box scenes and a post-card sunrise. There is nothing worse than a feeble ending, but what can one expect? Theophilus Panbury and Tiny Tim both said "Oh, hell." I'm very glad I saw Fantasia. There were wonderful passages, and the colour alone was enough to fill one with delight.

It is so cold here that I can hardly make the pen write, my fingers have lost their feeling. I cannot remember so cold a winter

191

for many years. They say there has been snow near the border. Mafeking wears yellow kid gloves these days and looks so comical that the lift-men laugh at him! Tomorrow I shall write again. This paper is by courtesy of the W.D.C.

SUNDAY. [27 June]

Agens is out playing tennis all day, and Father, being an Air-Raid-Warden of great importance, is out supervising one of those practices where all the men wear arm-bands and give orders to each other. Joe ("Basher") Foster has put up a bag of sand weighing about 2cwt under the house and he is punching this with great force. We worked out that if it comes back and hits him it will knowck (Good God, there wer — DOG of a MACHINE — there we go again) him our (out). You can see what I'm up against with this typewriter; still, it is remarkable that it still works, for two or three times a week it takes a thrashing from Father, whose typing is far from gentle. So if the pounding and dull thuds stop under the house I shall go down to make sure that Basher is not stretched out among his own blood, bits of skull and a few teeth.

You will be sorry to hear that Joe has "resigned" from his office of Scoutmaster. It is a shame to see one of the Prominent Figures of the Scouting World retire. The trouble was this: Joe had a tribe of "weaklings" (according to his fanatical standards) and he tried to "build them up". They resented it, and expressed a desire to remain unbuilt up and undisciplined. Now Scout Laws (so Joe tells me) forbid — quite rightly — the use of physical violence by people such as Joe. He has therefore abandoned the weaklings and will devote the extra time he has to building up his own muscles. His green shirt (you know the one — it belongs to his "usual clothes") was removed from his room and washed some time ago, but was not improved by washing. Joe has not yet "called" at War Damage. I think I must persuade him to come up and remove their clock: your story of the two men who removed a piano from the Bowling Club inspired me.

The sunshine was splendid until a few moments ago. Clouds have come up suddenly, but at lunchtime it was so warm that Joe and I ate our lunch on the veranda. Joe cooked himself a dirty big piece of steak and filled the kitchen with blue smoke in the process of cooking it. I would tell you what I had but it would probably break your heart to hear about it, and you have warned me before about boasting of . . . surrounded by . . . and . . . with . . . and plenty of . . . covered with . . .

. . . At lunchtime there wasn't a sky in the cloud – good God, I really wrote that, it's not a joke, my brain is getting out of hand – but now the wind has blown clouds and packed them tightly across the whole sky. How cold it is! I think there will be rain before evening.

I have bought a book by Eric Gill called "Beauty Looks after Herself", a series of essays on art and contemporary life. Gill is very sound, I think, and his own sculpture is lovely. Most books or essays about art make me sick, with their talk of nonsensical abstractions of one kind and another, ideology of pure thought-forms and so on. Gill says much the same as Maritain says in "Art and Scholasticism", but he is easier to read than Maritain.

Sometimes the uselessness of my days at W.D.C. distresses me so much that I feel like walking out on the spot. But if I did, I would probably be sent by the fools at Manpower to some equally futile concern. How in God's name can anyone take life there seriously? How can Mafeking "get up at night to make notes" on "work" that has no significance however one looks at it. The foolish and empty drivel that he talks, thinks and writes he tries to pass on to me as something real. Lord Christ, it is better to be a rubbish-collector or a dish-washer than to be what Mafeking is. I should dearly love to make a little speech to this effect and walk out, but what difference would it make? None at all. (Besides, I await the pleasure of being thrown out.) But I must stop this, it is not good. It is much better to laugh, and think how fine it is to be 23 and have coloured hair[1] and to be retained by an important govt. dept. in spite of bearded callers.

. . . I shall send back "Orlando"[2] soon. What an amazing

[1]The colour was red.
[2]*Orlando* by Virginia Woolf. See (54), footnote 1.

book! Its richness made me think of a colourful and closely patterned tapestry. It was all fine, but I liked the beginning best with the wonderful ice and the frozen bumboat woman and the Russian princess. It reminded me, with its interwoven themes, of a symphony. It had "everyzing", including the Good Queen herself. Thank you.

. . . As Agens is out I must get the tea for the family tonight. We are going to have . . . and . . . surrounded by . . . and . . ., not to mention . . . with . . . Don't you wish you were here?

With my love,
Gwen.

(59)   FOSTER'S MADHOUSE.
                                                  MONDAY, 1943.
                                                      [28 June]

My dear Tony,

I rather like this paper, and as the W.D.C. has thousands of sheets like this there is no reason why I shouldn't continue to write on it. A strange "tightening up" has taken place in W.D.C. these past few days. Bro. Walter has allowed himself a month's "sick leave", as I told you, and some important Cretin (probably Weitemeyer or Battersby) has been sending ludicrous "staff notes" round for the staff to note and sign . . .

In addition to sending round ridiculous notes the dignitary responsible ordered that anyone wanting anything from the storeroom should "ask Norman" first. People go and "ask Norman" for packets of envelopes, etc. There was some talk of locking the storeroom, so I went immediately to remove the key, but it wasn't there anyway and couldn't be found, and getting supplies of paper like this, brown paper and string, etc. is a simple matter for one who has been trained by the Rufo-Nanine agency.

. . . The President of the Bitches' Temperance League would be glorious in a drunken state. She is so gross and bloated that no-one loves her now except Father, who is blind to her faults. This morning I was awakened by Father's voice saying in the idiotic language which only Gretchen understands "Oozy dogger, little doozous, two this morning, two this morning, two this morning . . ."

"Two what?" I called out.

"Two cups of tea," replied Father.

True enough, the little beast is given large cups of hot tea as soon as she's let out of her kennel in the morning.

Daphne has left us for good, thank God. She did nothing but break things, and any praise I ever gave her shows my total inability to recognise a film-crazed moron at first glance. So we are doing our own work once more, and thank the Lord the beans don't have strings any more. I think we were having bean string trouble the last time you were here. The little dim-wit couldn't even mash potatoes, and her sweeping lacked zeal.

Anything I didn't know about sweeping, polishing, etc. (and that was plenty) I learned at the Convent, where the Mother Superior "took me in hand" the first morning. I can remember her gentle eyes as she told me about polishing the bake-house floor for the glory of God, and when I was half-hearted about the convent veranda she took the broom from me and did it herself, without saying anything at all, so that I felt thoroughly ashamed.

Thank you for sending "Another Country". I had forgotten it, and was glad to read it once more. I find it very difficult to imagine how I wrote it; I write "all at once"—that is, the whole thing is there and all I have to do is "get it down". Sometimes I am thinking about something—a situation, or an idea, even a phrase, and suddenly I see "in a flash" how it really is, and how it should be done, but most of the time I am rather dull, and the P.S. really does rob me of natural "flowing out" of ideas—I "twist and wither" as you say, like the plant out of reach of sunlight. (I look like it, don't I, says Tiny Tim.)

. . . Agens won at the tennis match yesterday, and has been in a wonderful mood ever since. She is really a fine player, and once nearly knocked out the local greengrocer's wife with one of her "star" shots. The unfortunate woman missed the ball entirely and it struck her on the head!

. . . After omitting the references to food in my last letter I find that you don't mind hearing about it after all. Father brought home a "dirty big" cauliflower the other night. It was so big that it was given a whole chair to itself in the kitchen. He also brought us a "dirty big" fish, a squire I believe, that Agens cooked excellently. Agens has some spectacular successes in cooking, and some equally spectacular failures when she's not in a good mood. She makes a delicious pudding called "Pavlova"—or rather she did, in the days when cream was plentiful. This airy sweet has a light shell filled with whipped passionfruit cream. We have been having mysterious soups, rich and thick, with Heaven knows what in them. We have had chickens, "surrounded by" vegetables, and wonderful pies with kidney, if you're lucky enough to get the kidney; some nights one gets nearly all kidney and other nights none at all. At lunchtime I have cheese, lettuce, tomatoes and such things and quantities of fruit. It gives me great pleasure to eat such things in winter, because they have an icy coldness that is proper to their nature—except cheese, of course. Sometimes I sit in the sun in All Ss. churchyard, and if it's raining or too windy I stay in the "tea-room" and make the dim-wits listen to my stories which are all wild, fantastic, gripping etc. and quite untrue, though I introduce real characters into them. Or else I tell them about my wishes for the collapse of civilisation and the public service with it.

"But if there were no public service," said a tea-girl, "what would you do for a living?"

Of course they think I'm joking; they cannot imagine a world without the public service, or something like it. God in Heaven! WEDNESDAY. [30 June]

I have noticed a great blossoming of chalk-marking on the walls of Brisbane during the past few weeks. The inevitable Foo is everywhere.

Outside a dreadful cafe: FOO EATS HERE
Beside a broken window: FOO THREW A BRICK
Outside the Gresham: FOO IS STAYING HERE
Other notices inform us that FOO HAS JOINED THE WAAAFS, FOO IS RIGHT HERE, FOO IS NO FOOL, FOO IS IN THE STEW.

196

Down in Roma Street the notices are often in the second person, and there is a very large one which says YOU ARE MAD. This has quite a fascinating effect on tram passengers. Two of my contemporaries looked at it the other day, and one remarked "I wonder what they meant?", and the other looked at it without a smile and said "Probably those niggers put it up." I didn't know the young ladies but they looked as if they'd fed on pies all their lives.

A little further along was the statement MOLLS GO WITH YANKS and it stayed there for two days, but this morning I noticed that some Censor of Public Notices had rubbed out the M, so that now it reads OLLS GO WITH YANKS.

Can you imagine the mentality of a person who'd rub out the M and leave the rest of the notice! I've often wondered who rubs out the notices on brick walls that are nobody's property — is it a pure-minded bill-poster, a Methodist clergyman, a member of the Racial Hygiene Society, or an old gentleman with Victorian morals?

. . . Here is a gem from the W.D.C.'s private and highly confidential Examination Manual, which I "borrowed" from M's drawer while he was at lunch.

It will be noted that each class is qualified as "apparent", the reason being that all enquiries should be approached from the angle that certain conditions "appear" to the Commission to exist. Such an approach is easier to abandon if contrary facts are demonstrated.

With my love,
Gwen.

Thursday, 1943.
Diocese of Creek Street.
Cretins' Rest Home.
[1 July]

My dear Tony,

BISHOP STOPS CLOCK.

Yesterday afternoon, at 5 to 4, I walked from the switch to the clock and stood in front of the clock. I gazed at the clock face intently for about two minutes. Everyone within range stopped work and looked at me, and at the clock, which was ticking away in an orderly manner.

Then I opened the little door under the clock, and looked seriously at the works inside for some moments. Everyone looked puzzled. I put my hand inside the clock and stopped the pendulum, then shut the little door and returned to the switch.

At 4.15 the clock still showed two minutes to four.

Presently the office girl set up a terrible howl: "The clock's stopped." Several people stopped work, and some examined their watches. "The clock's stopped," they said.

The office boy went up to the clock and was going to open it, but the Asst. Accountant shouted "Leave that clock alone, you don't know anything about it." The Asst. Accountant then went to have a look at it, but went away again.

I was waiting for someone to come down and accuse me of stopping the clock, but suddenly I realised my foolishness: NOBODY BELIEVED I HAD STOPPED IT. This is true.

Miss Banfield, the head typist, came quietly out from her little sheep-pen, wound up the clock, put the hands right and returned to her desk.

That is all. This little story is brought to you by courtesy of the Rufo-Nanine Cretinous Stories League . . .

Joe has reaped the reward of his crowbar-lifting, and other such fiendish sports. The other night he simply collapsed and has gone to bed. He swears that his illness (described by himself as being "crook in the guts") has nothing to do with crowbar-lifting and sand-bag punching, but I don't believe him. It is probably a judgement on his "crook" attitude to physical strength.

Joe, within living memory, has gone to two extremes; at the age of fourteen or so he was champion cream-bun-eater of the boys' Grammar School, and had a figure which made everyone ashamed of him. No "boys' suits" could be bought to fit him, and his tailors had to make extra large pants for him. He was a miniature edition of Father Foster, and looked like a walking barrel. I suppose it is the surviving pictures of those days which have driven him to fanatical exercises. He does not seek to destroy such pictures: on the contrary, he displays them, in a sort of "Look on this picture, and on this" attitude.

I can remember one "incident" during my fifth-form year at school which is worth recording. At the school "Sports Day" I was "put in charge of" the ice-cream stall. This shows a fantastic short-sightedness on the part of the authorities, and I have never yet discovered why they reposed such simple trust in me. But that is beside the point. The "ice-cream stall" was under the pavilion in the field, and simple arrangements existed for serving people over a small board as a counter. Joe, who knew of my influential position, was present. The actual scooping of the ice-cream was done by two assistants, who dug it out from cans, and passed the filled cones to me at the counter. Thus, I would call out, "Two, please," and two would "come forward". Joe presented himself at the counter at intervals of ten minutes or so. Needless to say no money was handed over from one Foster to another. Joe, pleased with his success, but tired of ice-cream, presented himself twice in the queue for free buns, but was flung out by a watchful maths. mistress, who spoke to him severely about greediness, and called him "you greedy little boy". Needless to say this had no effect at all on Joe's character.

THURSDAY EVENING CHEZ AGENS

As I was writing the above this afternoon a letter arrived from you in the late mail. It contained a portrait of me in a hat which filled me with joy: a militant hat, a glorious flag-flying hat, a hat . . . well, not every hat has a portcullis! Where did you get all the colours from? Have you an "official" supply for document-marking, or do you keep them privately for your secret hat-designing activities?

I have to go off and "take" choir practice now. I hope Ethel, the prim soprano, is absent, as I'm not in a fighting mood, though I'm pretty sure to be after five minutes' practice.

. . . It is late now. I'll write some more tomorrow.

FRIDYA (Friday) [2 July]

My Dear Tony,

This morning I felt rather sick, and I was just planning (at about 8 o'clock) to stay home and sit in the sun, when Agens said "You forget, the painters are here." They were, too, clanging tins and battering against walls. We are having the inside of the house painted, and some of the railings etc. So I decided to go out after all. I spent the morning playing with the adding machine, adding up fantastic sums of money, and after lunch I had a rest and wrote ridiculous rhymes about everyone in sight. Tonight I feel much better. Joe is up and about again, as well as ever . . .

Gretchen was at home today, and after the painters had painted the boards of the doors opening on to the veranda bright red, Gretchen walked on the wet paint and then in and out, so that her foot-prints are recorded in bright red paint on the veranda boards and the lounge-room floor.

There is a small group of some vulgar hot-gospelling society at the corner of our street tonight, playing cornets and banging tambourines. How I hate that racket! . . .

But here is a splendid incident: it happened at a wedding on Tuesday evening.

I arrived to find the church decked with great bowls of poinsettias. The guests were dressed in furs — I think all the richest people in Brisbane must have been there. I was most delighted, too, because they were a Cathedral congregation — the Dean was taking the wedding — and they behaved quietly. A splendid man in a suit just a little too tight for him was showing the guests to their pews (he had obviously been "hired" for the evening) and when I came in he tried to prevent me from going down the side aisle to the organ!

I had been warned that a singer was to "render" that dreadful song "Because", but when the ceremony started no singer had yet arrived. The bride was magnificent, and everything was proceeding in a dignified and proper manner when in staggered the singer, <u>drunk,</u> waving a brown-paper parcel of music.

He swayed to the organ and leaned against it. After several attempts to regain his beery breath (he had been running, or at least hurrying) he said in loud and commanding tones, "Me tram broke down." Everyone turned round to see what was going on, and he demanded a glass of water in still louder tones. So I took a glass from a cupboard at the back of the church and brought him some water from the churchyard tap. He spilt it all on the floor, put down the glass, and collapsed on to the seat. I took the music from him and set it up, turning over to page 3 to read it to myself. He got up again, and said in a dreadful whisper "Don't start there. Start here." And he turned the music back to page 1! He sat breathing heavily, and I thought he had collapsed, but when the couple went into the vestry he sprang suddenly to life, stood upright (though holding the organ for support) and said "Right." Off I went.

Well, I can describe him best by saying that he was a genuine singer of the Wolf school — the real thing, and no mistake. He "bloody well roared", as I heard a soldier say outside the lions' den at Taronga. The guests were spellbound at the volume that came from his voice, which was full of beery sobs:

"Be-he-ca-hause Go-hod ma-hade you-hoo mi-hine" he sang, and now and again would waver on this or that note and then go on again with alcoholic fervour.

He took a long deep breath before his last note, and held on to it in a way that no sober person ever could. The whole performance was unbelievable. It was the real stuff, a "Hesperus" performance. Oh Tony, I wish you'd been there!

After he'd finished he seized his music, wrapped it up clumsily and walked off unsteadily into the night.

Sometimes I wonder if it was only a dream.

In the week-end I'll answer your letter, which is full of

interesting thoughts, and I shall tell you various things about aunts, tomato-vines, hats, hell-fire, etc.

With my love,
Ginnie

(61)   CHEZ AGENS
                                                              Saturday, 1943
                                                                 [3 July]
My dear Tony,

Poor Agens is in bed with 'flu, and we are all "taking care of" her as she has to make a broadcast in the morning. (I'll write by hand for a time, as Joe wants to listen to a spy drama on the radio, and the typewriter is annoying him.) Well, tomorrow Agens is to talk on "The Opportunity Shop". She and Father (mostly Father) wrote a little speech about "The Opportunity Shop", how it began, what it sells and how fine an institution it is! I'm sorry I'll miss the broadcast but I'll be at High Mass. However I have every confidence in Agens, who used to broadcast regularly in the Housewives' Session, telling housewives in grim tones how to run model households, leaving Gwen and Joe home with 1/- to buy what dreadful food they cared to from a travelling pastrycook.

The wedding this afternoon was a large and vulgar affair with all the usual trappings. There were two bridesmaids, one blue and one pink, and a dreadful flower-girl "got-up" like a dolly varden in mauve silk; this terrible little creature walked in front of the bride, who had a lovely wedding gown and a "dirty-big" pink HORSESHOE dangling from her waist on pink ribbons. Clarice, the demon Contralto, bellowed out of tune as usual. A bar's rest is nothing to her, and she just howls at any old pace that happens to suit her.

SUNDAY [4 July]

I couldn't settle down to writing last night. Father carried the Little Dogger about and pushed her on to the paper, and when we tried to put her to bed she escaped, and when we caught her again her dressing-gown was missing, Agens called for hot lemon drinks,

202

people rang up, Diogenes dragged the cover off a fowl in the kitchen, Spondulix knocked over a vase and walked over some damp paint and Joe kept asking me questions, so finally I just gave up and read one of Agens' books from the library:

> He had the face of a Napoleon — a Caesar, but with the jaw of a prize-fighter and the eyes of a dreamer; a face, once seen, never to be forgotten.

In the book (by reading the last paragraph of each chapter) I found that an international spy-ring was easily cleaned up by the hero.

Agens, after a successful broadcast, was introduced to an American at the radio station; as he had nowhere to go she brought him home. He is an instrument-maker, and his name is Karl Thomas de Aquino! He claims to belong to the family of the great philosopher, but he's very stupid and I don't like him at all. I wish Agens hadn't brought him home; however he has fallen into Joe's clutches, and Joe is telling him the finer points of watch-making. Karl Thomas de Aquino is very Italian-looking and might easily be related to the saint. He and Joe have come out from the watch-making lecture and Agens is telling him all about BORERS, and how we had to cut our trees down because of them, the liar! "A Borer," says Agens, "is a kind of wood-worm."

I am listening to the Valkyries in the opera hour. You asked me once before if I like Wagner — Well, I've never seen him performed (remember what sort of town I live in) but he strikes me as being a bit Hesperussy, though on a grand scale. I find the music pretentious and devoid of content, but I should very much like to see how it appeals to me in connection with the stage setting . . .

I am easily terrified (this is proved by my reaction to the devils in Fantasia) and perhaps if I saw Wagner done properly I should change my opinion . . .

Now, about Aunts. You are lucky to have an Aunt to send you things. I have no Aunts in Australia, and my father's sisters in England are much older than he is, and have never seen me, nor do they send me things. Agens is an only child. I have acquired an Aunt by marriage—she married Father's brother Bill. Uncle Bill is a wonderful gardener, and he has only to touch a plant to make it grow for him. Every little shoot or plant he puts in the ground flourishes—Dad's father has the same power of making things grow, but I'm afraid the magic touch hasn't come to me. Bill's wife is a screaming madwoman—she studies astrology and I shall never forget the first day I saw her: when we were in Melbourne Agens took Joe and me to her place, and Aunt Dorothy opened the front door and said, at the top of her voice: "Is this Gwen? She's not like you. The Queen Mary's doomed." "What do you mean, doomed?" asked Agens. "She's doomed," shrieked Dorothy, "astrology tells you, she's doomed." (The Queen Mary we had seen two days before lying safely in Sydney Harbour.) Aunts are wonderful people—real aunts, I mean; think of Peter's "Aunt Edith". I am sorry not to have any. Uncle Bill used to take us out driving in his car, but Aunt Dorothy sat in the back "making night hideous" with her astrological predictions.

The thought of tomato-vines being watered carries me back to days at the convent. I had a whole bed of tomato plants under my care, and after lunch, when I had finished washing up, I used to go down and water them, sitting in the sun on a tree-stump and singing to myself. Sometimes I would hoe out the weeds growing near the path, or pick them from the wet soil in the beds with my hands. I shall never forget those days. How happy I was! I made a cupboard out of old fruit boxes for the bake-house, and mended a fence, and sawed wood. But these simple delights were all a natural part of my life there, and it would be absurd and illogical to attempt to recapture happiness by sawing wood under Agens' house, or making her a cupboard out of fruit-boxes. It seems very difficult to make people understand life in a convent, or in any religious order, but that is because our industrial system has deprived people of the joy of making things with their hands, and doing simple things not for the purpose of getting them over and done with as quickly as possible but because they are really part of one's life. I can remember the refectory in the long summer evenings, when the sunshine fell across the table before the sun disappeared behind the hills. Strange long-legged birds used to come and walk about the fields at the back of the convent, and there was a possum that made a terrible nuisance of itself at night, sliding over the roof and jumping around in the trees. There was a convent dog called Cuthbert, a half-witted dog who used to bite novices' heels when they were carrying jugs of milk.

I am interested in your remarks about individuality. It is a problem which seems to obsess a great many people, particularly artists of various kinds (mostly bad ones), because they confuse individuality with personality. The best thing I have read on the subject is by a Thomist, Fr Garrigou-Lagrange.

> To develop one's individuality is to live the egoistical life of the passions, to make oneself the centre of everything, and end finally by being the slave of a thousand passing goods which bring us a wretched momentary joy. Personality, on the contrary, increases as the soul rises above the sensible world and by intelligence and will binds itself more closely to what makes the life of the spirit.

Still, being young, I prefer being Gwen to watching the grass grow. (Though, as St Thomas might say, I must be before I can watch the grass grow—STOP THIS NONSENSE.)

We will write about hats, instead.

"Note: I have written to a leading Brisbane milliner ordering a special hat to be made to my own design, etc."

Ah, Hubert, wouldst thou put out mine eyes?[1] Are you telling the truth? Do you realise that if this is only a trick I will go to bed and stay there till the plaster falls down on me, like Mrs Clements?

. . . The decay of festivals is indeed a sad result of the world's mechanisation. How feeble most things are! There seems to be little spirit left in most people, and worse still, they resent any evidence of real life. A few dirty big bungers would enliven the W.D.C. temporarily at least. I must see to something of the sort

---

[1] *King John,* Act 4, Scene I.

on Guy Fawkes' Day. If you are in town by great good fortune, then I trust you will take part in any little ceremonies we can devise.

I must help Agens now. Tomorrow I'll write again.

With my love,
Gwen.

(62)   Sunshine Home for Cretins
                                              Monday, 1943
                                                 [5 July]
My dear Tony,

Last night the family was heartily sick of Thomas de Aquino and cunningly schemed to push him off to Evensong with me. So I turned him over to my scholastic friend Harold, who ground him to pieces with theology. When I got home I found Joe giving Agens a stern lecture on bringing home Americans after broadcasts, especially fools who didn't know anything about aeroplanes!

There were some amusing incidents yesterday afternoon when Joe asked the American: What physical training do you have in your army? The poor fellow, not realising he was talking to a fiend in human form, began doing some simple exercises, and Joe stood by laughing with fiendish glee. "This one," said Thomas de Aquino "is better if you do it with a stick." "Stick!!!" replied Joe with contempt, "I use a crowbar."

Joe took the weakling downstairs and showed him his 2cwt. "punch-ball" made of sand. "Try that," said Joe, but Aquinas would not, and sank in Joe's estimation to nil, nihil, nothing.

I feel very sorry for anyone who falls into Joe's clutches; his fanaticism is reaching unimaginable limits.

Today I have a sore throat; I daresay I have caught Agens' flu. I wish the painters would finish their work at home, so that I can stop home in peace and potter round at my leisure. Gretchen now has both her sides covered with red and cream paint. She is very ill this morning, and is believed to have eaten or drunk a quantity of brown paint left uncovered. Agens gave her some oil this morning, which she licked up with great relish.

. . . Peter wrote to me last week. Joyce has some kind of fever, and he is looking after his wife, child, home and parish all at once, so he has his hands full. Arthur Cran, the inquisitorial public servant, has been invited to be a godparent. That puts him in a difficult position, as he is a stern opponent of the marriage of the clergy, but would dearly like to be a godfather! He hasn't accepted Peter's offer yet, and keeps turning over the problem in his mind: whether he will assent outwardly to Peter's marriage and take part in ceremonies connected therewith, or whether he will maintain an attitude of disapproval and renounce the joys of being a godfather. Arthur came up to see me this morning and entered very mysteriously with his leather case, which has a dirty big lock. I took my own leather document-case to the counter, and we exchanged some gramophone records in a sinister fashion, sliding them into the dark compartments of our cases. Most of the people here are "dying" to know what I keep in my case, which I have always by me, but I won't show them. They try elementary tricks, such as asking "Can I have a look at the inside of your case, please? I'm thinking of getting one, and I'd like to see the way it expands." But I won't let them.

. . . The number of delightful hats in Brisbane at present is exceedingly small. The design and workmanship displayed in the majority on show indicate that the present race of hat-designers and makers has no imagination and little skill.

Today is a most depressing day—there is not a glimpse of the sun, and the light is hard and without warmth. The spirit of the W.D.C. weighs upon me.

I had a letter from a German Manfred Ritter, who is interned. He claims to have discovered several new theorems in mathematics, and has made a gadget which measures "the sun's altitude, sunrise, etc". (I don't know what the "etc" includes.) "Astronomy," he says, "is good clean fun and you can't get hurt." It sounds a bit like Heath Robinson!

TUESDAY, 1832. [6 July]

The inezact date and the pecualiar spelling are due to the fact that

I am in bed. I have moved the typewriter out to a small table beside the bed, and I am lying on my side, leaning on the right afm, arm while I type.

I woke up with a very sore throat, so I went to selep sleep again. Agens rang up W.D.C. and "regretted" that I wouldn't be in today.

The house is still being painted, and a very fat painter who wears a delightfully paint-spotted felt hat turned up in the front like the traditional village idiot, keeps poking his head out of Agens' bedroom, which is being pianted, and asking me if I think chocolate would be nicer than cream for the skirting, and things like that. I merely reply "Yes" to everything, and it will be interesting to see what Agens' romm is like when he has finished.

I am vaguely ill, not seriously, but I don't feel like doing anything at all energetic, and lying here weiting to you gives me great pleasure, though you may strike some unintelligible patches. I have a slight temperature. It id vrty pleasant here on the veranda, as I have the blinds up and can see the blue sky and the trees in the sunnshibe. (I wonder if James Joyce invented hisnew language by typing in bed,?)

A few moments before sje left for the "Opportunity Shop" Agens brought me out a letter from you which by good furtune was addressed ti grumes st. (to grimes St) Take your pick when there are alternative sets of words. So I find my day at home altogether delightfurl. Hell, says Tinny Tim,[1] where are these words coming from. The machine has a tendency to repeat let rs as it is not entirely under my conytrol. I thick Tinny Tim had better become a permanent charachter.

Your accusation that my attitude to evil was Protentant enrageedme. Who said I didn't believe in evil sopirits? (It's not must suse HEL?)
HELL It's not much use trying to make any convincing theological statements in ludicrous type.

---

[1] Originally a typographical error for Tiny Tim. This character and his variants became one of GH's recurrent aliases. He appeared again, much later, as Timothy Klein, one of the pseudonyms under which she published in the 1960s and 1970s.

Evil is a deprivation, it has no existence of its own. Evil spirits were in any case originally good spirits – the Devil was the first Protestant. I didn't say it had a <u>negative importance</u>; did I? Iddon't belittle it at all. Everything, insofar as it has existence, is good, that is, noting is created evil. I think you will find that Peter agrees with me in this. Do you know the lovely prayer

> Holy Michael Archangel, defend us in the day of battle; be our safeguard againstt the wickedness of the Devil. May God rebuke him, we humbly pray, and do thou, Prince of the heavenly host by the power of God, defend us from all wicked spirits who wander through the world for the ruin of souls.

Tinny Tim's arm collapsed, so he will continue in ink. We stole this pen from the W.D.C. yesterday. Our own pens are worn out. Stealing from the W.D.C. is too easy to give us much pleasure, but is is a step in the right direction: they are scrving a good cause in spite of themselves.

Evil is a tremendous problem in any of its forms. Some philosophies, especially Eastern philosophies, are based on its existence as a positive reality: really, it is a deprivation of being. Evil spirits certainly exist, but they were not created as evil spirits. When they set out to "ruin souls" they assume good forms or offer seemingly good things very cunningly. There is a story that S. Martin was by himself one day when the Devil came along in Our Lord's own form, and Martin was almost deceived, but said "If you are indeed the Lord Christ, show me the marks of the nails and spear." Of course the Devil couldn't, so he went away.

. . . I shall send you the words of "Then give me ale". Where are you likely to go if you leave Darwin? There are worse places than Darwin, I believe, and D.N.I. doesn't seem to have much idea of what would please you.

Can't you be an actor and a singer too? Your voice moves me very deeply, and I can remember its quality even when you are away. And as I have heard you only "out of practice", after being in Moresby or H.I.M. Opera House, I think you'd be splendid after some "disciplined and patient training". Whatever you do, don't give up singing. Your singing has the power of making one forget that one is in a room, and time simply dissolves away while you sing. Your singing sounds effortless and easy: I envy you — it must be fine to sing. I hope it won't be too long before I can see you act. Although the war cramps life, if it hadn't been for war perhaps I'd never have met you, and there would have been no WOLF in my life and perhaps no COOK in yours. I'm going to get up and see what Eliza has to say. I haven't tried the *sortes cookianae*[2] for a long time.

Cook is not very comforting to a sick person:

(1) Despair is in the father's tear
Deep anguish in his sigh;
The dreaded words have met his ear
His only one must die[3]

(2) Because the pages happen to have come loose from their binding, the book opened at the "Song of the Dying old Man to his Young Wife".

(3) Eliza tells some "dirty big" lies:
Build up the school-house well
Where Infancy and Youth
May hear wide echoes fall
From Knowledge, Hope and Truth.[4]

(Ah, Hubert!) . . .

WEDNESDAY. [7 July]
Tinny Tim feels a bit better today and is pottering around in his father's dressing-gown; his throat is exceedingly sore, and he has no appetite.

. . . Last Sunday someone told me a story about a certain Dr in Brisbane, who used to own the big house on the hill near Auchenflower Station. Do you remember it? — a grey stone house

[2]On the analogy of sortes virgilianae, sortes Biblicae or sacrae. See (4), footnote 2. GF and TR were in the habit of consulting the collected works of Eliza Cook on important occasions by opening the pages at random.
[3]These lines are from "The Only Daughter" by Eliza Cook.
[4]From "Good works" by Eliza Cook.

with trees all round. The Dr was mad, from all accounts, and is said to have committed murder, letting a youth take the blame. At his funeral the coffin was in a van drawn by horses; and they brought the body along River Road, on which the house stands. When they reached a small bridge near his house, the horses stopped dead. They were whipped. They refused to move and stood trembling. The driver lashed them, and they reared up but would not cross the bridge. There was nothing to be done, so they changed the horses. When the second team of horses came to the bridge, the same thing happened. They stopped dead, and neither whipping nor coaxing could make them pass the bridge. They changed the horses again. The third time they dragged the horses across.

That is all I know. There are amazing stories about the old Doctor and the murder. I wish I could find someone old enough to recount the story—most of the people who know anything about it have second-hand information. The part about the horses is true. Isn't it good! I think I shall use it in a story.

You were right about the inquisition: diplomatic relations no longer exist between myself and the parties concerned. They simply leave me alone, no matter what I do. Nobody will fight me. I was rebuked by a Church of England young lady (the one who'd die if you visited her) for saying "Good God," "God in Heaven," and other phrases like that. "Very well," I replied, "in future I shall substitute Reed as I do not wish to offend you." So whenever she is near I say "Reed in Heaven," or "Good Reed, where's my pencil," or "Thank Reed it's one o'clock." She does not speak to me now. Your suggestion that I should fight with M's secretary cannot be put into effect, as she has no weapons of her own left. Her only weapon, the threat of "reporting me", she knows to be quite ineffective. The assistant accountant complained to Roland Weitemeyer that I "frequently wrote letters" (Weitemeyer is in charge of the staff during Bro.'s "sick leave") and our friend of the dirty big pies told the asst.acc. to mind his own business, get on with his work, and never mind what I was doing as it was no concern of his . . . I have discovered that the pie-man is breaking his neck to get out and join the army. So you can see, there is nobody at all to fight with. The only thing to do seems to be to make myself as comfortable as possible and have a jolly good rest at the expense of the Government. May God preserve my spirit!

Tinny Tim is going back to bed. It pleases him to think that on Monday he hid a number of vital documents, and while he is lying in bed there will be frantic searches going on at the W.D.C. for them.

Well, Tony, I'm not very bright at present. When I'm feeling better I shall send you news of a great many things . . .

With my love,
Gwen.

(63)
FRIDAY NIGHT
GRIME STREET
[9 July]

My dear Tony,

I had absolutely a hell of an afternoon that wore my temper to nothing. I think I am cracking up — I suppose that you can't run indefinitely in a system quite against your nature. I'm in a good mood now — Agens gave me an excellent dinner and made some delicious biscuits and a LARGE apple pie. I am writing to you and listening to the wind and everything is fine. You seem to be in much better spirits from your latest letter, and I am glad your intake of oxygen has "irradiated" you.

But when I say I am cracking up, I mean it. There are subtle changes: my moods of buoyant incompetence and celestial indifference are giving way to more frequent ones of dissatisfied brooding and reflection on the essence of my surroundings during the day — calculated to destroy the spirit. Nothing is alive: there is no growth, only an atmosphere of emptiness of spirit. Out at the damned school I was ill-fed and had to cope with brains 50 years behind anything, but at least I never taught anybody anything from the beastly Grade books and I used to take the little boys out in the sun when we got tired of being inside. I used to draw on the board with coloured chalks, too. I remember one day when the Coadjutor Bishop (the school's official "Visitor") came out to "visit" us and found the board covered with appallingly mal-proportioned alligators. He asked my class (it was supposed to be a history-lesson) about King Alfred and the Cakes, and nobody could tell the old fool anything at all about the incident. Enough of this.

Last night was one of the loveliest nights I have ever known. It was full moon and there was a cold wind blowing. The clouds at first were swept out flat and shining, but presently the wind blew them together into one enormous cloud almost round in shape. There was only the full moon and the great round cloud and the brightest stars. The air was so clear and fine that everything stood out as sharply as in sunlight and the trees sparkled with cold light. The roofs of the houses shone all around. It was so beautiful that I could not sleep—I lay awake looking out at the trees and the cold sky.

When I heard that your singing teacher has a house in the mountains I thought of my old grandfather who is a hermit in the Dandenong range. Do you know what pleased me in Victoria—the apple-trees. He had apple-trees beside his little shack. It was wonderful to pick apples off the trees and eat them: Joe and I had never done that before.

On Sunday in the opera hour there is to be Dido and Aeneas. I shall listen and tell you about it.

With my love,
Gwen.

(64)
                                                    Crimes Lodge,
                                                    AUCHENBLUME
                                                    Saturday, 1943.
                                                    [10 July]
My dear Tony,

This is the War Damage Commission's paper, and this is Fred Hackleskinner[1] writing on it.

I'm feeling much better today; it is good to be well again. Tomorrow if I feel all right I'm going to spend the afternoon with Diana. I hope her people take me for a drive in the car — I love riding in cars because we've never had a car of our own: there is a story that when Father was learning to drive he ran into a chinaman, and developed a complex about cars.[2]

When I was a child we had a horse and cart (not at Auchenblume) and I remember that Father couldn't be "trusted" to drive — something always went wrong if he took the reins. Do you know the pleasure of riding in a sulky? I can remember beautiful rides through the country at a gentle pace. Motor cars were so rare then that our old horse, Don, made a terrible fuss when he saw one. The first person to have a car in our district at Mitchelton was Old Coar. That was in 1925, when Joe was born, and the first word Joe learnt to say was "coarcar", according to Agens — who may possibly have invented that to please Old Coar, and taught Joe to say it with great persistence in order to encourage Old Coar to take us for drives.

You wouldn't know Crimes Lodge now. Because of the painters, all the furniture has been shrouded in the front of the house, and the kitchen has been stripped bare: the plates, knives, forks, spoons, cups, saucers etc. have been put on the billiard table, and Agens runs round screaming WET PAINT if you go near anything. I didn't let them paint my room because of the trouble of taking everything off the walls and moving the books (anyway it doesn't need painting) and wicked Agens took advantage of this

[1] GF, another pseudonym.
[2] This is a true story. Dad never drove again. (GH)

214

and moved incredible numbers of vases (including wall-vases), ornaments and odds and ends into my room. There is hardly space to move in. You really don't know (I mean, you'd hardly credit) what there is in a house until it has to be moved somewhere else. Normally I'd enjoy the upside-downness of things and spend my time looking for forgotten treasures, but I've been so sick this week that I took little delight in "border incidents" that kept occurring between Agens and the painters: for instance, there was a conflict about the colour of a picture-rail in the lounge. The head painter was determined to have a brown one, and he started painting the rail brown when Agens came in and stopped him. She seized a dirty big vase, blue, decorated with orange and red flowers, and pointed to an obscure corner of one flower on the vase. "That," she said in a determined voice, "is the colour I want." The unhappy man squatted down among his cans of paint and Agens stood over him while he mixed the colour and kept pushing the vase into his unwilling view for him to "compare it with what's being mixed".

I don't share Agens' enthusiasm for paint. I don't think this house should ever have been painted, but the damage was done before we came here. The doors are of solid cedar, but some idiot plastered them with green paint before we arrived, and not only the doors but the whole house (outside) was a hideous green of unimaginable hue.

A large fat painter had a marvellous felt hat, entirely spotted with coloured paint. He wore this continually, and tucked the brim under in the front; as he always put his head round the corner before coming into a room the effect was delightful. He looked like a genial Rufo-Nanine Napoleon.

Now we come to part of your last letter: it would appear (to use a W.D.C. phrase) that you overestimate the number of my hats. In spite of the fact that I am an authority on headgear I have very few hats, and none that you could possibly condemn: here they are:

WINTER HATS

1. The Tale of Two Cities Hat. Brown felt, decorated with golden-

brown velvet, trimmed with velvet round the edge, and two velvet buttons.

2. Small green hat, plate-shaped with small crown, decorated with fancy velvet leaves and two small strips of felt in front, cunningly inserted through slits in the crown.

3. The Tower of Babel. I have already described this. It is decorated with veils and what I believe to be feathers of the common or household fowl, dyed shiny brown. An ideal hat for Saturday weddings. A corker.

SUMMER HATS

4. The Straw Boater. Need I say more?

5. Straw hat decorated with four bows of ribbon. Can't say what exactly, but it 'as sumzing. Same period as Straw Boater, but more chaste and godly. A vicarage hat.

6. Green velvet pixie's cap. Not really a hat at all. I use it to cover a gas bracket that can't be taken off my wall. No decoration, but I <u>could</u> easily decorate it.

7. Green cloth hat of great age. Shapeless. Simple. Ideal for gardening. Father sometimes wears this to dinner, without any particular reason.

There you are. All absolutely necessary. None superfluous. There aren't any hats in town at the moment that I care for. I'm waiting until summer-time. I have in mind a "come-into-the-garden-Maud" hat. I don't want a lot of hats any more than Rubinstein wants a lot of pianos. Here, too, I'm handicapped by the lack of seasons. There is no autumn and hardly any spring. In a snowy country one could have a Christmas hat with tiny fir trees.

. . . Your new tent-companion, Harold, seems to be an extraordinary person. Is he married? Or will he "go through life an old bachelor"? People who say that one "should marry" are very often unmarried themselves, I find.

I was amused to hear that greed is evident in your mess. If you want more than a "moderate portion" of anything, drive your fork violently into the hands reaching towards the dish. And remember, as the good book says, "Your knife is your personal implement."

. . . I found in my desk the other day part of a long poem called "The Baboon", which belongs to my "early period" (about 1938). Here's the beginning:

The big baboon
Waits for me
On Wednesdays
In the afternoon.
He has a voice like Swinburne's sea,
He never lives laborious days.

He has small hands
In spite of his size;
He's not very clean.
He understands
Only things he can see with his eyes
Not thinks of things that might have been.

The facts of life
(Such is his fate)
Demand that he
Should have a wife.
His lust he cannot moderate
With abstract thoughts on chastity.

O Ape, arise!
(No wife has he)
Demand a mate
With tender eyes
Full of baboonish mystery
Which none but you can penetrate.

Ah, Hubert! 1938 seems half a century ago.

With my love,
Gwen.

(65)   Crimes Lodge,
                                              AUCHENBLUME
                                              Monday.
                                              [12 July]

Dear Tony,

When I said Mafeking's Secretary was no good for fighting, I was
mistaken. This afternoon there was a wonderful public dust-up
between us, and I will get my commentator, Fred Hackleskinner,
to describe it for you.

The fight began when Harvey was "going through" the files
and found some of Bishop Foster's "work", that is, some
mysterious cards with real names and bogus information on them,
made out by the Bishop solely for her own pleasure and having
no connection with the Examining Dept.

HARVEY: What are these?
BISHOP: Leave them alone. I'm in charge of them. I know all
            about them. Don't touch them.
HARVEY: But I <u>must</u> know what they are. I <u>must</u> know.
BISHOP: All right, then. Go ahead.
HARVEY: What are they? Tell me what they are? How did they
            get in the current list?
BISHOP: Ah.
HARVEY: Miss Foster, I insist on knowing what these cards are.
BISHOP   (speaking in her "German style", clipping off words
            at the end, saying everything with annoying
            distinctness): It is entirely unnecessary for you to
            worry about them. They are in my care, their origins
            and destinations are alike known to me (and much
            more in that style).
HARVEY   (losing her temper): Miss Foster, I won't stand any
            more of this from you. I INSIST ON KNOWING ABOUT
            THESE CARDS.
BISHOP: Ah. Yes.
HARVEY: Don't you go on like that. You can't fool me. I can
            see right through you. I know all your tricks.
BISHOP   (innocently): Tricks? Tricks? Tricks? Oh, how can
            you say such a thing.

218

HARVEY: Don't you try that, either. You can't put that over.
BISHOP: Good. The affair is then concluded.
(The Bishop walked off and left Harvey, who stood with the cards in her hands, looking at them, rubbing her forehead as if trying to remember something.) After a few moments she called out angrily, "Miss Foster!"
BISHOP: Do you want me?
HARVEY: You didn't tell me what these cards are. I must know. I cannot have matters like these without knowing all about them.
BISHOP: They are my concern. Yes. Do not worry about them. They do not concern you. (This is the most infuriating thing to Harvey, as she cannot bear to think that the Bishop is getting any matters under her individual control.)
HARVEY: You make me furious. You're so stupid. Sometimes I get so annoyed with you I can hardly speak.
BISHOP: DEAR ME!
HARVEY: There you are, it's that kind of thing that enrages me. I've been in "a lot of" offices, but I've NEVER NEVER NEVER seen ANYONE carry on like you do.
    . . . It is impossible to describe Harvey's manner while she delivered the following speech. I will reproduce it in her own style as far as possible, but she was really trembling with rage and grief at the depravity of my character – I mean, Tony, this was the real stuff, for Harvey. This lecture took about 15 minutes, and I can only remember some of it.
    "I'll tell you some of the things you do, and remember, these are only a few. I actually saw you today SITTING ON THE FLOOR."
BISHOP: I was examining some Supplementary Pay-Roll Tax Interstate Registration Sheets. (That stopped her for a moment.)
    "I don't care what you were doing. The point is, that you were SITTING ON THE FLOOR. There isn't another business girl in Brisbane who'd sit on the floor. In all my life I've NEVER known anyone to do a thing like that in an office. NEVER. Suppose Mr Battersby had seen you?"

219

BISHOP: I daresay he has seen me sitting on the floor.

"Well, I can tell you that Mr Battersby has been noticing a great many things about you, and he's not at all pleased. But SITTING ON THE FLOOR! I can't imagine any normal person sitting on the floor. You're abnormal, that's what it is. Suppose anyone had come in to the counter. Think of the prestige of the Commission. What would they think if they saw one of the staff SITTING ON THE FLOOR. What would they think. And another thing: one day, actually while I was explaining something to you, you started swinging on the door! Just think for a moment, and tell me if anyone else here would swing on one of those doors while I was talking to them. You're abnormal. Everyone here knows you're not normal. There isn't a person here who thinks you're normal. You don't hear yourself talked about, but believe me, if you knew what they were saying about you you'd behave differently. You think I can't see through you, but I can. I've known people like you before. You'll come down to earth one day, with a mighty big (it should have been 'dirty big', shouldn't it?) bump. You think you can do just what you please. Work means nothing to you. You think it doesn't matter, but sometimes Robbie and I are worried to death by your attitude. You wouldn't care if the files never got attended to. You wouldn't care if the cards were all numbered wrongly. You just sit here and write letters, or some silly drivel . . . I feel sorry for your parents. I don't know how they put up with you. And the way you talk! I can't understand a word of what you're talking about, half the time. I've never heard such nonsense in all my life. And the way you go on about the Public Service makes me sick, simply sick. What do you stay here for, if you don't like it? Why don't you get out. How would you feel if you had to work with someone who didn't care about the systems you'd spent hours working out? And the mistakes you make! Millions of times I just fix them up myself and say nothing about it, because I know it's no use. Its no use at all talking to you, anyway, you simply don't understand a reasonable person's point of view. That's the whole trouble with you—you're not normal at all; you don't behave or talk like a normal person. You've been here long enough now to settle down, but you're one of the people who'll never settle down, you'll never make good, because you simply can't stick to your job; you're not interested in the Department, that's what it is, and I can tell you, I'm an easy person to work with, I flatter myself on that, so it's not as if I were hard to get on with. No, you must go your own way. You don't care what sort of a reputation the Commission gets. I <u>live</u> for my work, but you couldn't understand that. You'll never understand that. You don't even understand what I'm talking about; you'll never see my point of view. I saw right through you from the start. <u>Assistants</u> (<u>technically</u> I am Harvey's assistant) <u>I</u> never had assistants. You waste your time and get other people to do the work for you. But you'll go on just the same, whatever I say, so it's no use."

Well, Tony, Harvey is 35. Wouldn't it strike fear into anyone's heart to see what life can become. I didn't make it up, I simply record it . . .

I sent "Another Country" to Peter[1] and I'm enclosing his

---

[1]Peter Bennie's criticism which seems "very sound" is nevertheless parodied in the next letter. His letter reads, in part:

> The Vicarage,
> Imbil,
> 9.7.43

My dear Gwen,
Returning "Another Country" with very professional criticism.

Part 1 is rather good, I think. The traditional sympathetic interpretation of the child mind. I doubt whether it is realistic though. Children are not romanticists — that is one of the ill-effects of adolescence. They do not yearn for Arctic forests, fairies, for Wagnerian folk tales — they prefer food, bright colours and themselves . . . However, granted your psychology, part 1 is quite convincing and the word grouping and rhythm excellent. You convey your information quite effortlessly without distortion — and this is high compliment.

Your second part however is quite infantile. John remains an infant weeping incongruous tears about a purely romantic conception of Germany . . . I notice you avoid the story's most difficult effort-dialogue. Such touches as you have are banal. Next story you write, unless it is purely atmospheric, try to develop plot, dialogue and dramatic cause and effect — at the moment you haven't even event. However the main thing — capable writing — sentence construction, diction — choice of words — is all there, so keep going and sent me some more.

Send your best to the Editor, Meanjin Papers . . .

Turn up at the baptism, Friday, July 16, 2.30, St Johns if you care to and are recovered. Love, Peter.

221

criticism, which seems to be very sound: it really was rather infantile; and I hope Peter gives his infant food and bright colours and keeps it from "incongruous tears".

Now I'm going to make some butter for Agens: she has saved up a "dirty big" basin full of cream, and has been asking me every five minutes: "Wouldn't you like to make some butter?" "I thought you'd like to make butter, are you ready?" "There's all this cream here, I've left it for you, you'd like to make butter wouldn't you?"

I'll write again soon.

With my love,
Ginnie

(66)   Friday, 1943.
                                  Crimes Lodge, Auchenblume
                                                [16 July]

My dear Tony,

Peter rang me up at W.D.C. this morning, but I wasn't able to see him as he's going back to Imbil almost at once, although Joyce and the baby are staying here till the end of July. Arthur finally accepted the position of godfather, and said the baptism "went off well" . . .

Theophilus has been in a terrible mood for days: he has no ideas, he is unable to laugh, sing, play the zimbummer or write. It is partly living in a wooden house in extreme cold, I think. These houses are not built for the cold weather, and you know what condition 14 Crimes Street is in. Joe has made extensive plans for living in a flat of his own after the war—it is to have a sign outside WATCHES REPAIRED which Joe will take in immediately he sees anyone coming. He proposes to earn his living by ingenious dishonest methods. He says he is going to appear among the intellectuals of the gramophone society next week in disguise—it is very good to see him engaged in such gentle sport; probably he will work up to grand heights if once he starts "calling" on societies; I'm still trying to persuade him to come up and remove the War Damage clock.

I left you last time to make butter, but I didn't realise what

222

a job it would be. The dirty big bowl of cream was handed to me, and I wrapped myself in father's old dressing-gown and an apron and set to work. I beat it with an egg-beater until my arm ached, and nothing happened, except that Gretchen and the cats appeared and watched me with interest and greed. When I put the egg-beater down for a while Diogenes leapt on the table and put his whiskers in the cream, and father came in and said "Are you trying to make butter?" "Yes," I said, "I am." "Ah," said Father, "give the Dogger some cream."

With Father in the kitchen, Dogger saw her chances brightening, and the greed in her eyes grew more intense. "No," I said. "Poor little Dogger, poor little Dogger, just a little bit of cream?" "No!" "Give Dogger some cream." Dogger was picked up, and as she came nearer the cream Father could hardly hold her back. Finally I gave her the egg-beater to lick because its handle was loose, and got another egg-beater. I continued to beat the cream with vigour, but nothing happened. Agens came in, and after looking at the cream and tasting it said "You ought to beat it a bit harder." My arm felt as if it would drop off at any moment, so I rested for a time, and then set to work with some other implements including the potato-masher and cake-beater. After half-an-hour (with frequent rests for my weary arm) I saw the cream beginning almost imperceptibly to thicken, and just as it was about to become butter Agens came in, seized the beater, and "took over" with an air of triumph. Then, when the buttermilk came out, a scene occurred which has haunted me all through my life, whenever we have made butter: the buttermilk was poured away, and as it disappeared Agens cried out "Oh. Oh dear." Joe put his head in the kitchen to see what had gone wrong, and Agens continued "Oh dear. We should have kept the buttermilk for Gwen's freckles!" Ever since I have been a child people have been "meaning to save" buttermilk "for my freckles", but they always forget at the last moment. Whether buttermilk is really good for freckles I don't know, but my grandmother pursued me for many years with buttermilk always poured away at the last moment, and attributed the persistence of my freckles to the lack of applications of buttermilk.

We had a cow of our own at Mitchelton, called Daisy. (Ah, Hubert!) Grandfather (the hermit) drove her home from town one day as a "present", and Agens tells me that she had a horrible feeling when she saw old grandfather walking along the road with a lean and hungry cow. Grandfather's choice was a good one, though, for Daisy gave milk for many years and never "dried up" (which I believe cows do sometimes).

RUFO-NANINE SCHOOL OF WRITING

Mrs Herodias Smith, a pupil of Edeledel Edel,[1] wrote this after a course of five 6 guinea lessons:

> Sayed Bin Baba, Claude Sluce, Cuthbert Lai Foo and Jaffer Ahwang glimmered inevitably in the trumpet-toned memory of Lovie Garvey, who sank symmetrically on to her resplendent armchair, which Bargu Ah Mat and Bin Rassip had given Ellen Bin Juda on the previous Monday.

VERY PROFESSIONAL CRITICISM by Subidir Hooser, official Critic of the Rufo-Nanine Plasterers' and Certificate-Forgers' Association.

> The first line is rather good, I think. The character of Claude Sluce, while showing a lack of philosophical speculation, is presented without effort. The verbs are in the right places, and this is high compliment. Bargu Ah Mat, however, remains an infantile arm-chair donor. It is a pity that he has not read Vol. 11 of the Prologue to the Rufo-Nanine Studies in Arm-Chair Folk-Lore, Part 3. However the main thing, the spelling, is there.[2]

Tomorrow I'll write you something more like a letter — I'm very tired . . .

With my love,
Gwen.

[1] A red-bearded dwarf.
[2] See the letter of criticism by Peter Bennie attached to (65).

(67)

Crimes Lodge,
AUCHENBLUME
Saturday, 1943.
[17 July]

Dear Tony,

There is a little fruit-tree in bloom in a garden nearby—it is covered with delicate pink blossom, and is most comforting to see.

This afternoon Joe has been building himself a "room" on the veranda outside his own quarters. He has walked through the house continually carrying three-ply and long bits of wood, so that one had the impression of numbers of boys passing to and fro (do you remember Stanley Laurel and the wood in that delightful picture when Stan and Olly were in the army?) I see the downfall of our present conditions in 14 Crimes St., for as soon as Joe has finished his "room" he will start on another one, until the veranda is honeycombed with three-ply cells all for Joe's personal use. Joe claims that he doesn't get enough "peace" in the house, and says sternly that no one will be allowed to enter the new section. He overlooks the fact that when anyone stays with us he or she is "put into" the room that opens on to the veranda where Joe is shutting himself in with three-ply, so Joe may be disturbed by a peculiar great-aunt, a "distant" relation, a bearded sailor, or even Old Coar who turns up to live with us at odd moments. (He hasn't done this for several years, but he is quite capable of it.)

On Saturday afternoon it is difficult to write a connected letter—between paragraphs I have peeled potatoes, cleaned shoes, made a fruit salad and whipped cream and rescued the chops for tea from Gretchen.

You will be glad to hear that the nine grapefruit on the little tree that Agens cut in half are now ripe; not one was lost. I have just looked at them, and they made me feel that after all Nature is stronger than Agens, and can grow more trees than Agens can ever cut down.

Saturday has an air of being concentrated in the house—I mean, it is not a day (if one is at home here) for speculations on

225

the destiny of man, the degrees of knowledge or even the nine choirs of angels; no, one turns to the lemon-trees and the grapefruit, mending clothes, cutting flowers for the table, polishing with Nobby's Clear Veneer (which is lost, by the way; perhaps Gretchie drank it), and storing food in cupboards and jars. It has a pleasant sunshiny air, and is quite relaxing. This afternoon I listened to a Haydn symphony on the radio while I brushed and dried my hair, but now Hadyn has given place to Artie Shaw and Benny Goodman.

Do you ever notice how somctimes things—chairs, boxes, pictures, baskets—take on an individuality of their own and seem to be standing quietly aware of things? I don't know what causes this illusion, but it is very strange.

At night now the evening star is so bright that one can hardly believe it is real.

SUNDAY, 1943 [18 July]

Last night I didn't feel like writing; instead I read *War and Peace*. What a splendid book it is! Its greatness leaves one breathless. I'm only halfway through it; there's something about the first reading of a book that one can never recapture: one may love it better or know it more deeply later on, but there is something never quite the same. Sometimes I wish I had never read things simply so I could have the pleasure of reading them for the first time over again.

Agens has managed (Lord knows how) to burn the handles of most of our knives. "It would appear" that she left them on the stove, and the handles "caught on fire". It came as a shock to me to find that knife-handles were inflammable—somehow I still can't convince myself that it's possible. We are learning to juggle with the thin and irregular parts that remain, and doubtless will become so used to the new state of affairs that soon we'll take it for granted that knives should have their handles partly burnt away.

I think a new paragraph should be inserted in the book of etiquette, in the section that ends "your knife is your personal implement".

226

It is not permissible to comment on the fact that the handles on the knives given to you are partly burnt away. Should any of the burnt portions come off in your hand, drop them quietly on the floor and they will be removed by the servants. Do not make remarks about them to your neighbours at the table. As host or hostess, do not press burnt knives on your guests; if they wish to use their pen or hunting knives they should be allowed to do so. It is a good plan to have a servant handy with a small grindstone in case your guests find their own knives are not sharp enough.

I just opened your last letter to see if there was anything I hadn't answered, and threepence fell out. This is most encouraging! . . .

Would you still like the Schubert and the Wolf book sent up? Do not sent any stamps. You can include a postage stamp display in the hat instead. And can you get cigarettes? If you would like some I'll send them, as father has given me quite a lot he got from Americans – I have more than I need, and I don't know whether they are hard to get in the "bloody tropics". It is quite warm today, I think summer won't be too long now . . .

With my love,
Gwen.

(68)

Maison Foster,
Rue de Grimes
Auchenfleur,
Lundi. 1943
[19 July]

My dear Tony,

Bloody thou art, bloody will be thy end. (That refers to the machine.) This fine new ribbon was given to me by a leading city office. I did not ask for it, neither did I pay for it: yet I did not steal it (we are now in the realm of metaphysics and have left behind us the milk-livered ethics of the W.D.C.). Father is very pleased with the new ribbon; I warned him not to ask any questions, and he asked none, but gave me some chocolate. You will see that I am in much better form today: I'm afraid that yesterday I was terribly dull, but today I felt better and obtained for myself some blue paper and a new ribbon to write to you with, also a quantity of brown paper and some sticky labels. Such Rufo-Nanine conduct will doubtless please you.

Bro. Walter has returned from his "sick" leave, and has proved himself my master in one respect: I'm unable to take his letters at a speed that will annoy him, for he dictates so slowly that I could write everything out three times in long-hand. I sat down at his desk and moved things out of the way, altered the position of my chair five times, turned my notebook upside down, dropped my pencils, tied up my shoe-laces, and finally looked up at him expecting to see the expression of self-contained rage that delights me so, but instead Bro. was looking absently at the ceiling and kicking his heels gently on the floor. He continued to gaze at the ceiling for several minutes, and I thought he had fallen into a contemplative trance, but he "came to" and said "The Shire Clerk, er . . . just a minute . . . no, the Town Clerk. No, wait . . . er . . . just a minute . . . er . . ." and then he stared blankly at the letter in his hand for some more minutes. I drew a waitress, a railway engine and a daisy on my book. I did the shorthand outline for "State Controller" and turned it into a camel. Bro. continued to gaze vacantly before him. He revived, looked skywards, and began again "The Shire Clerk, Charleville. Dear Sir, . . . er . . . Estate of A.E.L. James . . . that's a heading, Miss Foster. Make that a heading. Just a moment, I think we'll leave that one. Cross that all out." Then he fell into another trance, and I drew a Controller-General. His average speed of dictation would be 10 words per five minutes, I think. At 12 o'clock I said loudly "I'm going to lunch now," and shut up my book and departed, leaving Bro. still gazing at the ceiling. Diana told me last week that she takes her Greek grammar in with her and keeps it in her lap to study while Bro. is dictating.

. . . Joe's room is finished now, and he sits there in solitary splendour for about 8 minutes every evening, then the silence in his own quarters overcomes him, and he comes out to join the family once more. As I foresaw, he has "plans on" other parts of the house, and heaven knows where his infernal three-ply walls will spring up next . . .

I have just said to Agens, who is sewing nearby, "What would you do if I burnt the Nuttall Encyclopaedia." Agens replied "I'd go mad." Hurrah! I love to see such devotion to books. It is good to know that when next Agens cuts down a tree I have power to drive her to madness . . .

STOP PRESS.

Dr Alexis Jemindar, of Woffelbuttel, claims to have discovered an Early Creek Street Man.[1] The skeleton was found intact 20 feet below the Primary Building, in a crouching position. One arm was abnormally developed, and the hand held a rough chisel-shaped instrument. Nearby were some stone tablets arranged in orderly piles, all bearing a mark at the bottom believed to have been made with the chisel-shaped instrument. Dr Jemindar says that the only translation he can arrive at is "BRING UP". Experts think that possibly some tribal chief wished the stones to be moved to a higher level.

(69)

Crimes Lodge,
AUCHENBLUME.
Thursday, 1943
[22 July]

Dear Tony,

Another letter from you! It is very good of you to write when you don't feel like it. The "Iron Tonic" has impressed me tremendously. It suggests the "Iron Maiden Corset Co." and Bismarck's motto.[2] You put me to shame—bed of pain, indeed it was not. It is one thing to have a burning head in the tropics and quite another to recline at ease on a pleasant veranda with trees outside and visits from a lunatic painter with a crazy hat. Iron Tonic. Yes. That has captured my fancy.

It is rather delightful to think that the Hippo was not

[1]See pp. 224–225 for illustrations.
[2]Blood and Iron.

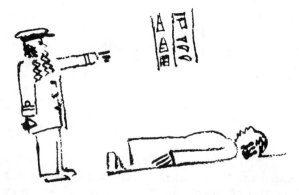

Early Creek Street Cave-drawings & Carvings [from letter 68].
Top: *The flight of Ma-fe King from the tax-collector. The artist has
depicted a scene which, according to legend, took place at the time of
the Winter Solstice (July, in Creek Street). Lettering reads: "Foo has
been here."*

Bottom: *Original now in Queensland Museum. This shows the
legendary To-Ni appearing in the form of a bearded sailor to a young
woman. Overcome by the vision, she falls dead. The inscription reads
"NO CALLERS". (In folk-lore, the visits of To-Ni caused utter
confusion in Creek Street.)*

230

Top: *Sacrificial Meal of the God Wei-Te-Meyer. The animal in the upper corner is believed to be a mammoth. The words read "Unclean Large" or "Unclean Big", though some scholars prefer "Dirty Large". The significance of the inscription is still a matter of uncertainty.*

Bottom: *Dr. Jemindar's latest discovery: Early Creek Street drawing of young maiden carrying sacrificial drink to the God Bat-Ters-Bee.*

discovered by you until such a late period. However it proves that the warning was unneeded, as you'd have discovered it long ago if you had eaten the peanuts all at once. Now I must warn you to be careful, extememly (Ah, Hubert) extremely careful with those you have, if any, as there WILL BE NO MORE. I have seen peanut toffee in small quantities, and I suppose a peanut-fiend would be able to extract peanuts with care, but penaust (away, away, mad ass) penauts (away, thou issue of a mangy dog) PEN

NEWS ITEM: A battered typewriter was found in Auchenblume last night on the railway-line. A young woman, obviously demented, had placed it there. She was found gibbering beside a train and six carriages derailed by the typewriter. When the typewriter was discovered by Haroun Cheswick, porter, the young woman screamed and began tearing at it again, swallowing two shift keys and the margin release before the authorities could prevent her. When questioned, she howled "Peanuts".

The hat, the glorious hat (created by TFR) shines in my dreams at night. Nuts too! What about a bottle of Iron Tonic hidden tastefully among bunches of daisies. I think the brim will have to be made of iron if it is to stand the weight of your creative fancies. Will it have flying buttresses? Perhaps it will be so delicately balanced that one onion (pickled) will disturb its angle, and it will become The Leaning Hat of Brisbane.

Iron Tonic (I cannot leave the subject) will make you thin and gaunt, and will probably reduce the rainbow hues of your splendid beard to iron-grey; once the damage is done, no quantities of peppermint creams will restore your colourful appearance, and no gallons of ice-cream will build up your figure. (Who is that? That is Cdr "Iron-Gut" McGeoch;[3] they say he sells his whiskers to wire merchants. What does he do with the money? With the money he buys hundreds of bottles of Iron Tonic. Does he drink nothing else? Nothing. TWENTY YEARS LATER: Mama, why is that man wearing an Iron Mask? Sh, dear, that is not an Iron Mask.

[3]Joe introduced Tony to one of his friends as Commander McGeogh (McGeoch) of the submarine *Penguin*.

That is his face. Whose face, Mamma? Cdr McGeoch's face, my dear; let that be a warning to you never to touch Iron Tonic.)

Yes, News. BISHOP FOSTER MOVED BACK TO SWITCH.

At 3.45 the "girl" came with a message that Mr Battersbee would like to see Miss Foster. Bishop Foster went in, sat down, and smiled in a friendly way, ready for war. Then Battersbee made a little speech, saying that Miss Carthew's hand was "bad". (Note: Carthew, Blanche Norma, would die if you visited her. Yes, that's the young lady!) To continue: Miss Carthew's hand was "bad" and she couldn't take shorthand, would Bishop Foster "like" to change places with her, and let Carthew be employed in the examining dept. until such time as her hand was better? (The poor girl has a sort of rheumatism, and gets "bad" hands at times.) Bishop was not very pleased, but Battersbee added, "You can go back to the switch, and we'll only give you shorthand in case of emergency." SWITCH! The switch is home to the Bishop. Tomorrow morning the Bishop resumes duties at the switch and once more will know all there is to be known of the interior workings of the W.D.C.

Oh Tony, I wish you could have been at the farewell scene with Mafeking. He's not at all pleased to have one of his "trained" assistants taken from him, and he worked out little plans for "sending work down to the switch".

Harvey is delighted that I'm going, and said so audibly. I shall not be able to stage any more three-round contests with her, but the delight of fighting doesn't compare with the celestial joy of having the dirty big switch under my hands. (Diana will be sitting next to me, at Blanche Carthew's table, and she can go to the wall phone and "chip in" when I have some good hook-ups.)

So Carthew's "bad hand" has earned a delightful rest for the Bishop. I don't know how long it will last — I wonder if I put a long-distance call in to Darwin what would happen? I am looking forward to taking notes from Battersbee: I wonder how he will stand up to my "Beg pardon?"

. . . As I retire to take some balmy sleep (or drowsy sleep) I think of your stiffening limbs: the Iron Tonic will get into your blood-stream and your limbs will really be "fettered" as the song says. (Father, what is that creaking sound? Quiet, boy, that is Cdr McGeoch getting out of bed. Father, what is that clanging noise? Sh, boy, that is Cdr Geoch walking to the cupboard for his morning drink of Iron Tonic. Father, do all you men drink Iron Tonic? No, indeed, boy, and I trust you never will touch a drop. No Father, this has been a lesson to me.)

FRIDAY

Joe is sick tonight . . . I've been rather sick all day—Joe and I are agreed that Agens' cooking must be to blame in some mysterious way, or perhaps we are "sickening for" something really spectacular, and then we shall stay in bed on the veranda listening to the little radio Father brings home for sick people to have beside their beds.

This morning I moved back to the switch, and the change was quite restful. A beautiful conversation occurred between a man (Bert, I think) and Battersbee.

BERT: Is that you, Bob?
BATTERSBEE: Yes, what is it?
BERT: Have you got a girl to spare?
BAT: No, she's out at the moment. Want anything?
BERT: Yeah, send her round when she comes back. I got a ham you can pick up this afternoon.

When the "girl" came back she was "buzzed for" and Battersbee, after keeping her waiting at the door for five minutes (a trick of his) send her out to pick up "a parcel" . . .

I left my "pixie-hat" in the dining-room yesterday and Father found it. He took a fancy to it at once, and wore it for the rest of the evening. When I came in last night I took it back to my room. This evening father began his dinner, and then suddenly rubbed his head and asked: "Where's my little hat?"

. . . By listening carefully to conversations all day I have my suspicions that the young lady's "bad hand" was used as an excuse to get Bishop Foster out of the Examining Dept. The general idea

234

seems to be that if I'm kept on my own I won't cause so much disturbance. Fools!

I do hope the Iron Tonic has made you feel better. I'll write again tomorrow.

> With my love,
> Gwen.

(70)
> Crimes Lodge,
> AUCHENBLUME
> Saturday, 1943
> [24 July]

Dear Tony,

I'm sitting on the veranda near the kitchen, and the sun is falling across me in strips from the blinds. It is a pleasant and bright afternoon; it would be fine if you were here, then perhaps we could go for a walk. I have no weddings this afternoon, so I am sitting in father's old dressing-gown, which has a magical effect, I can't say why. It is not a handsome garment, and it's much too large, but it has a soothing effect on me and seems never to wear out: I've had it for years already and I think it will last forever. It is really a family weakness, I think, to stick to old clothes—you know Joe's tastes.

There are many pickled onions in jars on a table nearby. Father bought a great many small onions and requested pickles, so Agens made him sit down and peel them all himself. He and the Dogger sat miserably in the dining-room with a large pile of onions and a growing pile of onion shells, but he will feel rewarded when he sees what Agens has done with them. The trouble is, however (we know this from experience) that Father will discover them before long and begin eating them before they are really pickled, so that when the time comes for eating them only empty jars of vinegar will remain . . .

RUFO-NANINE SCHOOL OF FORM-FILLING

Form 12567£4(a)iii for Public Servants, or Employees of the P.S.
1. If you want to go out for lunch five minutes early, do you
   (a) push on the hands of your clock 5 minutes

(b) pretend you are washing your hands and sneak out the side
    way
(c) go out five minutes early
(10 points for a & b, no points for c)
2. How many assistants have you?
   (a) one
   (b) two or more
   (c) none
   (5 points for a & c, ten points for b)
3. At what distance can you recognise a State Controller?
   (a) 300 yards
   (b) length of the office
   (c) not at all
   (10 points for a, 3¾ for b, none for c)
4. If you meet your boss in the lift, do you
   (a) raise your hat & say good morning
   (b) look sheepish
   (c) stamp hard on his foot
   (10 points for a, 2¼ for b, if your answer is c, deduct 20 from
   your score)
5. What do you have for lunch?
   (a) pies
   (b) dirty big pies
   (c) something else
   (5 points for a, 20 for b, none for c)
6. When your assistant, if any, sets fire to vital documents, will
   you
   (a) dismiss her
   (b) reward her
   (10 points for a, deduct 20 for b)
7. If you wanted to call on anyone would you
   (a) fill in an interview slip
   (b) wait outside till his/her lunch-hour
   (c) walk straight in, gesticulating
   (10 points for a, 6¾ for b, deduct 15 for c, and 25 if you peered
   in first)

If your score is 100, you can't count. If your score is 80, your name is Mafeking. 60–80 you will rise to be an assistant State Controller. 39¼ you will feel all funny whenever you see a sailor. 27¾ you are, and will remain, a Sunday School teacher. If your score is minus 55, you have been sacked already. If it is minus 65, you have a rainbow beard, and your conduct is most irregular.

Now, Tony, I'm going to tell you about Father's wonderful dream that he dreamt last Wednesday. (It is evening now, and Father and Agens and I are at home. Father and Agens are sitting in the dining-room, and I am typing in the "spare" room, which I've described to you before. Father has just told me his dream, and as he is quite close I can refer to him. I didn't believe him the first time he told me, but as the story progressed I was simply overcome: oh, if only you were here. Father's style is inimitable. But here is his dream.)

Father Foster's Dream
"THE TALKING CRAB"

I was standing in the shop when in came a drunken soldier with a crab; he put the crab on the counter, and said "This is for May."[1] Arnold Schwarz[2] took hold of the crab, and started pulling off its big claws. "Don't do that," I said, "it's like pulling the limbs off a child." At this point in came Arnold Schwarz's father, and Old Schwarz was nursing something in his arms. "You can talk," he said, "but you haven't got a crab like mine. It's a talking crab. It can talk, and read, and sing, and do anything at all. It's a wonderful talking crab." Sure enough, he had a crab, and it was a soft pink crab with little arms, hairy legs and lovely big blue eyes. I said "Hello," and the Talking Crab said "Hello." Its voice was like a little girl's and it had a slight lisp. "You must have been in shows," I said to the Crab. "Yes, I was," replied the Crab, "all over the world." Old Schwarz put the crab down, and Arnold picked it up and began to nurse it. Presently Arnold and Old Schwarz disappeared, and I found myself talking to the crab in

[1] A barmaid, a friend of my father. (GH)
[2] Another radio dealer, also a friend of my father. (GH)

237

a narrow laneway. The Crab was dressed up like a little girl of four or five in a pretty dress, and was leaning over the front of a little "Punch and Judy" stall . . . The Crab told me that her name was Doreen, and that she had been in shows all over the world. "There's a lot of money in me," said the Crab, "I wish you'd save up and buy me. I'd like to belong to you, not to Arnold. Why don't you buy me?" I determined to get the Crab for myself. The Crab said, "There's only one thing, I don't get enough to read. I wish I could get some good books to read." So I said to the Crab, "You wait here, I've got some good books in the back of the shop." I went off and began searching hurriedly through a great pile of books, and I remember selecting for the Crab "The Best Girl in the School" and some geography books. When I got back I was just in time to see Old Schwarz loading the Crab on to Arnold's truck. The truck drove away, and I followed it into Burnett Lane, where it stopped. The Crab was standing on the pavement, and around me was an enormous crowd of men with clerical collars and drooping moustaches. Arnold took hold of my arm, and Old Schwarz said "Here's Brother Foster, come to give his testimony." "No," I said, "I'll do no such thing." But Old Schwarz called out "Brother Foster is here. We will now sing a hymn." They sang a hymn, and the Crab joined in the singing. When I refused again to give my testimony, a man with four arms held me down. "Let go of me," I cried, and he held up two of his arms in the air and sang out "Look, I'm not touching you," but his other arms held me firmly. An old lady rushed out and folded up a Courier-Mail. She banged me on the head with it, and I woke up . . .

Father has made two drawings[3] of Doreen; you will agree, I am sure, that Doreen is Rufo-Nanine in character, and quite capable of saying Ting-a-ling-a-ling to anyone. I would love to get an earnest psycho-analyst on to Father's dream: the fact that Doreen tried to persuade Father to buy her is significant, and also his choice of "The Best Girl in the School" as reading-matter for

[3]Unfortunately, these drawings have been lost.

a Talking Crab. Knowing Father's inventive powers, I questioned him on many points of the story, but I am convinced that it is genuine. Of course before very long elaborations will creep in (as they do in his "murder stories") and by the time you are with us again the story will have increased in strangeness and fantasy. When you are having dinner with us, and when the interest has died down after your uttering ROCKHAMPTON, I shall ask Father to tell you the story. Tonight as he told it Father was wearing his red dressing-gown covered with dragons, and my green hat, pulled down on top of his head, added the right note of irresponsibility. He assured me that Doreen's "booth" is pictured exactly as he saw it in the dream . . .

SUNDAY AFTERNOON

Poor Agens is sick again, and has stayed in bed. When I got home I found that Father Foster had the lunch ready: we had soup, with various things in it, and the inside of a pie—Agens cooked the steak and kidney for it last night, and put it in the refrigerator, so Father "hotted it up" (do you know that silly joke: "Did you heat the rice pudding, Emily?"—"Oh no, Mum, hi 'otted it up for you.") and we had pie without the pastry. There was a cheese salad, and a wonderful fruit salad into which Father put oranges, mandarins, apples, bananas and preserved pineapple; we had this with cream, and father opened a dirty big bottle of stout (Mrs Bloom's favourite drink, wasn't it?) During this meal we played Dnieper Water-Power Station, by Meytuss, Steel Foundry, by Mossolov, and Russian Dance by Schostakovitsch. Lear would have called it highly prepossessing and efficacious. An enormous quantity of potatoes which Father put on too late for lunch will be eaten for tea. Stout is a funny drink, I don't know whether I like it. Its name is against it, seeming to suggest the last state of those who drink it continually . . .

I hope you are well and in good spirits.

With my love,
Gwen.

Grimy Street,
AUCHENBLUME.
Monday.
[26 July]

My dear Tony,

They're awfully casual about the mail at home here, and one has to "track down" any letters that arrive. I was peacefully drying dishes after dinner, when suddenly Agens remarked—Oh, I forgot, there's some mail for you in the hall. So I dashed off (what greater delight is there than receiving letters?) and found that there was nothing of the sort in the hall. I returned to Agens and demanded to know the whereabouts of my "correspondence". She said indifferently—Oh, I suppose it's somewhere around. I made her go and look for it, but she couldn't remember where she put it. Finally she found a parcel and a letter for me stuck behind an obscure flower-pot on the veranda, where I'd never have found it. It would appear that the postman came as the telephone rang, so she just put the mail down and forgot about it.

The parcel was *Claudius the God,* for which I thank you. I'm glad you enjoyed it; it is a grand book, and outweighs all the twopenny rubbish that is being turned out in ungodly quantities. I heartily approve of the mediaeval idea of burning harmful and needless books: for instance, when S. Bonaventure had completed his life of S. Francis, which he wrote after seeing those of the Saint's friends who were still alive, he ordered all other "lives" which were partly legend and were becoming a source of contention within the Order, to be destroyed whenever they were found. Wouldn't you join me in destroying all school-books and "commentaries on" various things? Of course, this is quite useless to wish for, as doubtless the publishers would win in the long run.

Your letter was full of interest. (Go on to page 3, this is only a long-winded scholastic dispute.) Our old friend the problem of evil is up for examination again, I see. I haven't made myself clear, it seems, and it appears that my choice of scholastic phrases was not happy. When I say that nothing is created evil, I don't mean that evil things have no existence—far from it. S. Augustine says that if things are "corrupt" they must first have been good. If a thing is evil, it must have existence to be evil. And existence comes first, that is to say, a thing must exist before it has any qualities (not in order of time, but metaphysically existence comes first). Your idea of evil and good as co-existent and co-eternal seems to me to contain the elements of a subtle pantheism as well as its obvious dualism. Zoroaster (the original) held that belief, and it is eastern rather than western. If, as you say, evil and good are co-eternal and co-existent "from all eternity" it seems that you must hold the idea that things (creatures) can be evil by nature.

I maintain that no creature is evil by nature. If it is evil it has fallen from goodness. The devil is a fallen angel. Evil spirits are good spirits who fell by pride and rebellion.

My mind recoils from dualism because I cannot accept the idea of uncreated evil. The doctrine of the Fall is a cosmic truth.

Uncreated good is another matter, and I won't bother to repeat the five arguments of St Thomas Aquinas, since you admit the existence of uncreated good. But if there is uncreated good, then it must be the source of all existence, since created being can only draw its existence (ultimately) from uncreated being. And it seems to me that once you admit uncreated good, you cannot admit uncreated evil.

You admit uncreated good: then you must admit uncreated being, for good cannot be separated from being, and this uncreated being must be pure actuality, for if it were not pure actuality, that is, if it were partly potentiality, there would have to be a cause greater than it to account for the composition of potentiality and act, and if this cause were not uncreated it would in turn depend on something else, and so on in infinite regress.

To put it more simply: evil is the corruption of something good. Uncreated good must be the source of created good. Uncreated being is the source of all created being. Evil, being the corruption of something good, cannot be in existence before good. Good must exist first.

Evil is a spiritual quality. There can obviously be no departure from good except by rational beings (I do not speak here of imperfection, which has arisen in creation as a result of the spiritual problem of evil). The drama of the universe, which you see as an eternal struggle between good and evil, is so indeed with the exception of "eternal" which I cannot admit, as I believe that the conflict is being played out in time, but has been won in eternity. That is to say, I believe, as the Creed says, that our Lord "shall come again in glory to judge both the quick and the dead; whose Kingdom shall have no end". The results of the struggle will be eternal, I believe, as in the end there will be for us beatitude or misery for all eternity. You say this yourself later on: "It's as if the battle was long ago won & lost, and that evil has been enslaved . . ." I can't reconcile that with your dualism.

The Church begins her year, in Advent, with the prayer "Almighty God, give us grace that we may cast away the works of darkness and put upon us the armour of light, now in the time of this mortal life", showing that she draws our attention first of all to the struggle with evil.

I'd much rather talk to you than write — I'm afraid my philosophical meanderings would drive anyone to drink. Sometimes I feel that I'd like to retire and study philosophy for seven years, but as von Hugel says, "What can one do with a learned woman — except drown her?" I agree with him. I shall devote the time to cooking.

TUESDAY. 1943 [27 July]

Today I bought the complete organ works of Bach. This enterprise has relieved me of the weight of accumulated money which I kept in a small box. The organ works look most impressive. Of course I can't play them, but I sat down tonight and thought, I am still fairly young, I'm quite likely to live for a long time, the war will be over one day, I shall have time perhaps to be an organist. I wonder, now, whether I shouldn't be an organist to justify my possession of so much organ mustic (I'll squeak and gibber if this damned machine starts throwing letters in of its own accord) organ music, but that is rather like a man deciding to be a writer because he has 1,000,000 sheets of folio foolscap, or a chef because he has several dozen white hats and aprons. At present there doesn't seem to be a good organ-teacher in Brisbane, as the city organist is doddering and the others are in the army. I have ordered a lot of organ records, so that I can read from the scores.

At present I seem to have no time for anything, but that is only the effect of spending all day in the pudding-like atmosphere of the W.D.C. It really is dulling my brain. However as you say, I'm learning a good deal. It has been a lesson to me. (Father, what is that strange vegetable over there? Sh, boy, that is not a vegetable, that is a Public Servant who has grown into his office chair. Pray, Father, is he endowed with reason? In the metaphysical order, yes, my boy, he has a rational soul. But in the practical order, my boy, it has been crippled; he does not live by reason. Ah, Father, let us repair to a beer-house; but can the unhappy man save himself? No, my boy, supra nos levari non possumus nisi per virtutem superiorem nos elevantem. Procedamus.[1])

Please forgive me if I write rubbish this time — I'm in need of utter relaxation. I shall tell you about the Tower of Babel's latest success.

I wore it to Evensong on Sunday night. I sat in the tram opposite an American sailor and his girl. The sailor regarded me with interest, and I gave him a Babylonian grin. The girl didn't look at all pleased, but it dawned on her that the object of attraction was the hat, which was causing slight trouble to an aged lady sitting next to me, as the veils kept blowing into her face. When the tram stopped the girl remarked in a voice obviously meant for me to hear: "I don't like that hat, do you?" I fixed her companion with a stern look, and he nodded his head, but didn't say anything.

I have a very old man called Mr Sneyd, one of the wax-moustache school, in the congregation, who is trying to marry me off to various people. He comes to see me on his way up the aisle after Mass, and tells me how he liked the hymns and the organ music, and passes remarks about my clothes. (Why is it

[1]We cannot rise above ourselves except through the help of a superior being.

that old men consider themselves free to say anything they like to young women? Old Coar has the same idea.) Mr Sneyd's favourite hat is the little green one decorated with non-botanical leaves, and when I don't wear it he says "Why don't you wear the green hat?" (even if I have a blue dress on) or "When are you going to wear the green hat again?" Then, after a few words on the subject of hymns, he remarks cunningly, "Arthur's a nice quiet boy, isn't he? Arthur's a steady young fellow. He's got a good job, too." "Yes, Mr Sneyd," replies wicked Gwen, "but he's not as clever as Harold." (Harold is the fanatical Thomist at the seminary.) This never fails to distress Mr Sneyd, as he can't bear Harold. One morning I pointed out a perfectly strange soldier and extolled his virtues, and poor Mr Sneyd was quite upset. Mr Sneyd sings all the hymns loudly out of tune, and "puts off" everyone near him. He expresses his opinions about the sermon in a loud voice, and makes scathing remarks about the poor intelligence of the clergy if they choose a hymn he doesn't know or like.

This morning it was so cold that the cold actually hurt – I went to Mass early, and the cold made my hands, feet and eyes ache. There was frost on the grass. On the altar they had great masses of yellow and orange poppies, which looked warm and full of light. Do you like poppies? They are strange and rather mysterious flowers, I think.

The colour has reminded me of your previous remarks about boiled lollies. I love them, and I am certainly a "lollie-sucker". Well-sucked boiled lollies have the beauty of clear glass, and they make me wish I could use them to ornament my person . . . Diana bought some delightful green ones the other day, and we ate them during the afternoon. They looked like emeralds.

Wednesday, 1943 [28 July]

Great White Chief of War Damage, Mr Hitchcock, was "scheduled to arrive" at the Cretins' Sunshine Home this morning from Sydney. The "girl" was sent out to buy buttered scones for his morning tea. But I learnt (remember, I'm "on the switch") that

244

he was to be late, and told Diana, who immediately went and ate all the scones.

. . . I'll write again tomorrow.

With my love,
Gwen.

(72)   Wednesday, 1943.
[28 July]

My dear Tony,
I was writing to you a while ago, but I shut up the letter, so I'll start another. It has begun to rain: there has been no rain for a long time, and it is good to hear the sound of it on the roof and smell the clean freshness of wet leaves. The rain fills me with sadness and makes me think of "Super flumina Babylonis: illic sedimus et flevimus dum recordaremur tui, Sion." Have you heard the Sistine choir singing Palestrina's setting? It is lovely, but full of sadness.

It is strange that out of all the so-called "modern" music dance tunes, crooners' wails, etc. a phrase or a few bars of music shines suddenly through the cloud of rubbish and moves one with unexpected power. It doesn't happen very often, but it does happen sometimes: there is a rumba they are playing now called "Sand in my shoes"; I don't suppose you ever listen to such things, but Joe is an "expert" on modern dance-bands and constantly tunes in to them, so I'm fairly familiar with the popular tunes. "Sand in my shoes" is no different in essence from any of the others, and it will die out as quickly, but it has moved me strangely. The words, utter commonplace rubbish, were moaned by a wooden-voiced fool, and the accompaniment was tricked out with flashy orchestration and cheap imitation of the "Spanish element", but the tune has haunted me . . .

Tomorrow I'll try to get the music and see what the tune is made of. If you happen to hear it, see if you agree with me that the tune "as zumzing".

Old Coar has just arrived, and has brought us a "dirty big"

245

bag full of violently coloured lollies – not boiled ones. There are strange jellies and an opaque kind of sweet ornamented with stripes of so fierce a colour that one almost fears to eat them. (Gretchen has been shut out from the card players because she is a nuisance, and she is pacing up and down the passage with fury. Her greedy eye saw the lollies being emptied into a large dish, and she realises that the feast is not for her. Father is weakening – I can hear him imploring Agens to "let the dogger in" but Agens knows too well how many lollies the greedy "dogger" can eat. Frustrated greed is terrible to see. I think Gretchie's reason is likely to collapse under the strain.) Old Coar has got a new and impressive green cap "to keep his head warm". It probably has a concealed mirror which reflects his partner's cards!

The problem of evil is so important, that I shall try to put my own belief in the matter more clearly – I'm afraid my last letter contained some very confused ramblings on the subject.

Evil exists – there can be no reasonable doubt of this: what is evil: is it something existing in its own right? No, it is the absence of good. It is therefore unnatural, that is to say, evil in a given subject is the absence of some good that belongs to the nature of the subject. The positive reality does not belong to the evil, but to the subject to which it attaches. Physical evil is (like blindness or lameness) the absence of a perfection proper to the nature of the subject. Moral evil arises because our human nature has the power to fail, the power to choose between what is right for man and what is not. Moral evil is in opposition to the end of our rational nature.

There cannot be two infinite beings, one good and another evil. If there are two such different beings, one must have a perfection that the other has not, therefore the latter is not infinite.

Evil spirits exist, and seek (because their will is turned away from good) to draw souls to evil, but their power is limited as they cannot force man to do evil but only persuade him if his will is weak . . .

FRIDAY [30 July]

Diana and I are profiting by the presence of the Controller

General. Every morning sandwiches and buttered scones are provided for the visitors (a couple of "members" have come with him) and when the girl has put them ready on a plate we go into the lunch room and eat some of them ("them" being scones, of course). They never eat much, and we take the plate from the girl as she comes back and eat the rest of the sandwiches and scones. It is good to have Diana sitting next to me. We have disputes on eastern philosophy and various other things. Diana has a fine brain, and is delightful to have as a companion. Her ambition is to be dancer, or to go to Tibet to study eastern philosophy. After the average "nice girl" she is doubly refreshing . . .

Your suggestion in the letter that arrived yesterday, that one should smile "broadly and vacantly at all passers-by" took hold of my fancy at once, but alas, prudence prevents me from carrying it out. As you say, it is not a pastime for girls. "Border incidents" would certainly occur if I tried it.

Your letter was full of fine incidents, particularly the Grouper falling off his chair, and Bill's[1] theft of the peanuts (in their shells). It is a matter of wonder to me that the Hackleskinner supply has not failed by this time: you must have exercised superhuman control in your peanut-eating . . .

It is late now, I shall go to bed.

Goodnight.

With my love,
Gwen.

---

[1]The first mention of F. W. (Bill) Harwood, GF's future husband, who was then a friend of TR and, like him, a lieutenant in the RANVR.

(73)

My dear Tony,

I'm feeling rather off colour, as I have another fiendish16 (a burning devil take this machine) sore throat, which I believe I have "caught" from my colleagues at W.D.C. However father has brought home a large bottle of rum, and I shall make myself an excellent drink of rum, ginger, lemon, honey and hot water which is beneficial to sore throats.

The idea of the rum-ginger-lemon combination overcame me, and I'm now sitting with a large drink beside me. Father has not a sore throat, but I think it has inspired him, and he has disappeared into the kitchen, probably to look for another lemon. No, wait, I was wrong. Father has returned with a knife, a d.b. basin and a quantity of pickled — wrong again, raw onions. They are the pickled-onions-to-be, and Agens will only make them on condition that Father does the peeling. He is sitting patiently at the table peeling onions; Agens is reading the Telegraph, and has remarked that if Father didn't eat pickled onions in such great quantities he wouldn't get the unpleasant job of peeling them so often . . .

PUBLIC EXAMINATIONS FOR PUBLIC SERVANTS

1st Paper

1. Write an essay (two pages of folio foolscap) on one of the following subjects:
   (a) State Controllers I have known
   (b) An imaginary conversation between a War Damage Certificate and a Bring-Up Sticker
   (c) The development of the Bring-Up System in Lower Tanganyika
   (d) Filing Cabinets in the Middle Ages.

2. Comment on the imagery and the stylistic devices used in the following:

(a) It should be noted that this enquiry does not relate to plant of which you are the hirer under hire-purchase agreement.

(b) Stock does not include any growing crops, growing trees or vines, livestock or wool in the possession of a wool-selling broker awaiting appraisement.

3. Paraphrase the following:
"Plant" means any plant.

4. Contrast the attitude of Mr Battersby towards lost correspondence with that of Mafeking Reed. Quote extensively from their letters as found in the General File.

5. Make any alterations you consider necessary in the following sentences:
(a) He cut the dirty big pie into two halves with a knife.
(b) Miss Foster & Miss Gill ate them scones.

6. By whom, and on what occasion, were the following lines spoken?
(a) Most irregular, taking her away from the switch!
(b) I don't think they should be allowed to have callers.

7. Write out at least sixteen lines, from memory, from the Preface to Sub-Section B of the National Security (War Damage to Property) Regulations, and fill in an interview slip in the name of an imaginary caller who wishes to see the Assistant Accountant about the matter contained therein.

2nd Paper (Biology)

1. Make sketches showing and naming the structures seen in the following:
(1) Forearm of a cancelled-stamp affixer
(2) Brain of an Examining Officer
(3) Left ear of a switch-attendant.

2. Give an account of the life-history of the Lesser Tea-Girl. In what way is its structure an advance of that of Protococcus?

3. Would you say that assistants belonged to Phylum Platyhelminthes (Flat-Worms) or to the Cestoda (Internal Parasites)?

SUNDAY. [1 August]

I'm feeling better today, though still not very well. Agens has spent the morning making enormous fruit cakes and great numbers of chocolate biscuits, but these do not arouse my appetite and I contemplate them in an entirely abstract fashion, as through a glass, darkly. This proves that I am ill.

A ludicrous scene has just taken place: the Local Sub-Committee of the West Moreton Boy Scouts or some such body (prominent in the Scouting world) commissioned me to "examine" scouts for the Auchenflower section in Music and Interpreters' badges. So far I have "examined" only two, one for music (a long time ago) and this afternoon a French-speaking Scout turned up to be examined for the Interpreters Badge—the scene was quite funny, and I'm sure you would have enjoyed it.

A large cheerful youth of about sixteen arrived and was "shown into" the sitting-room by Agens, who then came screaming and shouting at me through the hall. (I was just beginning to write "Sunday".) So I appeared in my official capacity in father's old dressing-gown, and grinned at the Scout, who grinned at me. Then out of my pocket I took "L'Ane et le Cheval", a simple story that I copied out of The Children's Encyclopaedia last night. This I gave to the youth, who sat in an arm-chair looking at it. I sank on to the large couch and began singing Au Clair de la Lune, to create the right atmosphere. The scout, a bright specimen, then took out a fountain pen and began writing out a translation of L'Ane et le Cheval and telling me at the same time of a soirée at L'Alliance Francaise which he had attended during the past week; the fact that impressed him most was that enormous quantities of cake were offered to visitors at the soirée. We then conducted a ludicrous conversation in school-book French. I asked him how he was, and he replied "Bon jour, Mlle, je vais a la gare. Il fait beau temps." When he had finished telling me that it was a windy day, that he liked M.Bing Crosby, that he went to school every day and that it is cold in winter, he told me with evident joy (in English) that one of his teachers had broken a rib and been removed to hospital and expressed anti-educational sentiments very pleasing to me. He returned home tired but happy, etc.

Joe and Roy are sitting smoking their foul pipes in the dining-room and playing "hot" records. They are discussing girls with great contempt and criticizing mercilessly the physical charms of their contemporary feminine acquaintances.

SCONE THIEVES AT LARGE

A new menace to the Public Service, the theft of scones and/or sandwiches intended for visiting dignitaries from other states, has arisen in Brisbane. Miss Dawn Galbraith, Tea-Girl at W.D.C., told the police: on Friday Miss Foster and Miss Gill seized a plate of sandwiches intended for Mr Hitchcock and picked out all the egg-and-lettuce and cheese, which they ate before I got back from taking Mr Crowle his tea. They also ate three scones each, and wiped the butter off those they left with their fingers and put it on the ones they were eating, so that the scones that Mr Hitchcock did get had hardly any butter on.

I don't feel like writing now, Tony, so I'll send you some more news of Bishop Foster and her notorious companion tomorrow.

With my love,
Gwen.

(74)   Sunshine Home for Cretins
                                                          [2 August]

My dear Tony,

This afternoon (Monday 1943) I have a letter from you, with a red and white label "OPENED BY CENSOR 1". At first I thought you had stuck it on to impress me, as I have no access to such labels, but it was stuck over your own delightful little stamp with the anchor on, so I suppose it was put on by some meddling fool who had to check up "Rufo-Nanine Agencies" and the mythical Hilda Hackenberg, a task which I should not envy a dim-witted censor. The mails seem to be badly managed at present: you have received a sheet of clippings I cut out in bed, but before that I sent you a letter telling you why I was in bed . . .

MONDAY NIGHT, CRIMES LODGE.

I bought for you today a small present which I trust will delight you — a book called ARTISTIC HOMES or HOW TO FURNISH WITH

TASTE. The date is not given, but the very first advertisement remarks that The Most Artistic Window Blinds are those of the Empire Patent Cloth (as supplied to Her Majesty at Buckingham Palace) . . .

The book is illustrated, with pictures of chairs leaning sideways, "Queen Anne" cabinets, a "Modern Gothic" sideboard and a wonderful music stool. ("Music stools," says the book, "should, above all, be firm and substantial.")

The style in general is beyond praise: "In establishments of sufficient pretensions to reserve a room as a library, the bulk of the books will of course be deposited there . . .".

Your letter pleased me: the explosion of sausages[1] was really wonderful. It is so good that I suspect you of inventing it for my delight — but no, it is obviously true. Oh, if only we could cause Mafeking and his colleagues to be showered with the contents of saus. & veg. cans! I could stand by and feed the "naked flame" with correspondence, and you could hurl tins into the fire. Blackcurrant jam suggests itself, and spaghetti. Praise the Gods, and make triumphant fires!

I see we are still at war on the subject of personality. It is not the thomist who has his terms mixed, my rainbow-bearded friend, it is Tony. Here, of course, I fall into the attitude of all supporters of thomism, who expect that everyone shall adopt their terminology and abide by it; what you say is "individuality" is what I mean by "personality". St Thomas says that "Persona significat id quod est perfectissimum in tota natura."[2] A person, in scholastic terms, is "a complete individual substance, intellectual in nature and master of its actions". (I am not a fanatical thomist, by any means; I am inclining more to S. Bonaventura — and Plato.) Now, since the word "individual" can belong to man or beast or plant, as Maritain says, individuality is not "the rare thing". No, indeed. It is significant that in the Godhead there are three Persons, not three individuals, and Our Lord is said to have

---

[1] The troops were sick of being fed on tinned sausages so they hurled the tins into the fire causing them to explode. (GH)

[2] The person (personality?) means that which is most perfect in the whole nature.

one Person uniting his two natures. Of course, it is all a matter of terminology, and you are no more bound to accept mine than I am bound to adopt that of the infallible Wittgenstein.[3] Individuality is concerned with matter, personality with spirit. Reverse your terminology, and I am in agreement with you.

"Only bad artists will take a deep interest in their own personalities." That is true, indeed. Maritain says, "But did the Saints 'develop their personality'? They found it without seeking, because they did not seek it, but God alone." He says also, "a total death is needed before we can find ourselves". That applies to artists as well as Saints, don't you think?

. . . (Harvey has threatened me with dismissal from the Examining Dept. if I cross her again, and I await the issue with pleasure, as I can reduce her to trembling rage in ten minutes. She told me this morning that she was "psychic" and could read my thoughts. The little "border incidents" with Harvey take place in public, and everyone stops work to listen.)

Diana, now in charge of the switch, has been doing very well. The other morning she rang up a firm of coffin manufacturers, in the person of "Miss Fitzpatrick", and inquired about a special large-size coffin, to be made to her order. (I was listening on another "line"!) The official said, "Would you be wanting a cheap job, Madam, or something more expensive?" "Something very good," said Diana. The official then gave her a description of several "American-type" coffins, which, he jokingly said, "can be used as glory-boxes." Diana held a serious and wonderfully conducted conversation with him on the prices of large coffins, and finally made an appointment to come round the following morning and inspect them.

Another delightful episode occurred when a woman mistook our number for that of the Rationing Commission. Diana in reply to "Is that the Rationing Commission," said "Yes," and immediately "hooked" me up on the wall phone. We assumed various voices and finally allowed the woman to tell her story to

[3]A surprisingly early mention of the philosopher who plays such an important part in GH's later thought and poetry.

a "high official". The woman was long-winded and very stupid, and gave a glorious number of details about her home and children. It appears that she read in the paper that prunes were to be sold during the week to mothers with children, and she went into a shop to get some, and they refused to sell her any on the ground that she wasn't a regular customer. "Madam," said Diana in a deep voice, "are prunes really necessary?" The woman went into a long and detailed description of the virtues of prunes, and was passed on to the "Prune Board". As an official of the "Prune Board" I questioned her on all points of the story in grave tones, and when we came to the shopkeeper's refusal I remarked "scandalous", "disgraceful". When she had finished, Diana said, "Madam, it is necessary for you to send details to The Prune Board, Rationing Commission, Parbury House, Eagle Street, Brisbane. Be sure you omit nothing. Your case will be dealt with as soon as the letter arrives." Wouldn't it be fun to be at the Rationing Comm. when the letter arrives – "Dear Sirs, with reference to our telephone conversation . . ." – no, that's not the style, it would run "Dear Sirs, I was talking to the Prune Board the other day and they said I was to tell you that I have three children, one is an infant in arms, and you can't get prunes anywhere . . ."

Tomorrow Diana is going to stutter and ring up Brisbane's leading speech doctor and ask him if he can do anything for her unfortunate complaint. She also plans to ring up various schools and ask how her little girls are getting on, and if her Cuthbert is progressing in his geometry. It should take them quite a time to "locate" Cuthbert . . .

When I showed Joe the cover from our latest brochure . . . he snorted with contempt. His comments were brief and scathing! "Type of plane, obsolete; not used in any country. Formation of planes in upper corner, absurd. Falling plane could not possibly be in that position with other planes behind it: by the time it had fallen that far they would be in front of it. Bursting bombs: ridiculous. Picture obviously drawn by fool who knows nothing about planes or bombs. Take it away." . . .

I was delighted at the thought of the vaudeville you enjoyed — such a contrast to that dreadful programme at the Cremorne. (May I express genuine sorrow for raising your hopes about electric-eyed apes?)

As I prophesied, Father discovered the pickled onions and began to eat them with his dinner tonight. They are still raw in the centre, but that is nothing to Father Foster; pickled onions are an advantage in one way though — he cannot feed them to the little Dogger. She hates them. It is sad to see cream, chocolates, cake, biscuits, etc. being fed to Dogger by her loving master, but it would be the last straw if she got pickled onions too. (Not that we will get many — by the time they are ready to eat Father will have eaten them all.)

I am filled with joy when I hear that you plan to restore life to the theatre; you have a fine quality (I don't know what it is) that makes me feel intensely alive — even your letters have this effect. The falseness of our age, and its weakness, have never touched you, and that is why you can stir people to life in spite of the rubbish that has clogged them so that the "seeds of eternal life" are buried and choked. Most people don't know they're alive at all, or else are possessed by crippling ideas. It is a fine thing to know that nothing can rob you of this power "to break down materialist tyranny" — nothing can, external circumstances don't matter at all, they can't touch you in essence. And your suffering now will be repaid. "Many a blow and biting sculpture Fashioned well those stones elect."[4]

It is Wednesday by now (1943) — not that I've been writing continuously, but I forgot to mention it before. I hope you are feeling better — or so bad that you'll get leave.

With my love,
Gwen.

---

[4] From the hymn "Blessed City" (urbs beata). See (19), footnote 3.

FRIDAY, 1943
Fostershaus,
Crimes Strasse,
Auchenblume.
[6 August]

My dear Tony,

I have bought myself a number of gramophone records to comfort me in my declining years. I have the Beethoven Quartet in F Major, Op. 135, Beethoven's first symphony (Toscanini conducting), the Brandenburg Concerto No. 2 in F, and some chorale preludes – In Dulci Jubilo, Nun Komm, der Heiden Heiland, Freut Euch, and Wachet Auf, all played by F. Power Biggs (who sounds as if he should make steam-engines, but is a fine organist).

The quartet is the most lovely of them – and it pleases me especially because I have been waiting to get it for a long time. Agens and I were at home together on Wednesday evening (sans Coar) and we sat listening to the quartet, eating preserved fruit and drinking coffee; there is much to be said for such a pleasant way of spending an evening. Greedy little Dogger was put to bed – she is in great disfavour because Father Foster's unimaginable love for her led him to give her approx.

½ lb. solid chocolate
2 doz. small chocolates
quantities of preserved cherries
many nuts, including almonds
cream
butter
blackcurrant tarts
apple jelly   etc. etc.

all in a few days. The greedy little bitch was also found on three occasions eating Diogenes' and Svasti's tea in addition to her own enormous meal. Can you remember how fat she was? Well, she's twice as fat now. When Father holds her up her stomach is horrible to see. The horrid little dachshund has come to associate parcels delivered from one member of the family to another with FOOD, and if she sees anyone giving Agens a small package her eyes light up with greed. It has become impossible to eat in comfort, for the Dogger is always close by, breathing heavily, a living lesson on the deadly sin of Gluttony. Can you suggest anything? It is impossible to change Father's attitude to her. Agens suggests that the quickest and surest way is to let him feed her to death, but I think that Dogger will live for many years, simply getting fatter and fatter.

Joe will be 18 on the 23rd of this month — aha, what month? 1943, of course.[1] He is laying cunning plans to join one of the services — as he's an apprentice, he has to be "released". I wonder if he will take his "clothes" with him — can't you imagine him appearing for inspection in the green shirt and the football shorts?

Did you see the new moon? It has been close to Venus in the evenings; as I come home in the tram I can see the hills just after sunset when the darkness is gathering, and the new moon appeared suddenly one evening when I didn't expect it. It is a great pity that the moon is lopsided half the time, but when it's new it is really lovely. I can't say that I approve ofthe moon's shape as it appearsso ofteh (This butcher's cur is venom-mouthed).[2] What is the use of trying to write about the moon on a machine like this!

You asked me some time ago about my being a writer, I believe (or, it would appera God in Heaven it would appear). If I decided to be a writer I should certainly long to be something else in about three months, so it seems better to do nothing at all about it. I'm trying to work out a scheme whereby I can have 10 free hours a day (after the war, after the war . . .) and sufficient money to buy

    preserved fruit
    hats
    gramophone records
    books.

[1]Joe's birthday: 23 August.
[2]Shakespeare, *Henry VIII,* Act I, Scene I.

I have the splendid idea of laying in enormous quantities of writing paper (all colours) string brown paper labels &c while I have access to them.

With the ten free hours I propose to

(a) practise the piano 3 hours
(b)   ”   ” organ 3 ”
(c) study philosophy, German, counterpoint and Rufo-Nanine activities, 3 hours
(d) dig in the garden, 1 hour.

Every two days I shall take a day off. Every two weeks I shall take a week off. During these holidays I shall visit leading Public Servants in disguise, write for free circulars, samples, recipes, diagrams, folders, leaflets, advertisements etc., fill in forms, write letters to the papers, go to the pictures, go to the mountains, mutter audibly at public meetings, musical afternoons, &c, get myself engaged as accompanist to "leading" singers and play Pop Goes the Weasel when they have a few bars' rest, write fake reminiscences for Ladies' Journals, carry off the Brisbane City Council's goldfish from public parks in an enamel bucket, get a job as "office girl" (I could easily do this in a short frock and a hair-ribbon) and cause a loud explosion in the tea-room, wrecking 34 cups & saucers, order enormous quantities of pies & cakes in the name of city offices, cook, apply for every job in the paper with fictitious references, walk through the street in complete disguise advertising a non-existent picture, study ecclesiastical history, lock-picking, ticket-forging and wood-carving, write stories, sail round the bay, watch workmen digging up pavements, grow trees, etc. It seems foolish to worry about money—it always turns up somehow if you are prepared to lie well enough about your qualifications. You, of course, will belong to the capitalistic class after the war, and will become unhinged if the moeny (money) standard collapses. Why don't you invest in diamonds, or property . . . It would be fine to have visiting cards printed—T.F.R., Capitalist.

Of course life takes the most unexpected turns, and I may yet find myself Mother Abbess of a Benedictine Convent, Queen of Persia, Director-General of Public Servants' Affiliated Musical Bodies, cheese-tester, the lady who has knives thrown at her in a sideshow, etc. (I seem to have a run of "etcs" tonight.)

It is late now, and I'm tired and incoherent.

Ting-a-ling-a-ling.

With my love,
Gwen.

(76)

SATURDAY, 1943.
Fosterschloss.
[7 August]

My dear Tony,

17m (Fire and brimstone!) I'm very sad to hear that you are sick. I can't imagine a worse place than N.T. to be ill in, especially when you are denied the joys of delirium. The doctor seems to be a half-wit. Is he the one who gave you Iron Tonic? I don't like the sound of "You should hear my brother on doctors." He's a doctor, isn't he? (Father's cousin, Byran damn Byran damn2 DAMN Bryan Foster is a doctor in Melb.) I'm unable to control the machine, as usual, though there is a certain satisfaction in the red type.

I have been rather sick this week — my throat has been sore. I don't think it's serious; Brisbane is most dirty and unhealthy at present and full of dirty big germs

Hesperus entreats thy light

3this line of poetry is brought to you by xxxxxx (thank God for the xs) courtesy of the Rufo-Nanine poetry distributors' Asscn.

This morning it was so sore that I couldn't swallow without intense pain, and as I was exceedingly hungry I allowed myself the delight of howling and groaning horribly, wandering through the dining-room and kitchen. The family were not at all sympathetic,

And her cheeks as the dawn of day

256 this line of poetry is brought to you etc . . .

259

In fact the only kind remark—"Are you feeling better this morning, darling," was addressed to Svasti, who refused his tea last night. Tonight I'm in good spirits because I spent the afternoon in bed, in luxurious ease. Today is the coldest day I've known this winter, indeed one of the coldest I can remember. And it rained! This was most comforting—I lay in bed and watched the soft rain on the trees and looked at the misty sky. It was good to see rain again after dry windy weather. I do hope you get leave, or are sent down from the tropics.

Robin (Dame Nellie)[1] turned up last night, and he and Joe have made the house shake to its unsteady foundations. The noise has increased about 500%, and the air rings with Nazi sentiments, heel-clicking, ruthless cries, bawdy songs, &c. Robin began to eat the moment he got in the house, and does not appear to have stopped since. He borught (brought) stories of the uncivilized state of Wallangarra, where he has been, which filled us with horror, but he looks even better than when we saw him last, so I think barbarism suits him. He repeatedly tells Joe not to join the army, but Joe wanders round as usual saying quietly to himself "L.A.C. Foster, J.B.", "Staff-Sergeant Foster, J.B.", "Major Foster", "Captain Foster"—and so on. Joe is determined to join up as soon as possible, and can be seen examining his muscles in front of a mirror frequently. The horrid boy has bought himself a terrible chest-developer with three large expanding springs. It has handles at both ends, and the idea appears to be to pull the thing out as far as possible. I have tried several times, but cannot move the springs apart at all. It gave me great joy to see Joe lift it above his head with a superior flourish, expand it, and let it go again: it caught a bunch of hair on top of his head, and ripped it clean out. Serve him right. Joe has a number of gymnasium apparatus catalogues and plans to buy the more fiendish devices as his muscles develop.

How cold it is! I'm wearing warm pyjamas, a woollen jacket, a winter coat and Father's dressing-gown, and still I'm not warm.

---

[1]Robin's nickname derived from his habit of saying farewell and coming back again.

I wish we could have fires in the sitting-room again, but the billiard table is too close to the fireplace, and if we moved the billiard table into the dining-room and put the dining table in the billiard room the dining table would be too far from the kitchen. I can remember sitting by the fire when I was young—but I've told you about those times, when Maria Marten and Dr Crippen haunted our dreams. Aha, guess what Father brought home tonight!9 (These absurd numbers appearing at times remind one of the silent films, when Episodes were flashed quickly on and off in the middle of a picture.) Father brought home *The Master's Violin*. We had a chance to study the picture at our leisure, and I can only say that it reveals more and more the longer one gazes at it! The style is in keeping with the picture, I assure you. Father also brought home another book

THE SHORELESS SEA by Mollie Panter-Downes.
First 2/- edition of this story of love, temptation, and triumph, described as a most extraordinary achievement <u>for a girl of only sixteen</u>.

Girl of only sixteen, mind you! The first page revealed that it couldn't have been written by anyone else. The style was so juicy and infantile that Father and I had a ludicrous reading session—we read in turn passages from *The Master's Violin* and *The Shoreless Sea* so as to form a connected but absurd narrative. It is terrible to see the mind of a sixteen-year-old girl at work on a novel. The frequent mention of buns, ices, chocolates and chicken reminded me of "dirty big pies". All the family snatched the book in turn and read from it—

"a drooping birch tree, solitary and exquisite as a line of Shelley in a drama, or a few bars of Debussy in a Beethoven Sonata". Gott in Himmel.
"her mind strayed longingly to Bath buns and ices."

"Her mind" is the mind of the "heroine", supposed to be a woman.[2] Hell.

[2] Rather unfair coming from a notorious scone and sandwich thief.

I've been reading some Irish short stories; there was a story by Joyce from *Dubliners* "A Painful Case"—I've never had a chance to read *Dubliners*, and the story I read has made me more anxious than ever to read it. There was fine writing by James Stephens and Sean O'Faolain.[3]

(77)   SUNDAY, 1943
                                                              [8 August]

My dear Tony,
This morning there wasn't acloud inthe There's something rotten in the State of Denmark. This line of drama is brought to you by courtesy of the Rufo-Nanine Tap-Fitters and Rug-Weavers' Dramatic Society.

This morning there wasn't a cloud in the sky, and all the leaves shone with a lovely freshness, though the tree-trunks were still dark from the rain. The air was so bright and cool that it seemed like cool water flowing against one's cheeks, and there was a feeling of lightness in everything. Everyone seemed to be feeling it—there is a poor old man with only one eye who stands near the church gate until it is time for Mass. Usually he tells me about his collapsed lung, but this morning he smiled and said he felt "wonderful".

Two bishops preached at All Saints' this morning. The Bishop of Carpentaria came to the 9.30 mass. He wore a BLACK chimere . . . Doubtless when I'm very old I shall write to the Church Times and say "Dear Sir, When I was a young girl I distinctly remember the Bishop of Carpentaria wore a black chimere." . . .

You will be amused to hear that Bro. Walter is a Rufo-Nanine shorthand dictator of the highest quality. I went in to his little den with my book for the second time, fully prepared to draw waitresses, state controllers, trains, etc., and suddenly Bro. began dictating at a tremendous speed. Just when I was going to stop him he stopped of his own accord and gazed at the ceiling for nearly two minutes. Then he came to life, seized a letter, and took

[3]The conclusion of this letter is missing.

262

a deep breath, and I was "poised" for a quick stretch of writing when he said "Ah," and sank back without warning, balancing his chair on two legs. I relaxed. He sprang at another letter. I seized my pencil. He relaxed. I began hitting my shoe against the table leg, and he looked absently at me, then said "Ah," again, and began dictating at great speed for about a minute. Then without warning he pushed back his chair, put a pen between his teeth, took a bundle of cardboard files from his desk and left the sheep-pen. I sat there idly for quite a while. He came in suddenly and said, "Ah, where were we?" then without waiting for a reply began dictating a long, ungrammatical and involved reply to some remote shire council at the speed of two or three words a minute or 95 words a minute, as the mood seized him. Every few sentences he changed his mind about a sentence three or four paragraphs back, and every few words he changed his mind about a word ten words back. Then he began saying sentences over twice or even three times. Sometimes he would stop and write something quite irrelevant on a little desk pad, then put the pen between his teeth and gaze fixedly at me, without seeing me. I can assure you that no Rufo-Nanine Dictator could have done better. The dictation was punctuated with sighs, groans and repeated mutterings — for instance, he said "Brisbane City Council" about six times under his breath, and while he is searching for anything he repeats it to himself: in looking for a certificate he mutters "certificate certificate certificate certificate certificate certificate" until he has found it.

He rang up his wife the other day, and I had trouble in "raising her". When he "got her" finally he said "Was you out, dear?" "No," said the good Mrs W., "I was hosing the garden." "Ah," replied Bro. "I thought you was out." Because it started to rain one day I arrived at work before 8.45, and Bro. delighted a lift full of people by saying loudly to me "Aha, good morning, Miss F., WAS YOU on the early tram?"

Bro. rings up a good many Plymouth Br. on the phone, and I can't understand the conversations at all. It seems to be a matter of "balance sheets" as if the Ply. Br.s were in possession of large sums of money or great properties. Their conversations, when not relating to Balance Sheets, are very mysterious. I must take some of them down for you. "Can you arrange to have those—er—those things I was wanting sent round?" "Can you get that for me—you know, we were discussing it the other night." Such sentences excite my curiosity. Believe me, I shall find out more about this! . . .

I do hope you are feeling better now, or that you have got leave.

With my love,
Ginnie.

(78)

Fostershaus.
Monday, 1943
11 a.m.
[9 August]

My dear Tony,

Note the time. I'm not on a "bed of pain", far from it. I'm taking a Rufo-Nanine Holiday, and I know that would please you: Mrs F. rang up and "regretted" etc., with a wicked look in her eye, that I wouldn't . . . aha. What a lovely day, too: I'm sitting typing in the kitchen, near the window where the sun comes in at this time of day. There is a tree just outside, and I can see the white clouds moving gently across the church. I can see people going on their errands up and down the street. There is a big silver cover on the table beside me, and its roundness reflects everything in absurd proportions—now I look like a full-bosomed prima donna, but if I lean a little towards it I look like a gnome. Agens is moving around in the kitchen, and her shape changes comically. The light shining behind this W.D.C. paper has turned it to a most delicate tint of blue. For the first time in a week my throat doesn't hurt when I swallow, so I have spent most of the morning eating various things. Preparations for lunch fill me with interest—I see we are to have some of Agens "special" soup, grilled chops, and ice-cream. Robin has gone to town, so I gave him a letter to post to you. At an early hour this morning he got up and put on innumerable "beer-hall" records with a BOM-pom-pom BOM-pom-pom bass . . .

Joe got up too, and roared out the "Hi-diddle-diddle" parts, and Gretchen (her German blood no doubt stirred by all this) ran up and down so furiously that 14 Crimes St. shook (As you know, it shakes even under Gretchen's weight. We weighed her – with difficulty – the other evening on our bathroom scales, and the distressing creature was well over 22lbs.)

I have been peeling potatoes for Agens, and there was one large one that delighted me; it was shaped like a hippopotamus, and I peeled it carefully so that the shape remained. Agens, after admiring it, cut it up ruthlessly to cook for lunch.

I wish you could be here – you would enjoy being on the sunny veranda with a bottle of your Iron Tonic. I feel rather guilty about writing to you of the Rufo-Nanine holiday, because it may throw into more unpleasant relief the misery of being ill in the "bloody tropics", as you so rightly term N.T.

Joe has got a Rufo-Nanine device he calls a cigarette-lighter. It is cylindrical in shape, and has a small wheel at the side which strikes sparks from a flint. The flame produced is out of all proportion to the gadget, and reaches 6 inches sometimes. If you turn the little wheel sharply, five times out of six nothing happens, but the sixth time the enormous flame shoots up suddenly and is quite likely to blacken nearly all the cigarettes you are trying to light.

I rang up Diana, and she tells me that nothing of vital interest has occurred at W.D.C. so far. She had been taking notes from Bro., who was in excellent form; he invents "headings for" letters halfway through, changes his mind, rubs out the letter, leaves the heading, writes a new letter under the old heading, cancels them both, then decides to have "selections from" the previous dictation. I think he deserves a medal! I hope he says to me tomorrow "Was you sick yesterday?"

Please take care of yourself: cannot you do something to

convince the authorities that you are really ill? I have just been humming to myself the impassioned melody of "The Shell",[1] and remembered the words

> The tidings crazed her simple brain
> > And smiling still she goes
> A mad-girl heedless of her pain
> > And reckless of her woes.

Can't you imagine me, unhinged, wandering in vacantly to W.D.C. each morning. Someone pushes open the door for me, and the office girl guides my hand while I sign the "book". They lead me to the switch, still smiling, and I sit down absently pulling all the plugs out and turning off the power. All day I sit there, reading (upside-down) a tattered copy of THE MASTER'S VIOLIN. Sometimes I wander up and down the office with large folders under my arm and a pen sideways between my teeth. If any callers come I smile sadly and uncomprehendingly at them and do not speak. I never make an intelligent remark at any time. Mafeking concludes that I have reformed and become "regular" in my attitude to the P.S. ("Such irregular conduct when she first came here," he remarks to Miss Harvey, who, overcome by my amiable docility, undertakes to "put me on" my tram after work.) Sometimes I sit for hours holding the telephone receiver up to my ear, smiling broadly all the time. My lack of intelligence and ingenuity is rewarded in the end by the Public Service Inspector himself, who arranges an increase of 1-6d. a week in my wages and refers to me as "a most reliable young woman". This goes on for many years until one night Harvey forgets to take me home, and I am found next morning by the cleaners, strangled (but still smiling vacantly) by the telephone cord. Of course my "crazed simple brain" might set in another way, so that whenever I was led to a musical instrument I played The Wolf. Or I might steal queer hats whenever I had the chance . . . Or my "simple" brain

---

[1] "The Shell": a Victorian song, words and music by Mrs Caroline Norton. See (2), footnote 3 (the words are not recalled entirely accurately).

might cause me to write Bro's. letters from shorthand exactly as they are given, something like this:

"The Town Clerk ah The Town Clerk wait a moment. Dear Sir. Er, where was I? The Town Clerk. Just a moment, Miss Foster, I think someone is looking for me at the counter. We thank you for your information of the 16th instant, no don't put that, just say we acknowledge your information, where's that certificate certificate certificate certificate certificate ah here it is. Don't forget the heading, make it non-payment of contributions. Why can't they remember to send their returns properly this is disgraceful . . ."

. . . I am glad you saw the full moon up in N.T. I'm never quite sure how the moon works or who can see it at any given time. Sometimes I don't like the moon – it's most annoyingly lopsided at times; I think it is loveliest when it is new, though I love moonlight in the winter. Is it cool at night where you are?

. . . Take care of the portrait of the Good Queen. I am sorry I could not frame it for you. Put her beside the Great and Good.[2] If you feel youself becoming delirious you should put them out of harm's way and PLEASE arrange for a witness of your delirium. I feel that when it does come the collapse of society as we know it now will be hastened.

With my love,
Ginnie.

(79)   Tuesday, 1943.
                                        Sunshine Home for Cretins.
                                                        [10 August]
My dear Tony,
Doubtless because of my pleasant Rufo-Nanine holiday yesterday I feel most depressed this morning, and not even scone thieves or the famous hat comfort me. What a hell of a place this is!

Last night Robin took me to the pictures. We saw "Commandos strike at dawn", a picture which showed Germans

---

[2]"The Good Queen" and "The Great and Good": Victoria and Albert.

267

arriving in Norway on American lorries, armed with American rifles, and tossing about American ammunition. The depravity of Joe's mind was illustrated by the way he tricked us over a newsreel: on Sunday evening Joe said "There's a wonderful newsreel on at the Elite before the picture. It shows a most complicated gadget made entirely out of wood. It has big wheels turning slowly, little wheels revolving quickly, shafts moving up and down, balls turning round, cogs moving—Oh! It's wonderful, Gwen, don't miss it. It's driven by a little electric motor. The wonderful thing about it is that it doesn't <u>do</u> anything—it just turns."

Of course I was most impressed with this, and asked "Has it got pistons?" "Yes," replied the wicked boy enthusiastically, "many pistons." He continued his description, telling us that the gadget was made entirely of wood and painting delightful pictures of its wooden complication and uselessness.

When we got to the Elite we waited in hope, but nothing of the sort was on any newsreel. Our disappointment—at least mine, was intense. Joe came out and stood beside my bed this morning, and I rebuked him sternly and bitterly, though congratulating him on his marvellous inventive powers. "You actually had me believing in your wooden gadget," I said. Joe was quite furious and swore that he could produce five witnesses to swear to the truth of his statements. He is going to get his friend Roy (the one who knew you first as Cdr McGeoch) to swear for him, but nothing will convince me now. I knew that his frightful exercises would have an evil effect on his brain. In two years he will be a menace to civilisation.

WEDNESDAY. [11 August]

It is raining again this morning. I feel most dissatisfied with my life at present—but that doesn't matter. The real danger is that one should feel satisfied—Mafeking probably feels satisfied. The cold rain seems to have got into my bones. I love rainy evenings.

I hope you are feeling better now.

With my love,
Ginnie.

Friday, 1943.
                                         [13 August]

Dearest Tony,

Your address on the latest letter was masterly! I'm glad to know
that the authorities recognise W.D. Comm and Prim Buildg. The
"girl" who brought me the letter was fascinated, and I'm sure she
showed it to everyone before I received it.

Your letter delighted me: I'm happy to know that you are well
again; last time you sounded so miserable that I was worried – I
attributed the rigidity to Iron Tonic, and I pictured you, stiff and
grinning like a Donaldson[1] drawing, sitting on your bed draining
a bottle of I.T. while Bill moved quietly through nearby tents
stealing more for you! (Does Bill ever steal from you? If he is
completely amoral, as you say, there's no reason why he
shouldn't.)

Yes, I know the Berlioz overture. Berlioz's orchestration is
lovely. Father, who gives me amazing things (do not forget that
he presented me with COOK'S POETICAL WORKS)[2] once gave me
a score of The Damnation of Faust, and – at the time I was rather
young, and was just beginning to play the piano – I had endless
hours of delight following the voice parts with one finger,
especially in the songs of Mephistopheles, who has some good
stuff in his part. That was the beginning of my love for Berlioz.
I don't know who has the score now; "it would appear" that I
have lent it to someone who hasn't returned it. Do you like the
Rakoczy March? Berlioz has orchestrated it in a most stirring
treatment and although it's played heaven knows how many times
it never fails to rouse me.

There is much in your letter that I'd like to write about, but
tonight I'm rather tired. In the week-end I'll write properly, but
now I'm talking to Agnes, eating PEARSONS ORIGINAL DIGESTIVE
BUTTERSCOTCH and beating back the fierce onslaughts of
Gretchen with one foot – it would take a genius to be profound

---

[1]Donaldson's comic drawings appeared in Smith's Weekly.
[2]Eliza Cook, of course.

in such circumstances. Agens tells me that as she came home from town she was waiting near a group of hot-gospellers standing in the light of a lantern at about 8.30 p.m. They appeared to be rather limited in their songs, Agens tells me, and sang

> We shall be changed in the twinkling of an eye
> We shall be changed in the twinkling of an eye
>   (pom diddely pom)
> We shall be changed in the twinkling of an eye

for nearly 10 minutes, to a very jolly tune (as Agens says, rather like "we joined the navy to see the world"). After that a weak-looking man with a shrill feminine voice shouted about "The Lion of Judah" until her tram came.

Agens has hung a print of some cypresses by Van Gogh in the lounge. The whole room is brighter now with its new paint, and we have cleared out the dreadful Muirhead Bones[3] – those scenes of desolation could only be lived with by people who had got so well used to them that they could ignore them – and have hung some coloured pictures including a charming little watercolour of a harbour with flat clear washes of colour over the piano.

I hope you like the room better to sing in now; it's much more cheerful now since we have taken the low-hanging billiard light away in the lower half where the billiard table is and allowed a decent light to shine on the shelves bearing Agens' collection of weird, curious, strange, hideous, hand-painted, 100 years old, bargain-sale, Japanese, Bavarian, odd, peculiar, artistic, useless, mended, broken, headless, handle-less, wooden, glass, plaster and china objects. I tried very hard to stop Agens putting Bones back, and I won in the piano half of the room, but Agens managed to hang a Bone in the billiard half – however it's not a desolated scene but rather a pleasant drawing of a town square.

---

[3]Muirhead Bone: one of the official British war artists. The "scenes of desolation" referred to were charcoal drawings of war. One was called "Over the Top". Another depicted the ruins of the Cathedral of Amiens. I found them depressing. The loss was mine. (GH)

The Bones have been hung in here—this is the room with the sewing machine, drum-kit, King Geo.V, linen cupboard, wicker baskets etc. Agens has managed to hang 3 dirty big war scenes on the wall. They are certainly fine work, but who wants to look at war scenes all the time! A couple of large chocolate-boxy scenes have been put on the floor in the corner where the saw stands. This is a Rufo-Nanine (rook.) room.

The letters are beginning to escape me, and even words are slipping away from my control. Before very long I'll be writing like Dylan Thomas. I "read" a short story of his this week—I forget what it was called—which sounded pleasantly apocalyptic. It was grammatical, the words were spelled aright, but brothers! the meaning escaped us. Mr Dylan Thomas has acquired a technique which I don't think is what is seems to be. Rubbish. That's not what I meant to say at all. No; let me try again (Rufo-Nanine Critics, to my aid!) I am likely to fall asleep, I think. Mt BURNING DEVILS. Mr Thomas' writing sounds apocalyptic, but is not. When you examine it closely it ¼s a confused mass of images and concepts jumbled together by chance connections—chance from the reader's point of view, anyhow. His early work was clearer, but now he writes stuff with great poetical associations but little content. An extraordinarily rich vocabulary fixes the attention of that part of the mind that responds to sensible and sensuous images, but there is nothing for the intellect to fasten on. It's like showing a hungry man pictures of a dinner, or letting him smell one cooking nearby. I saw a picture of Thomas in Lilliput. He looks gross, and appears to be seeing the world through a beery fog. It seems a pity that such rich words should have no bones behind them—I love the sound of "half-shaped moonlight", "owl-tongued", "melting garden", but there's little satisfaction for the mind in reading page after page of enchanting epithets.

What annoys me most about modern writing is its bonelessness. I have half a mind to take everyone to pieces tonight, but I haven't the energy. Brother Ass wants to go to bed.

I'll send your clothes to your Mother secured with Rufo-

Nanine slip-knots of the tightest construction. Your promises of stamps do not impress me in the least. You will receive a Rufo-Nanine bill for postage in due course:

To postage of clothes	stamps affixed	price
1 tunic	6d x 3d	4-9d.
3 h'dkfs	4 penny	1-6d.

I shall tie the clothes up in the week-end and post them on Monday. On Monday evening I shall write down the cost of postage in a firm, clear hand and send it to you by the next air-mail. If the stamps you promised me and failed to include do not arrive within ONE MONTH I shall send you a parcel of delicious fruit wrapped in transparent paper and secured with knots of so diabolical a nature THAT YOU CAN NEVER UNDO THEM. Six months later you will be walking round the spacious lawns at Goodna still trying to undo my knots.

. . . Show Bill "Artistic Homes" and see if he can steal a Modern Gothic Sideboard for you.

With my love,
Ginnie.

(81)
Fostershaus
Vigil of the Assumption
Saturday
[14 August]

My dear Tony,
Tomorrow is the feast of the Assumption of our Lady, one of the happiest feasts in all theyear. (See how this base machine is running words together!) It is an anniversary too, for it was on the day after the Assumption that I entered the convent two years ago. I arrived in a rush, with all my books in Father Foster's old beer-bags (those were the happy days when we bought the Foster beer in bags).

. . . This evening I played for "a big society" wedding. A great many socialites turned up. They looked very smart and their clothes were beautiful, but a certain air of grimness hungaround (base monster, why do you run workd words together?). One felt that tigerish sentiments were on the prowl! I had intended to wear the Tower of Babel, but I got a bit savage at the thought of Ethel's singing, and wore the French Revolution (father calls it "Jenny Lind") hat instead. (There was one marvellous hat there, with many flowers on it, and the whole business shrouded in light veils.) Beautiful young women walked (or rather glided) in. Some of them had been at school with me, and looked at me as through a glass, darkly. Ethel turned up early, and advertised herself as a "singer" by coming across to the organ at intervals and making remarks in an audible voice "in re" the song. The general tone of the affair was, as I said, grimly social. People "recognised" each other. Removed several degrees from the fishy atmosphere, it was as if people had assembled to see the prize big-game fisher of the season with her catch . . .

. . . The rain has gone now, and everthing is fresh and green. You seem to think I don't love rain, but I do, even if it makes me sad. That is because of something else. Falling asleep while the rain beats down outside is most comforting, and I love the sound of the rain among the leaves. When it rains I like to go without shoes, but people often walk on your feet in the tram and one cannot walk in town without shoes if it is at all dark because of broken bottles, etc. I remember a conversation with the young lady who would die if you called on her: it started about goloshes and shoes. I said that if it rained hard enough I took my shoes off and went bare-footed on the clean wet roads. "Oh dear," she replied, "I couldn't bear anyone to see me without shoes."

When I was a child we had wide fields around us, and one of my earliest memories is of the springy feeling of wet grass under my bare feet.

Rain is not the same here as it is in Melbourne. When I first arrived in Melbourne it rained for three days, and I thought it would never stop. Then the sun came out and I was amazed at the thinness of the sunshine. How fresh the air is down there!

Up here all through the summer that freshness lasts only for a time in the morning.

Tomorrow I shall write more.

(82)

The Assumption.
Sunday 1943.
[15 August]

My dear To-Ni,

I have just finished packing your uniform into a "stout" cardboard box. I managed to pack also a pair of shoes, about 1 doz. white shoe-laces, your gloves, the black socks, and some collars. Some of your past came to light as I examined the collars. Several of them have your name on, but some are labelled R. J. RIDDELL and one PRESCOT. The handkerchiefs revealed that you have no cause to accuse Bill: the nicest was clearly labelled in red EDW.F.COTTER. I suppose when you return from Darwin your clothing will be labelled BILL SALKELD, F.K., etc. By the time you get to Melbourne it will include J.R. FOSTER.

In the bag there are: several handkerchiefs, some shirts and underpants, a brush with not much hair on it, a white shoelace (got left out by mistake), a cheque-book without any leaves but only the part of the cheque you don't tear off, a small notebook urging me to buy somebody's superior rope cables and containing the names of Lorna & Dodo (obviously spies) and some laundry lists, a removable cap-cover and a prayer-book with the rubrics in red (which I have taken out because you said I might use it if I wished) and a brown shoe-lace. I'll send these to your mother when I find a suitable cardboard box — Agens and Joe recently "burnt off" all the cardboard boxes in the house except the stout one mentioned above which was on top of my wardrobe and escaped their notice. When questioned, Agens remarked that the boxes "were only using up space and nobody wanted them anyway".

. . . I am delighted to think that you're getting a GREEN STRIPE. It sounds typically Rufo-Nanine and will introduce new and wonderful complications in your "calls" at the W.1/2D.C.

274

(Damned Tripe-Visaged Machine).

I went to see "Tortilla Flat" at the Elite. The picture was most enjoyable and I was really very pleased with it. Joe's wooden gadget did not appear, but Diana saw it at her local theatre — and described it just as Joe did, with shanks, pistons, wheels, cogs etc. Diana (in reply to yours of 5th inst) is twenty-two and will be 23 in Decr. She is, as you say, a "gem"/. (Today this machine is experimenting with odd signs.)

. . . It is time to go to Evensong now.

> With my love,
> Gwen.

(83)   Monday 1943.
                                                        Auchenblume.
                                                        [16 August]

My dear Tony,

I was delighted to have another letter from you this morning containing news of the G.-G.'s visit[1] and its repercussions, also specimens of N.T. journalism . . .

. . . Today I posted the large Rufo-Nanine parcel. You will be depressed to hear that it cost 7/3. It delights me to think that the Rufo-Nanine bill reads:

	£	s.	d.
Seven shilling stamps @ 5/- each	35	10	9
Three penny stamps @ 1-6d. each	4	6	11
	138	25	13

Agens brought home a free pamphlet on HOW TO SAVE BUTTER. It remarks: "Now, more than ever before, pies, pasties, sausage rolls etc. should be provided instead of sandwiches."

It is interesting to watch the eating of pies in the W.D.C. lunch-room (this can be seen any day of the week, at any time between 12 and 2). Norman, the office boy, grabs his pie firmly in one hand and holds the paper bag under his chin to catch the drips.

---

[1]The G.-G.'s visit: the Governor-General's visit.

He is in favour of a juicy kind of pie from a cheap pastrycook.

The "girl", Dawn, simply eats her pie (which is gelatinous in texture) without any protection at all.

I have not seen Roland Weitemeyer eating his dirty big pies, but I have seen him eating: he was having his lunch "in" recently, and I thought he was having pies, so I strolled into his little sheep-pen. I found he was eating not pies, but a lunch apparently brought from home. He was eating a boiled egg, not hard, and not exactly soft, but at the revolting stage, semi-congealed, and some beetroot out of a jar. He ate these with a knife and fork, but I was determined to see more, so I sat down in a chair and spoke kindly to him while he ate a pear, which dripped all over his blotting paper. I feel confident that his method is substantially the same as Norman's; the blotting-paper, of course, has advantages which the non-absorbent paper bag has not.

THE WINNER

The pie-eating competition, however, is won by Miss Blanche N. Carthew (who'd die if you visited her). She arrives with five minutes to go, empties a pie out of a bag on to a saucer, and attacks it with a spoon. The pie is chopped with the edge of the tea-spoon and then conveyed to the mouth in haste. It is good towards the end of the meal, because the last few bites of pie have to be chased round the saucer. The gravy-scraping is also a notable feature of the affair.

The other girls eat their pies off saucers, but they are clumsy in comparison, and often pick up bits of pastry with their fingers, which as all members of the pie-eating public know, is not allowed. You must grab the whole pie, or none at all . . .

(84)
Crimes Lodge,
Auchenblume 1943.
[17 August]

Dearest To-Ni,

When I got your card (which conformed in size and shape with the blue border within which the address only may be written) telling me of your return, I became wild with joy and quite irresponsibly mad with delight. At first it seemed unreal, like a dream and I fell into a trance-like condition and gazed at the inhabitants of Sunshine Home for Cretins with a remote air, so that Norman the office boy became disturbed and asked me what was the matter with me. I read your letter again and again and kept pulling it out of my pocket to make sure it was real, until it fell apart where it was folded.

Oh Tony! I can't tell you how much it delights me to know I'll be hearing you sing again, and to have a bearded companion, the "naval friend", the "most irregular caller", the "sailor" in town once more.

The news is wonderful—you can't imagine my joy.

A new hat has been added to my collection. It is called the ADVENT HAT or TO-NI'S RETURN.

I feel sure it will meet with your heartiest condemnation. It is of green straw cunningly designed to deceive, as it is not the sort of hat at the side that you would imagine from looking at the front. It is decorated with white velvet flowers of a kind unknown to nature. They appear on one side, disappear, then reappear at the back. In shape it is a cross between a bell boy's cap and a Foreign Legion cap, but is quite unlike anything, really. Agens "discovered" it, and rang up the "switch" to say "There's a hat in X's arcade which would suit you, I think." I went down as soon a possibel (BURNING DEVILS, look at "possibel"—I had better resign from my professorship of English Expression) and when I saw it a voice within me said, "That is a hat designed to celebrate an unexpected return of a bearded sailor." It "'as zumzing", believe me.

Today another letter arrived containing a delightful story of the G.-G.'s boots. The absence of Rufo-Nanine agents is sad to think of. The letters A.R.N.A.[1] created a pleasing sensation. I saw the "girl" showing the letter to everyone in her path before she came to me. I'll continue this on the last page—this is written

---

[1] The Australian Rufo-Nanine Association.

after Monday 1943, but I want you to know how delighted I am at your return.

. . . I'm glad you are keeping the beard—it suits you immensely.

There are elections tomorrow. I found to my joy that among those to be voted for is one

McGEOCH, Robert Stewart.

I think I shall simply cross all the other names out and write HURRAH FOR McG. beside his name.

Tonight I have to do some typing for Father Foster, but in the weekend you shall have a letter about the following events

BISHOP FOSTER VISITS HER DOCTOR ⎫
CHICKEN-POX AT W.D.C. ⎬ entirely unconnected
NORMAN SWALLOWS PIN ⎭

With my love,
Gwendoline Nessie A.R.N.A.
(how does one rise to be a <u>fellow</u> of the R.N.A.?)

(85) SATURDAY 1943.
[21 August]

My dear Tony,

This afternoon I played at a wedding, so I wore the TONI'S RETURN hat, and it was definitely a success! The wedding was a remarkable affair, with two large bridesmaids and a small flower-girl. The bridesmaids were bedecked with pale violet lacy gowns; some ass had designed these gowns with a lace frill where a bustle would be; the bustle-like effect, combined with a tight bodice and the wrong headgear, was ludicrous. The little flower-girl was "got up" in a revolting garment. She did not quite realise what was wanted of her and was "helped" along the aisle by the fatter bridesmaid, not too gently. When they reached the chancel steps she was "jerked into place" by the other bridesmaid. There must be an agency in town that hires out flower-girls; this one was evidently untrained, or was perhaps hired at a reduced fee on account of being half-witted.

278

On Tuesday morning Bishop Foster was sitting at her stronghold, the switch, where she saw Norman gazing before him with an expression of the greatest imaginable alarm. Norman put his finger down his throat, pulled it out, coughed, hit his chest, coughed again, turned bright red and stood up in alarm.

"I have swallowed a pin," said Norman, almost inaudibly.

The Bishop was delighted. "Are you sure," she asked.

Norman was quite sure. He could hear a note of delight in the Bishop's voice, and it did not please him. But human comfort is necessary, and the Bishop was the nearest human. "Are you quite sure," repeated the Bishop.

"Yes," said Norman. He had two pins in his mouth, then he coughed, then he had only one.

"Ah," said the Bishop, with infinite glee, "this is serious."

The Bishop left the switch, and walked round the office, quietly telling everyone "Norman has swallowed a pin." Soon a little crowd gathered round the uncomfortable Norman near the switch. "How did you do it," "Why did you do it," "What on earth made you swallow a pin?" they asked.

The Bishop returned to the switch, and with a serious air phoned a nearby chemist.

The employees of the W.D.C. stood round while the Bishop spoke to the chemist:

BISHOP: Are you a chemist?

CHEMIST: Speaking.

BISHOP: It would appear that one of our staff has swallowed a pin. It is only a small pin. I daresay that is not at all serious.

(Voices around: "Of course it's serious.")

CHEMIST: Well, it depends. It could be.

BISHOP: The youth does not appear to be in any great pain. Indeed at the moment he appears to be normal.

(Voices around: "Ask him what we should do.")

The Chemist went into a long discussion on the possibilities of pin-points puncturing pin-swallowers, or lodging in their gizzards.

The listeners near the switch became impatient and kept whispering to the Bishop, "Ask him what we should do." Then the Chemist stopped for breath and the Bishop said "It was a very small, thin pin, really." The Chemist said "Yes, but even a small pin . . ." and gave another little talk on pins and their danger to the human frame. The listeners at the switch, unable to hear anything, became frenzied and began to poke the Bishop, which annoyed her, so she encouraged the Chemist to talk at great length. The Chemist recommended COTTON-WOOL SANDWICHES. The Bishop hung up.

"Oh," said frantic voices, "you didn't ask him what to do."

"Norman," said the Bishop, ignoring them, "you are to have cotton-wool sandwiches."

At once there was great activity. People rushed round looking for cotton-wool, but no one had any. The girl was sent out for some. Roland Weitemeyer came down to see what was up, and found Norman leaning on the tea-room door, next to the Bishop's quarters. When he heard of Norman's misfortune he said "Norman, you'd better let Mr Walter know what you've done." "Oh no," said Norman, "I don't want to tell him. He'll think I'm a dill." "You are a dill," replied Mr Weitemeyer.

The girl returned with the cotton-wool. The Bishop gave some brown bread from her lunch and supervised the making of a "dirty big" cotton-wool sandwich for Norman, and stayed with him while he ate it.

This story is brought to you by courtesy of the R.-N. Cretinous Stories League.

CHICKEN POX AT W.D.C.

Last Monday Iris, just before she went home, said to the girls around her, "I'm covered with funny little lumps. I wonder what they are?" "Chicken pox," said the Bishop, who'd had it years ago. (Joe and I caught it together, and Agens left us at home from school with instructions not to get up. As soon as she went to town we would get up and engage in chemical experiments, stand in draughts, get "over-heated" etc. and we got better very quickly.)

Iris went to her Dr on Monday evening, and he confirmed my diagnosis.

On Tuesday morning (this is before the pin-swallowing) Iris still had the "funny little lumps", but felt all right so she came in. She and Bro. were opening the mail in his office when suddenly there was the sound of a chair scraping back abruptly and Bro. rose to his feet crying "Chicken pox. Oh dear." He rushed in to Mr Battersbee, and words floated out "highly infectious . . . risk of infecting . . . staff all absent . . . never can tell who . . ." Then Bro. began rushing around aimlessly here and there, clapping his hands to his forehead and carrying a pen sideways in his teeth. Presently he began ringing up Battersbee and Weitemeyer, and they had serious little talks about the possibility of W.D.C. being "down with" chicken pox in a body. Anyone would think it was the plague come upon us. Bro. rang up Dr Stark and learned that chicken pox was infectious, and it was arranged that Iris should be sent home for a fortnight.

It was comical to see Bro. telling her this—he "kept his distance" as if she had been a leper, then returned to his desk and muttered quietly to himself for the rest of the morning.

PORTMANTEAU RHYME[1]

When Agens Foster's monstrous bag
    Fell open in the city
They found she had imprisoned there
    A turbulent Committee.

On Thursday evening a thought came to me: Why don't you go and see your doctor, Miss Foster? Why, I asked myself, do I need to see a doctor. You have another sore throat, said the voice. I hate seeing Drs but then I hate being ill, so I made up my mind to see my old Dr, Dr Greenham. Dr Eleanor Greenham "brought me into" the world. She is one of the fattest people I've

[1]Portmanteau Rhyme: E. C. Bentley, the inventor of the clerihew, wrote a series of "Portmanteau Rhymes" for *Punch*. The essential element was the inclusion of a reference to a bag.

ever seen, and generally dresses in mauve-coloured dresses of remarkable cut and style; once her hair was bright red, they tell me, but now it's snowy white. I sat in her waiting-room on Friday, and found to my delight that it was hung with innumerable pictures from floor to ceiling; they have been there for many years, but it's so long since I've been there that I was delighted and surprised. While I was waiting I made out a list for you to study, and I assure you that all the pictures were first-rate, of their kind. The Good Queen would have approved of them, I think.

> Picture of small chicken gazing at deformed puppy (front legs out of proportion) with the title "HELLO, WHO ARE YOU?"
>
> Picture of 2 queer youths in undergrad's gowns; possibly relatives.
>
> Photo of 1900 model car. About five wedding groups, all superb.
>
> View of refectory in a gloomy-looking college.
>
> Pastel drawing of 3 bananas, violently yellow; somebody's "early work". Drawing of kookaburra, possibly by same person.
>
> Group of 50 undergrads. Bunch of pansies, believed to be by painter of kookaburra and nearby "wild flowers", especially waratah.
>
> 2 babies (photo).
>
> "Views of" country roads and unidentified towns. Photo of stormy sky (hung upside down, I think).

Those are just a few of the wonderful wall-decorations, but you can see the general style. When the Dr appeared she didn't remember me, as it was nearly four years since I'd seen her, but when she had me at her mercy and began to ask what was wrong she looked closely and said "Well, I never!" "Yes," I said. "Here I am." The family history was recounted while she wrote down various things in unintelligible handwriting in a small book. "Well," she said at length, "what's the matter?" I told her, and she shone a dirty big torch down my throat and shook her head sadly and impressively. "We'll have to look at you, I think," she said, picking up her stethoscope. So I hung my clothes on a peg and lay down on her high table (how inactive or elderly patients get up on to it beats me — she must keep a body of strong nurses behind the scenes somewhere, or a Rufo-Nanine device for lifting people) and she listened to my heart, or whatever it is Drs do when they plant the stethoscope on you. She turned me over and back and knocked my ribs (possibly this was affection) and I meditated on the mysteries of medicine and thought, well, I wouldn't be any the wiser if this is only a dummy stethoscope. Indeed, we are at the mercy of Drs.

She has given me some tablets, called THE TABLETS on my chemist's label, and a bottle of stuff called

THE MIXTURE
There is no melody so sweet as relief from pain.
Take every four hours.

Joe was most amused by the phrase THE TABLETS & THE MIXTURE. The charming sentiment is printed on our chemist's labels; he is a prominent member of the Scouting World, and his name is Cecil W. Noble.

It is late now, I shall continue tomorrow. (Unless Dr G has made a mistake and the (I mean THE) TABLETS prove fatal.)
SUNDAY, 1943. [22 August]
It started raining after mass, and it is still raining heavily. Agens has been cooking various things in honour of Joe's 18th birthday, which is tomorrow. I gave him one of those "dirty big" jungle knives we were admiring in a window one evening on the way to that Hall of Deception, the Cremorne (electric-eyed apes being absent). Joe was most impressed, and has walked around all day sticking the knife into imaginary enemies, burying its point in the linoleum, rushing fiercely at wooden walls with the knife held in front of him and bringing its knuckle-duster handle down with force on inanimate objects. I do not think it was altogether a wise gift . . .

Joe has been thinking of nothing but military activities for a long time, and he is delightfully "ruthless" sometimes. He gave a masterly performance of a "typical" Nazi the other evening — Agens was sewing at the machine, and Joe said "There is the little mother. She is sewing." Agens stopped. "Sew on, little mother," said Joe, "or you will be dismantled."

When he goes away it will be strange without him.

MONDAY 1943. [23 August]

Today has been a lovely day. After the rain everything was clean and shining, and the air was cool and light. I feel really well, instead of being just "not sick". Oh, it was good to feel Brother Ass stepping lightly along instead of moving heavily at the mind's orders. My body, instead of being a weight to carry with me, is full of lightness to the very bones. While I was out walking at lunchtime it was so fine to be free from that vague feeling of heaviness that even slight ill-health brings that I smiled at everyone, irrespective of your warning. An Americal naval officer said "Hello, darling," and a truckfull of giggle-suited criminals whistled, but no repercussions followed. I went to Penneys to get myself some cheese for lunch, and walked sideways into a very small space at the cheese-counter; the girl served me at once — quite undeservingly — and a woman behind me remarked to her neighbour in a loud voice that it was a pity the way some people went on, pushing themselves in while others stood by but then young people never had any manners so what could you expect.

For Joe's birghday (what a funny-looking word) we had a "dirty big" cake made by Agens (noble creature) with a figure of Popeye on top. At first you would think that was symbolism on Agens' part, but Popeye's image is used (in war-time) on all birthday cakes and put back again in some secret recess in the kitchen whem (O, Villainy!) when the cake has been cut. Popeye is getting a little worn out; I don't think he will survive many birthdays. I didn't have a cake this year on account of a temporary shortage of materials so I propose to eat a great deal of Joe's . . . I hope you are feeling well and enjoying yourself immensely; I'll write again soon.

With my love,
Ginnie.

TUESDAY. 1943.
[24 August]

My dear To-Ni,

Joe is in wonderful spirits tonight: he passed the Air Force physical test as A1. (Voice from the pit: Crowbar, thou wert not in vain.)

The ghost of Sandow[1] rises from the floor, and presents Joe with a chest-expander.

Joe passed the trade test easily and is to be an aircraft instrument maker; I believe he is going to Melbourne before long, but I don't think he'll be there before you leave; perhaps you had better warn your mother that if a youthful fiend in human shape knocks at her door and requests the temporary use of a crowbar she is to refuse him admittance.

Of course various forms have had to be filled in, and ludicrous family scenes have occurred this evening as Agens, Joe, Father and I studied the forms carefully and suggested the best possible answers. It is wonderful to note how forms reduce quite competent people to a state of hesitancy. The departure of the household's only son will be about September 9th, I have just learnt, so he may have a chance to see you again before he goes. Joe is walking round smoking packets of cigarettes and playing "Beat me Daddy eight in a bar" on the gramophone. Agens is talking incessantly, mostly about the Opportunity Shop, and making violently green lollies, as in the excitement she poured twice the required quantity of creme-de-menthe into the saucepan.

I called at the Opportunity Shop at lunchtime and was quietly ordering some brown sandwiches when Agens rushed at me from the back of the shop (I didn't know she was there) screaming and gesticulating. "This is my daughter," she cried, "Mrs Brown, this is my daughter. This is Mrs Brown who makes all the dolls, Gwen." Ignoring my order Agens rushed at the sandwich-making helpers and said "I want some very nice sandwiches for my daughter." She stood over them while they made them, and kept relaying messages from me to the good workers—

---

[1] A professional strong man. He was said to be able to lift a horse.

"Do you want carrot and tomato?"

— Yes, please.

"Gwen wants some carrot & tomato & lettuce."

Then

"Would you like some egg?"

— Yes please.

"Gwen wants some egg & lettuce." (They had a surfeit of lettuce.) This went on while two old ladies, examining marmalade, looked at the scene in amazement. Agens ran around, served the old ladies, saw to my sandwiches, held conversations with everyone and counted money all at once. What a mother!

She rings me up unexpectedly at all hours of the day and starts off without waiting to announce who she is

"What do you think, Mrs Jenkins sold all that jam by 10 o'clock."

or "You know we had some black dolls, well . . ."

or "Mrs Hannah says she knows somebody whose sister died . . ."

Quite often I'm wandering around and someone else answers the phone, and they are amazed to hear these remarks hurled at them before they have time to say "War Damage Commission".

I bought a beautiful metronome last week — Agens discovered someone who knew someone etc. and got it for me, at such a terrible price that if she weren't my mother I should suspect her of profiteering; but I had to get one, and the music stores couldn't get one for me. As you may remember, my old metronome was a typically Rufo-Nanine affair that didn't tick at all under 70 and ticked in 3-4 time when it ticked at all . . .

This evening as I was reading an old magazine I came upon the following paragraph:

to prove that smoking was definitely harmful to the human constitution, a Melbourne doctor conducted the following test: — He fastened a leech to the arm of a heavy smoker; after a few minutes the leech dropped off dead. The doctor repeated the experiment. Again the leech dropped off dead. The doctor claimed that constant smoking had poisoned the man's blood-stream, which poisoned the leeches." . . .

THURSDAY After choir practice [26 August]
Fortune, that arrant whore, has deserted me. I was caught up today in one of the W.D.C.'s departmental "shuffles" and I am now BACK WITH MAFEKING.

I packed up my great leather bag, left the switch, and sailed brightly in to Mafeking who was blowing his nose and sniffing in his own disgusting way. "Here I am," I remarked with the utmost cordiality, "I've come back." Miss Harvey, who was standing nearby, gave me a look of unfathomable rage; in the caverns of her mind one could feel the tempests stirring again.

For the first hour I pretended I had forgotten everything about the Examining Dept.'s work, and pestered Mafeking till he almost dropped from weariness. Finally he gave me a wire basket full of things to "deal with".

I balanced the basket on my head and walked out and around the office with one hand on my hip. Harvey and Mafeking were standing by the filing cabinet when they saw me; "most irregular" was written plainly on their faces. Mafeking played right into my hands.

"Who the devil do you think you are," he asked.

"They call me the Jewel of Asia," I replied.

On the wall opposite to me I stuck up a little notice, saying

TAKE YOUR MEDICINE
9 a.m.   11 a.m.
1 p.m.   4 p.m.   5 p.m.

This was examined by the staff severally, and they asked me such questions as "What is that there for?", "Have you got to take medicine?", "Why did you put that notice up?", "Hasn't anyone said anything to you about taking that down?", "Do you think they would like you pinning things on the wall?" "Is that to remind you about your medicine?" etc. . . .

Agens and Joe are going to Mooloolaba for a holiday before Joe leaves. I shall be looking after Father Foster and 14 Grimes Street generally. Already I see Father (who beats me home in the evenings) cooking enough potatoes for seven large people, feeding the Dogger on cake and cream, hiding things in remote cupboards, bringing home 2lbs of prawns for Svasti, etc. Father's housekeeping is Rufo-Nanine. We have a wonderful time while Agens is away. Agens leaves on Sat., so I'll have some housekeeping stories for you very soon.

I hope you are well and happy.

With my love,
Gwen.

You claim that you will arrive on <u>September 8th, Thursday</u>. Nonsense, there is no such date[2] — a typically Rufo-Nanine arrival may therefore be expected!

(87)

Crimes Lodge,
Auchenblume.
Saturday.
[28 August]

Dear Tony,

Thank you for your letter which arrived this morning. I envy you your trip to the Dandenongs; my grandfather the hermit lives in the mountains — he must be nearly ninety now, but I remember how fresh and rosy his skin looked when I saw him last; perhaps it is the clear mountain air.

Thank you also for the enormous sum of money you sent in postal notes; they are probably Rufo-Nanine forgeries. I think a couple of letters failed to catch you in Darwin, but perhaps you have read of my scheme to send you a parcel of delicious fruit tied up with diabolical Rufo-Nanine slip-knots — it will not now be carried out. I sent to Darwin the week you left some Pearson's Original Digestive Butterscotch. If this catches you up somewhere it will seem a funny parcel; a Smith's Weekly will also probably find you several months hence, but it will merely be out of date. The Original Digestive Butterscotch will be in a horrible condition with bits of paper and string and cardboard embedded in the lollie.

I'm very tired tonight as Agens left with Joe this morning for

---

[2] Quite right. There was no such date in 1943. 8 September was a Wednesday.

Mooloolaba and I am now a semi-official Agens. I found some strange things collected in odd places when I was "cleaning out" this afternoon, including an ash-tray full of razor-blades, a gin-glass with a newspaper cutting about the price of vegetables, a cardboard box with the words "CATS ELEPHANTS MONKEYS TORTOISES" written in Agens' handwriting on the lid and a jar of yellow fluid labelled Strawberry Conserve. I found a bottle of peroxide and dipped some of my hair in it, but no results at all are apparent. I can only conclude that my hair is indelibly coloured; it will be funny if it turns yellow in parts next week.

Father and I had dinner on our own; we had soup—Lear would call my soup highly efficacious and mysterious—grilled steak with plenty of vegetables, and pancakes. I played for a wedding late this evening—at 7.30. It was a strange wedding. Only the bride & groom and the groom's mother were there, and of course the verger and the priest. I liked it much better than the "social" weddings (pick that damn train up, can't you?). After the wedding I met Harold (the clerical crank) and another friend of mine from the theological college in the churchyard; they came home with me for some supper. Harold ate enormous quantities of toast and talked incessantly of ecclesiastical and scholastic matters in a loud voice . . .

SUNDAY. [29 August]

It is a lovely day here. It would be spring, if we had such a season in Queensland. Crimes Lodge, with its creaking timbers, is in an unsteady mood; the floor shakes more than ever and boards are bending away from each other in an alarming way. I hope I do not have to invite you to sing amidst a heap of ruined timbers. Last night I lay awake and truly the house groaned and creaked so loudly that I know that when it does collapse not a post will be left standing.

I have been most unhappy for some time; I think it would help if I could tell you about it, but all my words seem to have deserted me. (Rufo-Nanine Writers' Aid Society, to the rescue!) It is this: I know quite clearly that what I am doing now is not what I should be doing—that is, I am unsettled and restless because I haven't really found what I should be doing with my life. I feel that I am corked up in a bottle, and this is because I'm not really doing what I should be doing, whatever it may be. Sometimes, remembering the close discipline of my days in the convent, I wonder if I have a vocation to the religious life, but I don't think so.

Life for me is easy and pleasant — as indeed it is for anyone who is twenty-three with coloured hair[1] (ting-a-ling-a-ling, etc.) but that is not enough. However the answer to my own question: What should I be doing? escapes and eludes me. Now that I have said this I shall tell you again how much I look forward to your company.

That is a stroke of good fortune — your return — I am intensely grateful for. It makes me happy already to think of your singing, for I know how it makes heaviness melt away. You are a lucky devil, to be able to sing like that.

It is understood OF COURSE that you take me to the circus if it comes here. The muttering goat, oh, the muttering goat! The muttering goat has restored my faith in the electric-eyed ape, which I firmly believe will re-appear.

Father is sitting next to Gretchen, sewing on a button. I suppose I ought to go to his rescue, but soon it will be time to get tea and I want to write a little more before I go to Evensong. Father Foster is the world's best button-tearer-offer; he simply ignores buttons and acts as if they weren't there at all. They fly off in all directions while he is dressing and he shouts for Agens to come and sew them on in a hurry.

It is very pleasant in the dining-room now; the sun is coming in through the window and it lights up all the wooden chairs and walls and the flowers on the table.

This afternoon I heard someone singing Beethoven's "Adelaide". It is the first song I really knew: when I was quite young I was sent to stay with Old Coar, who let me play his gramophone incessantly. He had a collection of records made

[1]Red, of course.

about 1920, and among them was "Adelaide" which captured my fancy although it was made by a sobbing tenor with a squeaky orchestra. It was Old Coar's birthday last Wednesday evening: he is 84!

AFTER EVENSONG:

It must be about a year now since I first met you. How quickly the year has gone, and yet it seems to be a much longer time in some ways. You have made me very happy. (Hurrah, cry innumerable red-bearded dwarfs.)

It is late now and very peaceful.

With my love,
Gwen.

(88)   Sunshine Home for Cretins
                                            Tuesday 1943.
                                            [31 August]

My dear Tony,

The last time I wrote (Sunday 1943) I was worried about my vocation but today I'm much happier and as usual not at all worried. I can always write. There was rain during the night, and it has begun to rain again today. Light rain was falling as I walked about during the lunch-hour, bareheaded, as T.P.[1] says it is foolish to wear a hat and carry an umbrella to protect it. The rain was most refreshing to feel in my face.

I enjoyed myself immensely in my capacity of official food-buyer (or rather food-controller) for Crimes Lodge. Even the rascally prices the dishonest greengrocers charge for vegetables and fruit did not greatly disturb my pleasure.

The new bottle of medicine I have from my Dr has a peculiar effect — like drinking alcohol on an empty stomach. Perhaps it contains Iron. It might even be Iron Tonic. As soon as I have a dose my head spins slightly. If I did not fear the result I should take the whole bottle at once.

The examining dept (to which I am still attached) has lost its

[1]Theophulus Panbury. See (45).

291

fighting spirit. Mafeking and Harvey simply refuse to fight and this is in sad contrast to the glorious battles that once shook the foundations of W.D.C. I said in a most superior tone this morning, to Harvey, "I have absolutely no faith in your system of red ticks; it is a waste of time." Instead of rising like the Furies she replied "Oh well, it is subject to the human element, you know."

CRIMES LODGE

This battered sheet of paper was put in my pocket as Roland Weitemeyer came looking for a stenographer. "What are you doing," he asked. I took the paper out of the typewriter, put it carefully in a file, and said "Well, I've nearly finished, as a matter of fact. I'll be free in about half an hour." He went away and I put the letter back in the typewriter, but before long he returned, so I put it in my pocket. He then asked Mafeking's permission to "borrow" me for his "mail". I have a new and most annoying trick; it is this: every few lines I stop and say, "Wait a minute, let me read this back to you." Then I read back what I have written, and say "Does that sound right to you?" Four times out of five they alter it!

Mafeking's lack of spirit is painful to see; I think he has given me up as too irregular to correct. One of my latest amusements is to stir up departmental strife; you would enjoy the results. I am "in charge of" a great deal of stupid correspondence and as I am filing it I look out for mistakes (which are pretty frequent). Mafeking seized a file this afternoon which Bro. had forgotten to mark BRING UP and raged magnificently at Bro., who put his pen sideways in his mouth and shook his head blankly. (How these Christians love one another!) . . .

It is still raining heavily. It was a wonderfully dramatic evening; the sky was massed with thick rolling clouds and looked like a dark fathomless sea; everything was drained of colour and light, as if the earth would soon be dead and cold.

I rang up Agens at the Mooloolaba Hotel not long ago. She and I held a ludicrous conversation, for although she "came through" perfectly she could hardly hear me, and I had to shout at the top of my voice, and the ordinary familiar words exchanged between members of a family sound ridiculous when shouted as loudly as possible.

Joe has to report (with a toothbrush) at the RAAF depot on the morning of Thursday 9th September. (Rufo-Nanine calendars, please ignore.) It is still not clear to me whether you are coming on Wed. 8 or Thur. 9, but if it is Thur. Joe won't see you — though I suppose he will if he's sent to Sandgate for a while. I haven't told the family of your return yet — last time Agens insisted that she knew of it before I did, so I shall surprise her. I called at the Opp. Shop today and there was a "rush" to serve me. Probably the good ladies thought I had been sent by Agens as an agent to report on them during her absence.

Well, To-Ni, this isn't much of a letter, but I have various things to do in Crimes Lodge (Nobby's Clear Veneer, where art thou?) Did I tell you of Agens' wonderful remark to Father when he asked her why she had so many potatoes stored away. She replied, quite seriously, "Oh, I always keep a couple of bags of potatoes ahead of myself." . . .

With my love,
Ginnie.

(89)   Aucking-flour.
                                                Friday, 1943.
                                              [3 September]

My dear Tony,
Thank you for your letter (written after midnight, 1943), which arrived this afternoon at the Sunshine Home for Cretins. I'm glad to know how happy a time you are having in Melbourne.

WAR DAMAGE NEWS
"AUDACITY OF TEN MEN," SAYS MAFEKING
In a recent contest between Mafeking and Ginnie Foster, "the Jewel of Asia", Miss Foster won on points. The contest came to an end when "Ginnie" proved conclusively that something she was blamed for losing had never existed. (She did this by eliminating all existent records and references.) "That Girl has the audacity

of ten men," said Mafeking wearily to his stenographer. "She would talk her way out of gaol," he added.

SAXTON, CHIEF ACCOUNTANT, TO VISIT BRISBANE WARDAMAGE

Mr Saxton . . . is to visit Brisbane Wardamage next week at about the time of the arrival of To-Ni (Scourge of the Public Service). Mr Saxton is reported to wear a white coat in the office and to chew incessantly medicated jubes and lozenges, carrying about with him an air of mild disinfectant. His reactions to "callers" of any kind are said to be terrible. When interviewed, Miss "Ginnie" Foster remarked: I propose to persuade a great number of cranks, lunaticks, maniacs, bedlamites, ravers, fanatics, hypochondriacs, in fact all people queer, crazed, infatuate, addled, deranged, insane, moonstruck, demented, daft, frenzied, delirious, frantic, raving, deluded, unsound, eccentric, cracked, imbecile, non compos, possessed and unhinged to visit the office of the War Damage Commission frequently during Mr Saxton's working hours . . .

BISHOP FOSTER PUTS CLOCK FAST

This is a border incident which will please you: this afternoon I was walking by the clock just after 4.30 and pushed the minute hand seven minutes on as I passed. Nobody saw me. At about 10 to five, when the public servants begin to keep their eyes on the clock, the Asst.Acct. stood up and remarked "That clock is fast." "No it isn't," replied a voice. "You're slow." Several people looked at the clock and put their watches fast. The whole of Wardamage stopped work seven minutes early, which would give the figures below:

No. of persons employed: 18
"   "   minutes lost   18 x 7 = 126, i.e. 2 hours 6 mins.

When this is discovered Bishop Foster will be tried under the National Security (War Damage to Clocks) Regulations.

. . . Father's company has been delightful. He has blossomed in the early morning, singing wonderful songs of the Ting-a-ling type endlessly and telling me, at breakfast, stories of his childhood in Nottingham and of his lusty youth spent with bright companions in the ale-houses round the market square.

Agens is returning tomorrow with the "fast-departing" Joseph.

I will not write any more; I look forward with great joy to your return.

With my love,
Ginnie.